THE **UNCONNECTED**

Steve Jones
General Editor

Vol. 69

The Digital Formations series is part of
the Peter Lang Media and Communication list.
Every volume is peer reviewed and meets
the highest quality standards for content and production.

PETER LANG
New York • Washington, D.C./Baltimore • Bern
Frankfurt • Berlin • Brussels • Vienna • Oxford

THE **UNCONNECTED**

Social Justice, Participation, and Engagement in the Information Society

EDITORS
Paul M. A. Baker
Jarice Hanson
Jeremy Hunsinger

PETER LANG
New York • Washington, D.C./Baltimore • Bern
Frankfurt • Berlin • Brussels • Vienna • Oxford

Library of Congress Cataloging-in-Publication Data

The unconnected: social justice, participation, and engagement in the
information society / edited by Paul M. A. Baker, Jarice Hanson, Jeremy Hunsinger.
p. cm. — (Digital formations; v. 69)
Includes bibliographical references and index.
1. Digital divide. 2. Social justice. 3. Information society.
4. Information technology—Social aspects. I. Baker, Paul M. A.
II. Hanson, Jarice. III. Hunsinger, Jeremy.
HM851.U525   303.48'33—dc23   2012014098
ISBN 978-1-4331-1142-6 (hardcover)
ISBN 978-1-4331-1143-3 (paperback)
ISBN 978-1-4539-0897-6 (e-book)
ISSN 1526-3169

Bibliographic information published by **Die Deutsche Nationalbibliothek**.
Die Deutsche Nationalbibliothek lists this publication in the "Deutsche
Nationalbibliografie"; detailed bibliographic data is available
on the Internet at http://dnb.d-nb.de/.

© 2013 Peter Lang Publishing, Inc., New York
29 Broadway, 18th floor, New York, NY 10006
www.peterlang.com

TABLE OF CONTENTS

Paul M. A. Baker, Jarice Hanson, and Jeremy Hunsinger

The term, the "digital divide," used to mean the difference between the "haves" and "have-nots" when it came to issues of access to communication and information technologies. As the cost of computers and other digital technologies dropped and more private and public distribution systems proliferated, social institutions—from school systems to the federal government—crafted policies aimed toward a bridging of the digital divide. Access to the Internet and the information and knowledge it made available was expressed as a critical social objective, and this thinking guided many social, economic, and political policies in the late 20th century.

Today, for all intents and purposes, in both the United States and in much of the developed world, we have declared "mission accomplished" over the digital divide. But as has recently been the case in other regimes, it appears that our victory may be a shallow one. If we consider access to the information environment simply in terms of *connectivity*, we have been relatively successful, but if we are concerned about a more robust idea of access as entailing *participation* in society, including complex relationships among individuals as citizens and participants, and as consumers of information in all manifestations, we have grossly missed the mark. This book examines the problems of addressing the digital divide when we closely examine those people who remain *unconnected*—the untouchables or *untouched* within the information society. Some remain untouched because of access or ability issues that also reflect race, disability, class, geography, and socioeconomic status, but others may be prevented from participation by factors of religion, language, philosophy, or culture, or simply by disinterest.

A second, but equally important factor, is that the *city* is changing as a location for economic and social activity. Social location and dislocation in urban areas around the world have upset the traditional "balance" of economic, cultural, and social capital that dominated the twentieth century and established the city as the place for social interaction, population diversity, and identity. In 2000, 50% of the world's population lived in cities, but it is predicted that by 2040, that number will increase to 70%, and 20% of those people will be squatters.[1] Matters of the digital divide are then further complicated as cities become either welcoming or unwelcoming to different publics, and issues of the "right to communicate"[2] affect matters of public policy, such as free Internet connections, access to information services, and municipal wireless plans and systems.

In this collection of essays written by noted experts in public policy, civic engagement, communication, urban planning, and political science, we examine the social, economic, and political contexts of the failure to reach the unconnected, and the importance of including these people in a dynamic, engaged civic democracy. Additionally we consider the role of the polis—or city state marked by a sense of "community"—in engaging the unconnected and the future of the polis as population shifts in urban, suburban, and rural areas change the playing field for digital communications.

Public policy, the engagement of the commonwealth, or the manifestation of public interest, offers a variety of approaches toward enabling the voice of persons who cannot speak up or represent themselves. One objective of public policy is to ensure that communication and information flow in an age of multi-media and differential access to wired and wireless technologies are both accessible and universal in nature. It is sometimes difficult to understand whether the digital divide creates a bifurcated society when the effects of new technology are not

---

[1] UN Report: State of the World's Cities Report: 2004/2005 http://www.unhabitat.org/mediacentre/sowckit.asp

[2] The right to communicate was first proposed by Jean D'Arcy in 1969 and became a component of the United Nations' 1948 Universal Declaration of Human Rights. In particular, Article 19 stated: "The time will come when the Universal Declaration of Human Rights will have to encompass a more extensive right than man's right to information.... This is the right of man to communicate. This is the angle from which the future development of communication will have to be considered to be understood."

completely known or whether extant inequities are amplified by the leveraging effect of these technologies. Would people who don't have home access to computers travel, if possible, to public libraries to use the Internet if they don't know what the Internet could offer them? What will it take to go beyond formulations of simple connectivity to the more complex constructs of accessibility (writ broadly) and engagement? It is difficult to design for that which you cannot imagine.

Similarly, we ask how we can plan, construct, and develop policy for the connected information society, the wired community, or any number of similarly coined clever parsings when we are still not clear on what constitutes engagement with, or participation in, an information society. Ideals of the information society and a sense of community that are assumed for all who have access often become more cloudy when we address the additional problems of class, race, and ability of the unconnected, the nature of social justice, and the policy and philosophical approaches that address the barriers to full community participation and engagement (social and civic). In the chapters in this book, authors survey the landscape of the unconnected; they address problems, potential solutions, and progress made, in certain cases, toward understanding the dimensions of policy discourse. Even more importantly, the authors paint a portrait of the dimensions of the unconnected in a society that assumes connectivity and purposeful action.

Modern literature involving access to information technologies and the potential for civic involvement began to appear in the 1980s and has evolved over the past 25 years. Some of this literature reflects views that see the opportunity for connectivity to more information technology as creating a utopian environment in which greater access for all will lead to equal access to government, giving a voice to the formerly voiceless, eliminating physical barriers for the disabled and elderly, and providing access to power for those of a socio-economic group or class that has been underserved. Dystopian literature often projects corporate control over technology, content, and systems of distribution that force greater consumerism upon an unthinking public.

Another significant theme in modern literature focuses on virtual cyberworlds, where either utopia or dystopia reigns in the form of a "community" that is not grounded in notions of *place*, but rather in commonality of interest. In this articulation of the information society, the notion of "engagement" depends on the motivation (or interest) of the user and tends to ignore the socially constructed world necessary for day-to-day involvement in the real world. Interestingly, however, these three avenues toward understanding the problems and the scope of engagement in an "information society" have brought us to the brink of a new understanding of the relationship of technology, policy, and civic engagement for those who can actively participate and those who cannot.

Even for those who may have nominal access to information, there are barriers to full engagement in the information society. These barriers exist not only in terms of connection but also in terms of the awareness needed to be able to engage in symbolic manipulation of information and the purposive nature of that information for social cohesion (personal and public). In fact, it can be argued that a superficial connectivity perversely accentuates the condition of the unconnected. An information society, be it a city, a community, or a nation, consists of layers of connection, meaning communication and engagement, in a mélange with the physical world, which presents a variety of opportunities for engagement that is simultaneously visible and invisible, proximate and virtual.

In addition to examining the context of the unconnected, this book explores the intersections of practical policy-making and execution of public policies toward groups of people that remain "unconnected" in the information society by choice. What leads these people to choose to remain unconnected, and what impact does this have on their ability to participate in democracy?

Organization of the Book

Each of the essays included in the book uses an organizational heuristic for development of a coherent body of readings that help readers understand the theoretical and practical aspects that influence the transition from a position in western democracy that defines "civic engagement" as public action to a social world in which information technology is both a tool and a participant in social change. We have grouped these essays into four categories:

- Context—Explanation of the environment in which the community exists. This ranges from the social structure of the city (which encompasses the community), to the regulatory regimes (state/national/international).
- Conduit—Infrastructure that both supports the community per se (roads, pipes, wires), as well as the infrastructure over which content and information flows.
- Content—Information, text of the law, political communications, zoning ordinances, and alternative modes of transmitting content.
- Communication—That which flows from the use/influence of content. Linkage to organization of communication, organizational behavior, and individual action.

While the chapters in this book focus on experiences in western society, the nature of telecommunication and the use of the Internet as the locus for a type of community action extend the possibility for examples to other cultures in world regions. Many nations are now developing "Technology Centers" to study the impact of technology, policy, and social use. Additionally, many colleges and universities have been drawn to the issues of *social justice* as an organizing principle for outreach and social learning; this book fits the model of real-world practice that has a strong theoretical base, with a social and pedagogical practicality. We take the principle of social justice as the nexus of responsible public policy, communication, and information infrastructures, and as the necessary link to what has been called "the right to communicate."

Section 1

Context

Chapter 1:
Connectedness and Political Attitudes and Behavior

Costas Panagopoulos

Throughout the chapters in this book, several themes become apparent. In particular, themes related to the manifestation of different political behaviors, the existence or re-interpretation of what constitutes "the digital divide," and the distinction of what it means to be digitally "connected" to a larger, democratic polis form the key elements that are examined through the lens of different authors and communicative contexts. To provide both background and a way of proceeding logically through these chapters, I analyze survey data collected by the 2008 *American National Election Study* (ANES). The issues that arise in this study are developed in future chapters, but the purpose of this chapter is to identify key issues that demonstrate the intersections of connectedness (or unconnectedness), the digital divide, and the impact these issues have on human behavior in a democracy.

Several authors have recently opined that the digital divide no longer exists, that it has either been closed by the creation of effective policies that have enabled more individuals to have access to the physical connectivity that makes Internet access more widely available or that the divide has been bridged by the availability of lower-cost technologies and greater attention to making educational, political, and community groups knowledgeable about ways to improve their access to civic matters. By painting the large canvas of the digital divide with such broad brushstrokes, they endanger the very elements that contribute to the issue of the evolution of social and technical change. S 10o, in an effort to bring readers to each of the following chapters with common discursive ground, I will identify the issues, through an analysis of the 2008 *American National Election Study*.

Introduction

There remains considerable debate about the extent to which there exists a digital divide in the United States. In this chapter, I will explore this question empirically using survey evidence collected in 2008. The evidence I present suggests that a digital divide persists and that some groups of citizens are systematically disadvantaged in terms of online access. Given the persistence of a digital divide, it is important to consider the implication for politics and democracy. Differences in political attitudes and behavior attributable to access to information and communications technologies can potentially have important consequences for democratic societies. The main focus of this chapter is to explore whether differences in access to the Internet can affect a wide range of behaviors, including electoral participation, voting behavior, and civic engagement. I will also investigate whether "connected" citizens differ from the "unconnected" in terms of their political attitudes on a wide range of policy areas and reform proposals.

The data utilized for the analyses that follow in this chapter were collected by the *American National Election Study* (ANES) in 2008. The ANES has collected data on Americans' political attitudes, preferences, and behaviors routinely during election cycles since 1948. In 2008, the ANES probed respondents about their access to the Internet. Self-reported access to the Internet using this survey item is adopted as my measure of "connectedness." Respondents who answered in the affirmative are considered to be "connected," while others are considered "unconnected." Overall, weighted responses to this survey item indicate that three in four Americans (76 percent) in 2008 reported having access to the Internet (connected) while the remaining one-quarter (24 percent) did not report having access to the Internet (unconnected).

Is There (Still) a Digital Divide in America?

My first task is to examine whether or not specific demographic characteristics are systematically related to self-reported Internet access. To conduct this analysis, I use probit regression to explain connectedness as a function of key demographic and political traits including age, race, gender, education, income, partisanship, and ideology. The dependent variable in this analysis is coded 1 if respondents reported having access to the Internet (connected), 0 otherwise. The results of the analysis are presented in Table 1.1. The coefficients reported in Table 1.1 represent the marginal impact of each of the traits I examined on connectedness.

Table 1.1: *Who Has Internet Access?*

	Connectedness
Age	-.01 (.001)***
Female	.01 (.02)
Democrat	-.02 (.04)
Republican	.01 (.04)
Ideology (Conservatism)	-.01 (.01)
Black	-.07 (.03)**
Latino	-.06 (.03)**
Other race	-.08 (.06)
Education	.03 (.01)***
Income	.02 (.002)***
N	1,935
Log Pseudo-likelihood:	-485.696
Pseudo R-squared	.34

Note. Probit regression. Dependent variable is self-reported Internet access (2008 ANES). Numbers represent marginal effect of corresponding characteristic. Standard errors in parentheses. **denotes statistical significance at the $p<.05$ level; ***denotes statistical significance at the $p<.01$ level.

The evidence presented in Table 1.1 suggests access to the Internet is systematically linked to some characteristics but not to others. Controlling for all of the other variables included in the empirical model I estimate, I found that age is significantly related to connectedness. All else equal, older Americans report being less connected compared to younger Americans. This is perhaps intuitive, given young Americans' proclivity to embrace new technology. I also found that race is significantly related to Internet access. Blacks and Latinos are significantly less connected compared to white Americans, with all else equal. Members of other races (including Asians, for example) do not report significantly different levels of connectedness compared to whites, however. Connectedness is also significantly related to income and education. All else equal, more educated and more affluent Americans are more likely to report having access to the Internet. There is no evidence, however, that gender influences connectedness; all else equal, women are as likely as men to report having access to the Internet.

Despite strong evidence that key demographic traits are related to connectedness, there is scant evidence that political attitudes are related to self-reported Internet access once we control for respondents' demographics. Overall, the evidence presented in Table 1.1 shows that there is no link between partisan identification and connectedness; self-identified Democrats and Republicans were equally likely to report having access to the Internet compared to self-identified Independents, ceteris paribus. Similarly, respondents' ideology is unrelated to Internet access; holding other variables constant, conservatives were no more likely than liberals in the survey to report having Internet access.

Overall, I interpret the evidence presented in Table 1.1 to imply that there persists a digital divide for some Americans. Connectedness is significantly related to key demographic characteristics including age, race, education, and income. On the other hand, gender and political attitudes such as partisanship and ideology do not affect connectedness. To what extent is connectedness related to political attitudes and behavior more generally?

Connectedness and Political Attitudes

The ANES questions respondents about a wide range of policy preferences and political attitudes. Can we observe differences in respondents' preferences on key policy questions and general political attitudes? I examined respondents' positions on 21 separate survey items about political attitudes and policy preferences. In Table 1.2, mean distributions of responses to each survey item are identified separately for connected and unconnected respondents. The final column in Table 1.2 presents a test statistic that indicates (if less than .05) that differences in means between connected and unconnected respondents are statistically significant at conventional levels.

Table 1.2: *Connectedness and Political Attitudes (Mean Levels)*

Political Attitude	Unconnected	Connected	Prob>F
Ideology (1–7 scale)	4.38	4.27	.24
Very Interested in Campaign	31.2	30.6	.86
Iraq Worth Cost	18.1	27.0	.00
Favor Universal Health Care	63.1	56.7	.09
Increase Social Security Spending	53.6	50.8	.28
Increase Welfare Spending	56.7	53.2	.18
Increase Foreign Aid Spending	57.8	47.3	.00
Increase Spending on War on Terror	54.2	47.6	.00
Favor Lower Emissions Standards	80.2	87.0	.02
Favor Death Penalty	69.3	70.4	.66
Favor More Difficult to Buy Gun	50.7	46.5	.10
Favor Gays in Military	70.0	81.9	.00
Allow Gay Marriage	29.7	41.1	.00
Favor Deficit Reduction	65.2	77.4	.00
Raising Taxes to Reduce Deficit	13.2	23.2	.00
Cut Military Spend to Reduce Deficit	31.8	41.3	.00
Increase Immigration Levels in U.S.	13.1	14.6	.41
Never Permit Abortion	26.7	11.1	.00
Favor Social Security in Stock Market	23.1	38.1	.00
Approve Handling War Iraq	21.6	30.5	.00
Trust Government (at least most of time)	34.3	29.4	.14

Source: 2008 ANES; Analyzed by author

The ANES asks respondents to rate their overall ideology using a seven-point scale ranging from very liberal to very conservative. Table 1.2 shows that the mean ideology on this seven-point scale was 4.38 for connected respondents and 4.27 for the unconnected. The difference in mean level of ideology was not statistically significant. Connected respondents expressed no greater interest in the presidential campaign in 2008 compared to unconnected respondents.

To compare the policy preferences of connected and unconnected Americans, responses to several survey items that probed respondents about their positions on key policies in 2008 were analyzed. The initial evidence implies significant differences may exist in some policy domains but not others.

The data indicate that Americans who reported having access to the Internet were more likely to believe that fighting the war in Iraq was "worth the cost," compared to those who were unconnected. Twenty-seven percent of those connected held this view compared to 18 percent of those who were unconnected. On the issue of universal health care, Americans with access to the Internet were somewhat less supportive compared to those without access; 57 percent of those connected favored universal health care in 2008 compared to 63 percent of those who were unconnected.

With respect to increasing spending on Social Security and welfare, there were no statistically significant differences between connected and unconnected responses. By contrast, unconnected Americans were significantly more likely to favor increased spending on foreign aid and the War on Terror in 2008 compared to connected respondents. Connected respondents were significantly more inclined to favor lower emissions standards, permitting gays to serve in the military, allowing gay marriage, deficit reduction, raising taxes to reduce the deficit, cutting military spending to reduce the deficit, and allowing Social Security funds to be invested in the stock market, compared to unconnected Americans. Connected Americans also expressed higher levels of approval of the handling of the war in Iraq in 2008, compared to the unconnected. By contrast, those who reported having no access to the Internet were significantly more likely, compared to those connected, to believe abortion should never be permitted. I find no significant differences in overall levels of trust in government or on policy questions relating to immigration levels, capital punishment, or gun control, between the connected and the unconnected.

These initial results are compelling, suggesting significant differences between connected and unconnected citizens on the lion's share of policy issues asked about by the ANES in 2008. A more rigorous analysis, however, would enable us to determine whether these differences persist even after taking respondents' demographic and political characteristics into account. To advance such an analysis, I estimated separate probit regression models to explain responses to each of the attitudinal questions discussed above as a function of respondents' connectedness, while controlling for their age, gender, race, partisanship, ideology, income, and education levels. The results of the analysis are presented in Table 1.3. The coefficients reported in Table 1.3 represent the marginal impact of connectedness on self-reported preferences examined while controlling for respondents' key attitudinal and demographic attributes.

Table 1.3: *Explaining Political Attitudes*

	Connected(Marginal Impact of Connectedness)
Ideology (Conservatism) (OLS)	-.08 (.11)
(excluded in analysis explaining ideology)	
Very Interested in Campaign	-.04 (.06)
Iraq Worth Cost	.03 (.04)
Favor Universal Health Care	.13 (.08)
Increase Social Security Spending	-.04 (.06)
Increase Welfare Spending	.03 (.05)
Increase Foreign Aid Spending	-.07 (.05)
Increase Spending on War on Terror	-.004 (.05)
Favor Lower Emissions Standards	.09 (.06)*
Favor Death Penalty	.04 (.05)
Favor More Difficult to Buy Gun	-.05 (.04)
Favor Gays in Military	.07 (.04)
Allow Gay Marriage	-.02 (.05)
Favor Deficit Reduction	.02 (.04)
Raise Taxes to Reduce Deficit	.08 (.03)**
Cut Military Spending to Reduce Deficit	.03 (.05)
Increase Immigration Levels in U.S.	-.01 (.04)
Never Permit Abortion	-.13 (.05)***
Favor Social Security in Stock Market	.06 (.04)
Approve Handling Iraq War	.05 (.04)
Trust Government (at least most of time)	-.06 (.06)

Note. Probit regression (weighted) (unless otherwise indicated). Figures represent marginal impact of having Internet access (dprobit). Dependent variable is coded 1 if respondent reported supporting each position, 0 otherwise (unless otherwise indicated). Standard errors in parentheses. *denotes statistical significance at the $p<.10$ level using two-tailed tests; **denotes statistical significance at the $p<.05$ level; ***denotes statistical significance at the $p<.01$ level. Control variables included in all analyses: age, gender, race, party ID, ideology, income, education. Source: 2008 ANES.

The evidence reveals that, after controlling for key political and demographic variables, most of the differences in policy preferences between connected and unconnected citizens vanish. In fact, the only differences in policy preferences that persisted are limited to three policy questions:

- Connected citizens were significantly more favorably disposed to lower emissions standards compared to unconnected respondents.
- Connected citizens were more favorably disposed to raising taxes to reduce the deficit compared to unconnected respondents.
- Connected citizens were more likely to believe abortion should never be permitted compared to their connected counterparts, all else equal.

After closer inspection, the evidence presented in Table 1.3 suggests differences in political attitudes and policy preferences attributable to connectedness may be fewer than expected. What about political behavior though?

Connectedness and Political Behavior

Self-reported political activity varied between connected and unconnected citizens in 2008. I investigated six types of political behaviors:

- Voting.
- Volunteering or contributing to a campaign.
- Attending a political meeting or speech.
- Talking to someone about voting for or against a candidate in the 2008 election.
- Displaying a campaign button, sign, or bumper sticker.
- Contacting an elected official (in the year prior).

Self-reported levels of each of these activities are presented separately for connected and unconnected respondents in Table 1.4. Across all forms of political behavior in 2008 there were significant differences in mean levels of activity. The pattern is striking:

- Connected citizens are more likely to report engaging in all of these activities compared to unconnected Americans.
- The self-reported voter turnout rate in the 2008 election was about 20 percentage points higher for connected citizens compared to unconnected Americans, for example.

- Connected citizens were about three times more likely to contribute to a political campaign in 2008, about twice as likely to volunteer for a campaign, more than twice as likely to attend a political meeting or speech, and much more likely to report displaying a campaign button, sign, or bumper sticker, compared to unconnected citizens.

- Those reporting having Internet access were also more than three times as likely as those unconnected to report contacting an elected official in the year prior year.

The data presented in Table 1.4 suggest connected Americans were consistently more likely to engage in political activity compared to unconnected citizens. To what extent do these differences persist even after controlling for respondents' demographic and political traits?

Table 1.4: *Connectedness and Political Behavior (Mean Levels)*

Political Behavior	Unconnected	Connected	Prob>F
Contributed	5.9	17.8	.00
Voted 2008	62.8	82.1	.00
Volunteered Campaign 2008	2.4	4.6	.02
Talked Someone Voting for/against	34.5	48.6	.00
Went to Political Meeting/Speech	4.1	9.9	.00
Displayed Button/Sign/Bumper Sticker	12.3	19.6	.00
Contacted Elected Official (past year)	7.0	22.1	.00

Source: 2008 ANES

Most of the differences in policy preferences dissipated once these factors were simultaneously taken into account. To examine this question, I used probit regression to explain respondents' self-reported political activities across the range of behaviors described above as a function of connectedness while controlling for respondents' age, gender, race, partisanship, ideology, income, and education levels. The results of the analyses are presented in Table 1.5. The coefficients reported in Table 1.5 represent the marginal impact of connectedness on engaging on each activity examined while controlling for respondents' key attitudinal and demographic attributes. Overall, connectedness exerts a significant, independent effect on political behavior in six out of seven activity dimensions. Connected citizens are significantly more likely to engage in all activities (with the exception of talking to someone about voting for or against a candidate) compared to unconnected citizens even after controlling for the range of traits described above.

Table 1.5: Explaining Political Behavior

Contributed	.11 (.02)***
Voted	.18 (.04)***
Volunteered Campaign	.02 (.01)*
Talked Someone Voting for/against	.07 (.05)
Went to Political Meeting/Speech	.05 (.02)**
Campaign Button/Sign/Bumper Sticker	.07 (.03)**
Contacted Elected Official (past year)	.12 (.03)***

Note. Probit regression (weighted). Figures represent marginal impact of having Internet access (dprobit). Dependent variable is coded 1 if respondent reported engaging in each activity, 0 otherwise. Standard errors in parentheses. *denotes statiscal significance at the p<.10 level using two-tailed tests; **denotes statistical significance at the p<.05 level; ***denotes statistical significance at the p<.01 level. Control variables included in all analyses: age, gender, race, party ID, ideology, income, education. Source: 2008 ANES.

Discussion and Conclusion

The evidence presented in this chapter shows mixed results. Overall, the examination of survey data collected in 2008 suggests the digital divide remains palpable in America. Some citizens are systematically disadvantaged with respect to Internet access compared to others. There are significant differences in political attitudes and behaviors between connected and unconnected citizens. On the plus side, the results of the analyses showed that connected and unconnected citizens are, on the whole, rather similar with regard to their policy preferences across a wide range of issues. That said, some differences did emerge, and a few persisted even after controlling for respondents' other characteristics.

Potentially problematic from the standpoint of democratic participation are the findings reported with respect to political participation. Unconnected citizens are simply disengaged from the political process compared to those who are connected. Given that there are at least some differences between connected and unconnected citizens in terms of policy preferences, such differential rates of participation have the capacity to render connected citizens' policy positions more influential in the political process compared to the preferences espoused by those unconnected. Such imbalances, rooted directly in citizens' levels of connectedness, could conceivably compromise democracy in America. This is especially true if they become exacerbated in the years ahead. It is thus crucial to remain vigilant to patterns that may emerge and to pursue policy proposals or reforms that seek to promote greater equity in political engagement.

Summary

When we approach another election year, it may be useful to keep the findings of the 2008 study uppermost in our minds. While questions concerning the meaning and impact of those citizens who are connected versus the unconnected are still a part of our culture and will be for some time, we should proceed cautiously as we create research milestones that situate social factors in historical perspective.

As each of the chapters in this collection outline connectedness and unconnectedness play an important part in understanding who is empowered to act, behave, or develop attitudes that reflect their own situation vis-à-vis larger society in general. Perhaps there is no larger overarching question in the United States today that deals with empowerment through online access and activity.

While the nations of the world experience differential access, connectivity, and skill necessary for political and personal empowerment, the range of issues related to social justice becomes a larger, heavier burden to uphold. As evidenced in this chapter, an empirical examination of the factors that investigate the intersections of technology, the digital divide, social justice, and connectedness provides important insights to understand who will be a part of the global dialog and who may be left behind.

References

American National Election Study. (2008). Retrieved from http://electionstudies.org/studypages/2008prepost/2008prepost.htm

Epstein, D., Nisbet, E. C., & Gillespie, T. (2011, March). Who's responsible for the digital divide? Public perceptions and policy implications. *The Information Society*, 27(2), 92–104.

National Telecommunications and Information Administration. (2011). *Digital nation: Expanding Internet usage* (November). Retrieved from http://www.ntia.doc.gov/files/ntia/publications/ntia_internet_use_report_februar y_2011.pdf

Norris, P. (2001). *Digital divide: Civic engagement, information poverty, and the Internet worldwide.* New York, NY: Cambridge University Press.

Vehovar, V., Sicherl, P., Hüsing, T., & Dolničar, V. (2006, November–December). Methodological challenges of digital divide measurements. *The Information Society* 22(5), 279–90.

Chapter 2:
Understanding the Multi-Dimensionality of the Digital Divide: Empirical Evidence from Italy

J. Ramon Gil-Garcia, Natalie C. Helbig, and Enrico Ferro

Introduction

Since the 1990s, scholars and practitioners have recognized the importance of studying the patterns of inequalities of access to technology and information across members of diverse social groups in their daily lives (Selwyn, 2002). The term, "digital divide," was coined to describe this phenomenon. The digital divide has been conceptualized in different ways, from characterizing it as simply an inequality of access to computers and the Internet, to characterizing it as a much more complex social phenomenon encompassing social, political, and economic factors. A fairly comprehensive examination of the literature reveals the difficulty in describing all of the different meanings and relationships among concepts such as technology, information, information and communication technologies, and the Internet (Dewan & Riggins, 2005). ICTs can be considered amplifiers of existing political, social, and economic trends (Ostling 2010); as a consequence, the presence of digital divides may lead to an exacerbation of the disparities present in today's society. In this respect, policy makers are thus responsible for carefully monitoring and understanding the nature and dynamics of such divides. Timely and effective corrective measures may in fact be needed to use ICTs as a lever for the promotion of widespread and homogeneous socioeconomic development. Such policy intelligence activity needs to be evidence based and rely on quantitative and longitudinal studies.

In this chapter, we thus explore the relationships between multiple factors, access to the Internet, and the extent of Internet use, using data from the Piedmont region in Italy. We argue that computer and Internet access does not automatically lead to meaningful and extensive use of the Internet, and there are several other important determinants. The digital divide is not only about access but also about other characteristics that define the social opportunities of an individual such as gender, education, employment status, IT skills, and an ability to speak foreign languages, among others. In addition, this chapter operationalizes Internet access and Internet use using multiple variables and concepts instead of a dichotomous variable.

The chapter is divided into several sections. Based on a review of existing academic literature, a section is devoted to describing two of the most recognizable approaches to studying the digital divide: an access divide and a multi-dimensional divide. This section is followed by the presentation of relevant hypotheses that have been developed based on each view. The concluding sections are devoted to analysis. In one, we briefly present the research design and methods used including the main characteristics of the respondents and an explanation of the operationalization of the dependent variables. In the next, we present the logistic and multiple linear regression models to empirically test the two views and discuss the results. It seems clear that the multi-dimensional view provides a better explanation of both Internet access and Internet use. Finally, we conclude with suggestions for future areas of research on this topic.

Characterizing the Digital Divide: Approaches and Assumptions

Throughout the last 15 years, many different conceptualizations of the digital divide have emerged. Two common approaches to understanding the digital divide—an access divide and a multi-dimensional digital divide—are discussed below (Helbig, Gil-Garcia, & Ferro, 2009; Dewan & Riggins, 2005). Hypotheses are developed based on the factors and relationships found in the literature on each view.

Access Digital Divide

One stream of research focuses on access to technologies. Simply stated, the gap exists solely because of an "access to technology problem" and scholars tend to frame the divide as an inherent delay in the diffusion of technology among different geographic areas and social groups (Adriani & Becchetti, 2003; Compaine, 2001). One assumption is that "once online, there is no gap" (Walsh et al., 2003 p. 281). In addition, individuals are assumed to use the Internet for the same purposes (Walsh et al., 2003). Driven by these basic assumptions, scholars studying the divide from this viewpoint often equate Internet access with Internet use (DiMaggio & Hargittai, 2001). Likewise, remedies to lessen the gap rely heavily on market forces being able to eventually close the gap over time; government intervention through policy or other means is not necessary. If government intervention is suggested, from this view, public policies should foster only Internet access, since use depends on, and is derived almost exclusively from, access.

Thus, one of the main assumptions of this approach is that only Internet access has a direct effect on Internet use. Therefore, the research endeavor is to identify and test how different factors affect Internet access and thus, Internet use. In general terms, many scholars confirm that access to the Internet and computers is strongly correlated with socio-economic status (Bimber, 2000; Selwyn, 2002), and three main factors have been associated with access: income, age, and education (Hoffman, Novak, & Schlosser, 2000; Mossberger, Tolbert, & Stansbury, 2003; Robinson et al., 2003). Additional factors associated with Internet access include attitudes toward technology, race/ethnicity, geography (i.e., rural versus urban), and gender (Bimber, 2000; Ferro et al., 2005; Mossberger et al., 2003). Relevant hypotheses based on the view that the only access matters are:

H1: Income has a positive effect on access to the Internet.
H2: Age has a negative effect on access to the Internet.
H3: Education has a positive effect on access to the Internet.
H4: Attitude about technology has a positive effect on access to the Internet.

H5: Race/ethnicity has a significant effect on access to the Internet.

H6: Geography has a significant effect on access to the Internet.

H7: Gender has a significant effect on access to the Internet.

H8: Access to the Internet has a positive effect on use of the Internet.

A Multi-Dimensional Digital Divide

Another stream of research suggests access to technology is an essential building block for use of ICTs, but that the types of use and patterns of use are equally important and should be considered distinct in analyses (Servon, 2002; Norris, 2001). This view treats access to the ICTs and use of ICTs as something different. DiMaggio and Hargittai (2001) argued:

> As the technology penetrates into every crevice of society, the pressing question will be not "who can find a network connection at home, work, or in a library or community center from which to log on?" but instead, "What are people doing, and what are they able to do, when they go on-line?" (p. 3–4)

Public policy interventions are seen as one of the many ways to close the gap with respect to access and use (Chinn & Fairlie, 2004; Cole, et al., 2004; Mossberger et al., 2003). This stream of research focuses on a variety of contributing dimensions of the divide such as race/ethnicity, income, skills, geography, cultural content, education, and training, as impacting access and use. These factors have been identified in other research as having a long tradition of engendering inequalities, and it is argued that the digital divide simply mirrors the issues of socioeconomic inequality in general (Castells, 2001; Norris, 2001; Warschauer, 2003; Hargittai, 2010).

This view examines both the micro and macro levels of analysis (Dewan & Riggins, 2005). For example, Norris (2001) suggested the digital divide should be understood as macro dimensions with three distinct levels: global, social, and democratic. These three levels are defined as a global divide (or the divergence of Internet access between industrialized and developing nations), a social divide (or the gap between the information-rich and information-poor), and a democratic divide (which is the difference between those who do, and do not use a variety of digital means to engage in public life). Whereas Servon (2002) identified important micro dimensions such as individual training and literacy, and cultural content of Web pages, DiMaggio and Hargittai (2001) combined micro and macro dimensions to provide a list of five factors of digital inequality, including equipment, autonomy of use, skill, social support, and the purpose for which the technology is employed.

The driving assumption in this line of research is that the divide is about access to and use of ICTs, and both are influenced by a number of factors (race, gender, income, education, skill, etc.) There is no consensus among scholars concerning which factors predict ICTs' use; however, it is clear that they agree there are many factors that do, and some are discussed below. Robinson et al. (2003) found education is more consistently associated with increases in Internet use (including types of sites visited, uses made of the Internet, and political engagement), and the higher your education level, the more likely you are to use the Internet. Hargittai (2002) argued that skill, defined as "the ability to efficiently and effectively find information on the Web," determines the likelihood of using the medium to the person's maximum benefit (p. 3). Kennedy et al. (2003) suggested that people with children use the Internet less than people without children and highlighted the arguments for a "gendered approach" to understanding use (Bimber, 2000). Hollifield and Donnermeyer (2003) found that employment by a company has a positive relationship with an individual's adoption of technology. Mossberger et al., (2003) found that use is not related to race when controlling for access. "Place" effects or geography are also important factors of use, such as the differences between urban and rural users, and even regional users (Shelley, Thrane, & Shulman, 2006; Ferro,et al., 2005; Mossberger et al., 2003; Bimber, 2000). Therefore, hypotheses concerning use of and access to the Internet according to the multi-dimensional perspective are the following:

H9: Income has a positive effect on use of the Internet.
H10: Age has a negative effect on use of the Internet.
H11: Education has a positive effect on use of the Internet.
H12: Attitude about technology has a positive effect on use of the Internet.

H13: Race/ethnicity does not have a significant effect on use of the Internet.

H14: Geography (or place) has a relationship to use of the Internet.

H15: Gender has a significant effect on use of the Internet.

H16: Speaking English has a positive effect on access to the Internet.

H17: Speaking English has a positive effect on use of the Internet.

H18: Having a PC at home has a positive effect on access to the Internet.

H19: Having a PC at home has a positive effect on use of the Internet.

H20: PC use has a positive effect on access to the Internet.

H21: PC use has a positive effect on use of the Internet.

H22: Information technology skills have a positive effect on access to the Internet.

H23: Information technology skills have a positive effect on use of the Internet.

H24: Size of household has a significant effect on access to the Internet.

H25: Size of household has a significant effect on use of the Internet.

H26: Employment status has a significant effect on access to the Internet.

H27: Employment status has a significant effect on use of the Internet.

H28: Individual Internet experience has a positive effect on use of the Internet.

H29: Household Internet experience has a positive effect on use of the Internet.

Research Design and Methods

This chapter is based on a survey of 2206 Italians who live in the region of Piedmont. The sample used for the purpose of this paper was created from a database provided by the Italian National Statistical Institute (ISTAT), whose data refer to the periodical census carried out in 2001. The entire data set was collected via Computer Aided Telephone Interviews (CATI), meaning that people without a fixed line are not represented in the sample. The stratified sample was created using a differentiated probability approach in order to over-represent segments with a higher variance in terms of technology adoption and usage (i.e., young versus older people). The variables adopted for the stratification of the sample were: age, gender, and size of town of residence. Following the guidelines provided by the European Statistical Institute, people less than 16 years old were excluded from the sample. Respondents were asked questions about computer ownership, Internet access, and Internet use, among others. Relevant individual demographics and household characteristics were also collected.

Characteristics of the Respondents

Table 2.1 presents some relevant characteristics of individual respondents and their households. The average age of participants is 48 years, and the sample is almost equally split between men (49%) and women (51%). Almost three-fifths of the population (59%) have dependent children, making the average household size slightly less than three persons (2.83). Approximately eight out of ten (45%) have a primary and secondary education, while 38% have an upper-secondary education. Occupation among respondents varied; nearly one-third (31%) identified themselves as employed. The majority of respondents live in either a town (47%) or village (48%). Forty-four percent speak English. Over half of respondents (61%) have a personal computer (PC) at home, about half of them (50%) have Internet access, and slightly less than half (44%) use the Internet.

Table 2.1: *Characteristics of the Individual Respondents and Households*

Variables	Mean	Standard Deviation	Minimum	Maximum
Age	47.67	18.704	16	92
Gender (Female = 1)	0.51	0.500	0	1
Occupation (Employee = 1)	0.31	0.461	0	1
Occupation (Self Employed = 1)	0.10	0.302	0	1
Occupation (Unemployed = 1)	0.06	0.232	0	1
Occupation (Student = 1)	0.10	0.295	0	1
Occupation (Other = 1)	0.44	0.496	0	1
Education (None = 1)	0.05	0.220	0	1

Education (Primary/Sec. = 1)	0.45	0.498	0	1
Education (Upper Secondary = 1)	0.38	0.487	0	1
Education (Tertiary = 1)	0.11	0.318	0	1
Other Language (English = 1)	0.44	0.497	0	1
Internet Use = 1	0.44	0.496	0	1
PC Use = 1	0.53	0.499	0	1
Household Size	2.83	1.189	1	10
Dependent Children	0.59	0.860	0	8
PC at Home = 1	0.61	0.489	0	1
Internet Access = 1	0.50	0.500	0	1
Location (City = 1)	0.06	0.235	0	1
Location (Town = 1)	0.47	0.499	0	1
Location (Village = 1)	0.48	0.500	0	1

Operationalization of Dependent Variables

Generally, Internet access and Internet use are studied as dependent variables, and their operationalization varies from study to study (DiMaggio & Hargittai, 2001). In the last two decades, the sophistication and reach of information and communication technologies (ICTs) and applications has broadened—ICTs include any communication device (such as a computer hooked up to the Internet, radio, satellite systems, cellular phones, etc.) used to communicate with and to access information. While digital divide research has investigated a fair number of different types of technology and connections, there has been a tendency, at least in the United States, to operationalize the term ICT to mean either personal computers (e.g., hardware and software) or the Internet. Clearly, this is one limitation of existing empirical studies. Neil Selwyn (2002) argued that scholars need to reconsider what is meant by ICTs. According to Selwyn, ICTs are a "heterogeneous range of technologies, types of information and resources—not all necessarily analogous to each other" (p. 7).

Warschauer (2003) found that the two most common models of access to technologies are those based on devices and conduits. Access in the sense of a device refers to physical access to a computer or other device, whereas access in the sense of a conduit implies a connection to a "supply line that provides something on a regular basis" (p. 33). For example, Mossberger et al. (2003) used various measures such as access to a computer at home, home access to the Internet, and an e-mail account, to operationalize Internet access. Ferro et al. (2005) used specific access types (i.e., modem or broadband). The way access is characterized often depends on the nature of the complex public problems in need of investigation, and also on the availability of data. This study uses three measures of Internet access: (a) the number of locations where an individual can access the Internet, (b) the number of devices an individual uses to access the Internet, and (c) a dichotomous variable representing whether the individual has access to the Internet or not.

On the other hand, Internet use is also operationalized in different ways in previous literature (Hargittai & Hinnant, 2008). Generally, studies examine the frequency of use and type of use. Bimber (2000) looked at the frequency of Internet use ranging from never to daily. Kennedy, Wellman, and Klement (2003) looked at types of Internet use (i.e., what people actually do when they are on line: meeting new people, searching for information, participating in recreational activities such as games, and engaging in commerce). Some scholars examine capital-enhancing uses or activities that lead to more informed political participation, career enhancement, or general knowledge about finances and health, or explore user typologies (such as netizens, utilitarians, experimenters, or newcomers) for what activities people are exploring online (Hargittai & Hinnant, 2008). This study employs two measures of Internet use: (a) a dichotomous variable representing whether an individual uses the Internet, and (b) the number of distinctive activities that an individual uses the Internet for (extent of use).

Analysis and Main Findings

Based on linear and logistic regression models, this section presents the results of testing the access divide and the multi-dimensional divide views. Overall, it seems that the additional variables suggested by the multi-dimensional view significantly improve the explanatory power of the models. Therefore, other factors, such as gender, employment status, IT skills, PC use, and ability to speak other languages, are important determinants of Internet access and Internet use. The following sections present and describe the results for several specifica-tions of the models for Internet access and Internet use.

Table 2.2: *Determinants of Internet Access (Number of Locations)*

Independent Variables	Access Divide Model		Multi-Dimensional Divide Model	
	Coefficient	T-Statistic	Coefficient	T-Statistic
Constant	0.069	(0.331)	0.497	(2.487)
Income	<0.001***	(4.863)	<0.001*	(1.697)
Age	-0.016***	(-12.940)	-0.001	(-0.346)
Education	0.252***	(8.638)	0.088***	(3.151)
Attitude towards Computers	0.110***	(8.444)	0.049***	(4.048)
Nationality (Italian = 1)	0.103	(0.737)	-0.064	(-0.524)
Location (Town = 1)	-0.027	(-0.323)	-0.069	(-0.929)
Location (Village = 1)	-0.045	(-0.537)	-0.070	(-0.948)
Gender (Female = 1)	-0.149***	(-3.864)	-0.072**	(-2.087)
Other Language (English)			0.093**	(2.178)
PC at Home			0.131***	(2.813)
PC Use			0.706***	(13.267)
IT Skills			0.137***	(3.151)
Household Size			-0.028*	(-1.697)
Occupation (Employee = 1)			-0.588***	(-7.644)
Occupation (Self Employed = 1)			-0.609***	(-6.639)
Occupation (Unemployed = 1)			-0.598***	(-5.662)
Occupation (Other = 1)			-0.774***	(-8.307)
R-square	0.396		0.542	
Adjusted R-square	0.393		0.536	
F-statistic	110.712***		92.956***	

Note. Those coefficients followed by * are significant at the 10% level, those followed by ** are significant at the 5% level, and those followed by *** are significant at the 1% level.

Determinants of Internet Access

Table 2.2 shows the results of an access divide model and a multi-dimensional model using number of locations for accessing Internet as the dependent variable. Examples of locations were home, office, and school. Income is positively associated with Internet access in both specifications: People with higher incomes tend to have access to the Internet in more locations. Age is significant and negatively associated with Internet access in the access divide model but is not significant when controlling for other variables suggested by the multi-dimensional divide view. This suggests that age has an indirect effect on Internet access, and some of the variables included in the multi-dimensional view are mediators between age and access to the Internet. Education and attitudes toward computers have a positive effect on Internet access: Individuals with more formal education and better attitudes toward computers have access to the Internet in more locations. Being female is negatively associated with Internet access: Women have access to the Internet in fewer locations.

Several of the additional variables in the multi-dimensional divide model were also statistically significant. For instance, speaking English is positively associated with Internet access. Having a PC at home and individual use of a PC are positively associated with Internet access. Being involved in an IT training course is positively associated with Internet access. Household size is negatively associated with Internet access. Employment status is a significant predictor of Internet access. For example, individuals who reported to be employed, self-employed, or unemployed have access to the Internet in fewer locations than students. Finally, there is an important adjusted R-square improvement from 0.393 to 0.536, which indicates that the multi-dimensional model explains about 14.3% more of the variance in Internet access than the access divide model.

Table 2.3: *Determinants of Internet Access (Number of Devices)*

Independent Variables	Access Divide Model		Multi-Dimensional Divide Model	
	Coefficient	T-Statistic	Coefficient	T-Statistic
Constant	-0.343**	(-2.232)	-0.217	(-1.537)
Income	<0.001***	(7.675)	<0.001***	(3.813)
Age	-0.009***	(-10.483)	0.002*	(1.776)
Education	0.174***	(8.139)	0.033*	(1.700)
Attitude towards Computers	0.093***	(9.705)	0.038***	(4.450)
Nationality (Italian = 1)	0.164	(1.603)	0.028	(0.319)
Location (Town = 1)	0.079	(1.290)	0.031	(0.593)
Location (Village = 1)	0.049	(0.803)	0.013	(0.240)
Gender (Female = 1)	-0.109***	(-3.860)	-0.047*	(-1.916)
Other Language (English)			0.120***	(3.966)
PC at Home			0.105***	(3.191)
PC Use			0.630***	(16.756)
IT Skills			0.083***	(2.685)
Household Size			0.003	(0.235)
Occupation (Employee = 1)			-0.258***	(-4.744)
Occupation (Self Employed = 1)			-0.264***	(-4.070)

Occupation (Unemployed = 1)	-0.231***	(-3.101)
Occupation (Other = 1)	-0.338***	(-5.132)
R-square	0.407	0.580
Adjusted R-square	0.403	0.575
F-statistic	115.712***	108.750***

Note. Those coefficients followed by * are significant at the 10% level, those followed by ** are significant at the 5% level, and those followed by *** are significant at the 1% level.

Table 2.3 presents the results of an access divide model and a multi-dimensional divide model using the number of devices for Internet access as the dependent variable. Income is positively associated to Internet access: Individuals with higher incomes have more devices to access the Internet. Age is significantly associated with Internet access, but in the access divide model the relationship is negative and in the multi-dimensional model it is positive. Without controlling for some important variables such as speaking other languages PC use, or IT skills, younger individuals tend to have more devices to access the Internet. However, when including all these important variables, older individuals have access to the Internet through more devices. Education and attitude towards computers are positively associated with Internet access. Being female is negatively associated with Internet access measured as the number of devices to access the Internet: Women have fewer devices with which to access to the Internet.

Similar to the previous specifications, several variables related to the multi-dimensional divide were found to be important determinants. Speaking English is positively associated with Internet access. Having a PC at home, and individual use of a PC, are positively associated with Internet access. Information technology skills as represented by an IT training course are positively associated with Internet access. Finally, employment status is a significant determinant of Internet access. Again, all other occupations have fewer devices with which to access the Internet than students. Overall, there was an improvement in adjusted R-square from 0.403 to 0.580, which represents an improvement of 17.7%.

Table 2.4: *Determinants of Internet Access (Dummy Variable)*

Independent Variables	Access Divide Model		Multi-Dimensional Divide Model	
	Coefficient	T-Statistic	Coefficient	T-Statistic
Constant	-3.584***	(22.614)	-23.913	(<0.001)
Income	0.001***	(59.409)	<0.001***	(6.901)
Age	-0.038***	(79.853)	0.013	(1.851)
Education	0.524***	(26.298)	0.080	(0.228)
Attitude towards Computers	0.320***	(44.754)	0.275***	(15.018)
Nationality (Italian = 1)	0.620	(1.555)	-0.115	(0.019)
Location (Town = 1)	0.683**	(5.094)	0.440	(0.954)
Location (Village = 1)	0.636**	(4.460)	0.595	(1.743)
Gender (Female = 1)	-0.160	(1.356)	-0.041	(0.037)
Other Language (English)			0.287	(1.454)
PC at Home			22.011	(<0.001)
PC Use			0.790***	(8.918)
IT Skills			-0.429*	(3.092)
Household Size			0.086	(0.723)
Occupation (Employee = 1)			-0.688	(1.692)
Occupation (Self Employed = 1)			-1.366**	(5.463)
Occupation (Unemployed = 1)			-1.113	(2.621)
Occupation (Other = 1)			-1.538***	(6.809)
-2 Log likelihood	1326.973		625.152	
Cox & Snell R-square	0.328		0.601	
Nagelkerke R-square	0.438		0.802	
Chi-square	534.653***		1233.653***	

Note: Wald-statistics are in parentheses under coefficient values. Those coefficients followed by * are significant at the 10% level, those followed by ** are significant at the 5% level, and those followed by *** are significant at the 1% level.

Table 2.4 shows the results of access divide and multi-dimensional divide logistic regression models, where access was measured as a dichotomous variable (having access or not having access to the Internet). Again, income is positively associated with Internet access: individuals with higher incomes are more likely to have Internet access. Age is negatively associated with Internet access in the access divide model and not statistically significant in the multi-dimensional divide model. Education is positively associated with Internet access in the access divide model but not significant in the multi-dimensional divide model. Once controlling for some important variables such as speaking other languages, PC use, IT skills, and occupation, education does not have an effect on the likelihood of an individual having access to the Internet. Attitude towards computers was positively associated with Internet access. Location (city, town, or village) was a significant determinant of Internet access: Individuals living in towns and villages are more likely to have Internet access than individuals living in cities.

Again, similar to previous specifications, some variables related to the multi-dimensional view were also significant. For instance, PC use was positively associated with Internet access. IT skills were a significant determinant of Internet access, but the sign was negative. Finally, employment status seems to be an important variable, but significant differences were found only between students and self-employed and students and others (which includes, for example, retired individuals). The Cox and Snell R-square improved from 0.328 to 0.601, and the Nagelkerke R-square went from 0.438 to 0.802, suggesting that the additional variables in the multi-dimensional model have an important impact on the percentage of variance explained.

Determinants of Internet Use

Following a similar logic as with Internet access, this section presents the results from several specifications of Internet use models. Overall, the multi-dimensional divide models have greater explanatory power and untangle the complex relationships in a more specific manner. Table 2.5 presents the results of three models using the extent of Internet use as the dependent variable. The extent of use is operationalized as the number of activities an individual performs using the Internet. The first regression model is based purely in the access divide view and therefore considers Internet access as the only relevant factor affecting Internet use directly. The second model includes the factors mentioned in the access divide view but tests direct relationships from all of them to Internet use. Finally, the third model incorporates additional variables related to the multi-dimensional divide view.

Overall, there is an important improvement in adjusted R-square, which went from 0.371 in the access divide model to 0.528 in the extended access divide model, and then to 0.697 in the multi-dimensional divide model. Internet access is positively associated with Internet use in all specifications. Income is positively associated with

Internet use in the extended access divide model but becomes statistically insignificant once other variables have been controlled for. This suggests that once controlling for other important variables such as speaking other languages, PC use, PC use at home, and individual internet experience has been controlled for. Income is not an important determinant of the extent of Internet use. Age is negatively associated with Internet use: older individuals tend to use the Internet for fewer activities than younger individuals. Education and attitude towards computers are positively associated with Internet use: individuals with more formal education and better attitudes toward computers use the Internet for more activities. Being female is negatively associated with Internet use: according to this study, women use the Internet for fewer activities than men.

Similar to Internet access, there were several variables related to the multi-dimensional divide model that were significantly associated to Internet use. For example, speaking English was positively associated with Internet use: individuals who can speak English use the Internet for a greater number of activities. Having a PC at home was negatively associated with Internet use, but individual use of a PC was positively associated with Internet use. Similarly, individual Internet experience was positively associated with the extent of Internet use, but household Internet experience was negatively associated with the extent of individual Internet use. Using a PC tends to lead to Internet use, and using the Internet appears to positively affect the number of activities an individual uses the Internet for. The more experienced users will then use the Internet for more activities in their lives.

Table 2.5: *Determinants of Internet Use (Extent of Use)*

Independent Variables	Access Divide Model		Access Divide Model (Extended)		Multi-Dimensional Divide Model	
	Coefficient	T-Statistic	Coefficient	T-Statistic	Coefficient	T-Statistic
Constant	0.376***	(6.545)	-0.824*	(-1.650)	-0.117	(-0.265)
Internet Access	2.929***	(35.882)	1.842***	(16.408)	1.488***	(9.426)
Income			<0.001***	(2.881)	<0.001	(0.912)
Age			-0.023***	(-7.644)	-0.007**	(-1.964)
Education			0.550***	(7.801)	0.138**	(2.229)
Attitude towards Computers			0.253***	(7.906)	0.099***	(3.706)

Nationality (Italian = 1)			0.276	(0.831)	-0.035	(-0.132)
Location (Town = 1)			0.050	(0.249)	0.051	(0.315)
Location (Village = 1)			-0.012	(-0.060)	0.023	(0.140)
Gender (Female = 1)			-0.554***	(-5.980)	-0.285***	(-3.737)
Other Language (English)					0.201**	(2.120)
PC at Home					-0.484***	(-3.461)
PC Use					1.160***	(9.275)
IT Skills					-0.099	(-1.023)
Household Size					-0.025	(-0.660)
Occupation (Employee = 1)					-0.083	(-0.489)
Occupation (Self Employed = 1)					-0.228	(-1.120)
Occupation (Unemployed = 1)					0.133	(0.570)
Occupation (Other = 1)					-0.184	(-0.891)
Individual Internet Experience					0.368***	(18.430)
Household Internet Experience					-0.089***	(-3.548)
R-square	0.371		0.532		0.701	
Adjusted R-square	0.371		0.528		0.697	
F-statistic	1287.531***		168.124***		152.547***	

Note. Those coefficients followed by * are significant at the 10% level, those followed by ** are significant at the 5% level, and those followed by *** are significant at the 1% level.

Table 2.6 shows the results of the same three models, but using a dichotomous variable to represent Internet use. Similar to the previous set of models, income is positively associated with Internet use in the extended access divide model but is not significant in the multi-dimensional divide model. The explanation is similar: once controlling for other important variables such as speaking other languages, PC use, PC at home, and occupation, income is not an important determinant of the extent of Internet use. Age is negatively associated with Internet use in the extended access divide model but is not significant once one has controlled for other factors. This suggests that age is important in terms of the number of activities an individual uses the Internet for, but it is not necessarily important to explain whether an individual uses the Internet for at least one activity. Education and attitude toward computers are positively associated with Internet use. Being female is negatively associated with Internet use: women are less likely to use the Internet than men.

Several variables related to the multi-dimensional view were also found as important determinants of Internet use. Speaking English is positively associated with Internet use. Individual PC use is positively associated with Internet use, but having a PC at home has a negative effect on Internet use. Employment status is an important determinant of Internet use. Three of the four dummy variables representing employment status were statistically significant, indicating that individuals who are employed, self-employed, or other, are less likely to use the Internet than students. Finally, similar to the previous specifications, household Internet experience has a negative effect on individual Internet use. Having the Internet for a longer period at home negatively affects the likelihood of an individual using the Internet, given that this individual has never before used the Internet.

Table 2.6: *Determinants of Internet Use (Dummy Variable)*

Independent Variables	Access Divide Model		Access Divide Model (Extended)		Multi-Dimensional Divide Model	
	Coefficient	Wald-statistics	Coefficient	Wald-statistics	Coefficient	Wald-statistics
Constant	-2.035***	(465.236)	-5.940***	(32.128)	-7.143***	(19.617)
Internet Access	3.258***	(749.617)	2.783***	(205.766)	2.837***	(48.038)
Income			<0.001**	(5.931)	<0.001	(0.051)
Age			-0.052***	(70.439)	-0.008	(0.568)
Education			0.937***	(45.866)	0.467***	(6.569)
Attitude towards Computers			0.558***	(68.804)	0.457***	(26.508)
Nationality (Italian = 1)			0.878	(1.708)	0.278	(0.073)
Location (Town = 1)			0.085	(0.042)	-0.158	(0.084)
Location (Village = 1)			0.044	(0.011)	0.056	(0.011)
Gender (Female = 1)			-0.712***	(14.491)	-0.428*	(3.028)
Other Language (English)					0.617**	(6.060)

PC at Home			-0.690*	(3.553)
PC Use			4.320***	(129.331)
IT Skills			0.014	(0.003)
Household Size			0.037	(0.109)
Occupation (Employee = 1)			-1.418**	(4.360)
Occupation (Self Employed = 1)			-1.391*	(3.467)
Occupation (Unemployed = 1)			-0.612	(0.524)
Occupation (Other = 1)			-1.680**	(5.007)
Household Internet Experience			-7.143***	(19.617)
-2 Log likelihood	1946.887	791.166	512.667	
Cox & Snell R-square	0.381	0.544	0.628	
Nagelkerke R-square	0.511	0.728	0.841	
Chi-square	1046.738***	1055.026***	1312.777***	

Note. Those coefficients followed by * are significant at the 10% level, those followed by ** are significant at the 5% level, and those followed by *** are significant at the 1% level.

Overall, the explanatory power of the different specifications improved from a Cox and Snell R-square of 0.381 in the access divide model to 0.544 in the extended access divide model, and then to 0.628 in the multi-dimensional divide model. Similar improvements can be observed in the Nagelkerke R-square, where values went from 0.511 to 0.728 and then to 0.841, respectively.

Conclusions

The results of this study provide evidence that multiple variables are important in explaining Internet access and use. Internet access is necessary for Internet use, but it is not the only important factor for an extensive and meaningful use of the Internet. For instance, income is an important determinant of Internet access (measured as a dichotomous variable and number of devices). Individuals need financial resources to buy the necessary equipment for accessing the Internet. However, income is not as important a determinant of Internet use, at least not when controlling for Internet access, availability of equipment, and location. Similarly, IT skills are an important predictor of Internet access but not of Internet use. However, education, which creates a broader set of capabilities, is very important for both Internet access and use. Attitude towards computers, employment status, gender, PC use experience, and the ability to speak English are important determinants of both Internet access and Internet use. Finally, there seems to be a reinforcing dynamic regarding Internet use: the more experience an individual has with the Internet, the more activities this individual performs using it. In contrast, the longer the period of having Internet at home and not using it, the lower the likelihood of an individual starting to use it.

The results show that Internet access is the most important determinant of Internet use. However, other variables are also important, and characterizing the digital divide as being only about access offers a limited understanding of this phenomenon. In fact, it seems clear from the results of this research that once online, not everybody uses the Internet for the same reasons and performs the same activities. For instance, females use the Internet for a smaller number of activities than males. Individuals with more formal education and who can speak English use the Internet for a greater number of activities. Finally, individuals with more experience using a PC and the Internet itself also use the Internet to perform more activities. This is consistent with other studies. For example, Hargittai (2010) found, even when controlling for basic Internet access, among a group of young adults, socioeconomic status is an important predicator of how people are incorporating the Web into their everyday lives, with those from more privileged backgrounds using it in more informed ways for a larger number of activities. (p. 92)

An access divide view also limits the capability of governments to develop appropriate policies that address other interrelated inequalities. In fact, public policies regarding the digital divide need to be re-framed and re-examined given the changes over the last 15 years in technology and patterns of ICT use. These policies should also take into consideration that virtual inequalities are the result of other inequalities in terms of education, gender, income, ability to speak foreign languages, IT skills, employment status, etc. The complexity of the associated social problems and their implications for the success of digital divide policies and programs needs to be fully understood, and future research should explore these relationships.

More recently, there has been a call to re-theorize technology and its relationship to race, gender, citizenship, and culture (Helbig, Gil-Garcia, Ferro, 2009; James, 2008; Mossberger et al., 2006; Shelly et al., 2006; Kennedy et al., 2003; Castells, 2001). In this line of research, government policy and programs are seen as a viable way of closing various inequality gaps. Scholars suggest that efforts to address different divides should begin by understanding the needs and problems of those who are most disadvantaged (Crenshaw, 1989; Kennedy et al., 2003; Servon, 2002; Hines et al., 2001). Similarly, Shelly et al. (2006) concluded, "Programmes and training must be sensitive to marginalised citizens' needs and real-life concerns" (p. 240). Future research should explore how the relationships between Internet access, Internet use, and their outcomes, are similar or different for different social groups, representing multiple and very different situations and perspectives.

From a policy maker point of view the awareness of the complexity inherent in the digital divide represents a prerequisite for the implementation of corrective and effective actions. Nevertheless, many challenges still need to be overcome. Firstly, moving the focus of government policies away from the expansion of the existing network coverage to demand stimulation poses a number of challenges having to do with the way government agencies are organized. As a matter of fact, demand stimulation actions cut across agencies' competences (education, professional training, unemployment, social services, etc.) and require a higher level of inter-agency coordination and collaboration for the implementation of an integrated policy strategy. Secondly, the significant variance present in society in terms of interests, skills, and education often results in very different policy needs. Such heterogeneity requires policy makers to engage in a more profound relationship with the citizenry in order to identify and respond to the different needs. Therefore, a single-offer expansion strategy will no longer suffice and should be replaced by a carefully targeted portfolio of policy actions.

Acknowledgments

The authors want to thank the valuable comments and suggestions from Luis F. Luna-Reyes, Paul Baker, and John Bertot in previous versions of this chapter. A previous version of this study was presented at the Fifth International Conference on Electronic Government, organized by DEXA, September 4–8, Krakow, Poland, 2006. The study was also partially supported by the National Science Foundation under grant No. 0131923 and grant No. 0630239. The views and conclusions expressed in this chapter are those of the authors alone and do not necessarily reflect the views of NSF.

References

Adriani, F., & Becchetti, L. (2003). *Does the digital divide matter? The role of ICT in cross-country level and growth estimates.* CEIS Tor Vergata. doi: 10.1080/1043859042000304043

Bimber, B. (2000). Measuring the gender gap on the Internet. *Social Science Quarterly, 81*(3).

Castells, M. (2001). *The Internet galaxy. Reflections on the Internet, business, and society.* New York, NY: Oxford University Press.

Chinn, M. D., & Fairlie, R. W. (2004). *The determinants of the global digital divide: A cross-country analysis of computer and Internet penetration.* Economic Growth Center, Yale University. doi: 10.1093/oep/gpl024

Cole, J. I., Susman, M., Schramm, P., Lunn, R., Aquino, J. (2004). The digital future report. USC Center for the Digital Future. Retrieved from http://www.digitalcenter.org/downloads/DigitalFutureReport-Year4-2004.pdf

Compaine, B. M. (2001, July). *Re-examining the digital divide. Internet and Telecom Consortium,* MIT. Retrieved from http://hdl.handle.net/1721.1/1521

Compaine, B. M. (Ed.). (2001). *The digital divide: Facing a crisis or creating a myth?* Cambridge, MA: MIT Press.

Crenshaw, K. (1999). Demarginalizing the intersection of race and sex: A black feminist critique of antidiscrimination doctrine, feminist theory, and antiracist politics. In K. T. Bartlett & R. Kennedy (Eds.), *Feminist legal theory: Readings in law and gender.* Boulder, CO: Westview Press.

Dewan, S., & Riggins, F.J. (2005). The digital divide: Current and future research directions. *Journal of the Association of Information Systems*, 6 (12), 298-337.

DiMaggio, P., & Hargittai, E. (2001). From the "digital divide" to digital inequality: Studying Internet use as penetration increases. Working Paper 15, Center for the Arts and Cultural Policy Studies, Woodrow Wilson School, Princeton University. Retrieved from http://www.princeton.edu/~artspol/workpap/WP15%20-20DiMaggio%2BHargittai.pdf

Ferro, E., Cantamessa, M., Paolucci, E. (2005). Urban versus regional divide: Comparing and classifying digital divide. TCGOV'05 *Proceedings of the 2005 International Conference on E-Government: Towards Electronic Democracy, 3416*, 81-90. doi: 10.1007/978-3-540-32257-3_8

Hargittai, E. & Hinnant, A. (2008). Digital inequality: Differences in young adults' use of the Internet. *Communication Research, 35* (5), 602-621.

Hargittai, E. (2010). Digital na(t)ives?: Variations in Internet skills and uses among members of the 'net generation.' *Sociological Inquiry, 80* (1), 92-113.

Hargittai, E. (2002). Second-level digital divide: Differences in people's online skills. *First Monday, 7*(4).

Helbig, N., Gil-Garcia, J. R., & Ferro, E. (2009). Understanding the complexity of electronic government: Implications from the digital divide literature. *Government Information Quarterly, 26*(1), 89-97.

Hines, A.H., Nelson, A., & Tu, T.L. N. (2001). Hidden circuits. 1-12, In Nelson, A., Tu, T.L. & Hines, A.H. (eds.), Technicolor. NY: New York University Press.

Hoffman, D. L., Novak, T. P., & Schlosser, A. (2000). The evolution of the digital divide: How gaps in Internet access may impact electronic commerce. *Journal of Computer-Mediated Communication, 5*(3).

Hollifield, A. C., & Donnermeyer, J. F. (2003). Creating demand: Influencing information technology diffusion in rural communities. *Government Information Quarterly, 20*, 135-150.

James, J. (2008). Digital divide complacency: Misconceptions and dangers. *Information Society, 24*, (1), 54-61.

Kennedy, T., Wellman, B., & Klement, K. (2003). Gendering the digital divide. *IT & Society, 1*(5), 72-96.

Mack, C.S., Thrane, L.E., and Shulman, S.W., (2006). Generational differences in information technology use and political involvement. *International Journal of Electronic Government Research, 2* (1), 36-53.

Mossberger, K., Tolbert, C. J., & Stansbury, M. (2003). *Virtual inequality: Beyond the digital divide*. Washington, DC: Georgetown University Press.

Norris, P. (2001). *Digital divide: Civic engagement, information poverty, and the Internet worldwide*. New York, NY: Cambridge University Press.

Ostling, A. (2010). ICT in politics: From peaks of inflated expectations to voids of disillusionment. *European Journal of e Practice, 9*. Retrieved from http://eui.academia.edu/AlinaOstling/Papers/637297/ICT_in_politics_fro m_peaks_of_inflated_expectations_to_voids_of_disillusionment

Robinson, J. P., DiMaggio, P., & Hargittai, E. (2003). New social survey perspectives on the digital divide. *IT & Society, 1*(5), 1–22.

Selwyn, N. (2002). Defining the "digital divide": Developing a theoretical understanding of inequalities in the information age. Cardiff University School of Social Sciences Occasional Paper 49, 330–967.

Servon, L. J. (2002). *Bridging the digital divide: Technology, community, and public policy*. Oxford, England: Blackwell.

Walsh, E.O., Gazala, M.E., and Ham, C. (2003). The truth about the digital divide. 279-284. In Compaign, B.M., (ed.), Re-examining the digital divide: Facing a crisis or creating a myth? Cambridge, MA: MIT Press.

Warschauer, M. (2003). *Technology and social inclusion: Rethinking the digital divide*. Cambridge, MA: MIT Press.

Gerard Goggin

Introduction

People with disabilities constitute a very diverse group across the world, varying according to impairment type, cultural notions of disability, the place of disability in societies, class, gender, status, and education. Estimates vary, but people with disabilities, especially in Western countries, are usually believed to number up to 20% of the world's population. For various reasons, developing countries report lower prevalence of disability, and so "a worldwide estimate of about a 10%–12% rate of disability seems reasonable" (World Bank, 2009; also Mont, 2007). There is an "intricate" link between disability and poverty, with people with disabilities being "among the poorest of the poor" (Mont & Loeb, 2008; Braithwaite & Mont, 2009). In developing countries especially, disability poses challenges for education, for instance, with disability "a stronger correlate of non-enrolment in school than either gender or class" (Lord et al., 2010, p. 2).

Disability, then, is a significant social category. Although much research is needed regarding disability and information technology, there is significant evidence to show that people with disabilities loom large among the unconnected.

It was during the early 1990s that disability came to be seriously discussed as an issue for justice, participation, and engagement in the information society and began to be incorporated and given serious attention in policy and research. This occurred slowly, with the broadening of debates beyond the narrow digital divide concept (Katz & Rice, 2002; Warschauer, 2004). Some scholars postulated a "disability digital divide" (Brewer, 2001, p. 66.4) or "disability divide" (Dobransky & Hargittai, 2006), "calling to attention the fact that there are aspects of the digital divide that are specific to individuals with disabilities" (Bricout, Baker, Ward, & Moon, 2009, p. 157).

If disability was a late inclusion in notions of participation and digital technologies, especially the Internet, that went under the US-influenced "digital divide," then it was even more of a laggard, or outlier, in accounts of the information society. The information society, we recall, stems from the Japanese high-technology concepts of the 1970s and the French appropriation of this (Webster, 2006). The information society has been an important way of imagining the relationships between society and information and communication technologies during the 1990s and 2000s. It is in this period that disability has been admitted into planning and visions for the information society—and its notional inclusion has posed challenges and highlighted the need to rethink not only the terms of inclusion (Clear, 2000) but the imaginary of the information society itself.

A development that shifted the terrain for conceptualizing disability and information technology came with the wide-ranging conceptualization of justice and participation to be found in civil society contributions to the World Summit on the Information Society. Then came the high-water mark of aspirations for connecting disability, which, for the present, remains the declaration of the United Nations Convention on the Rights of Persons with Disability, adopted in December 2006 (hereafter the UN Disability Convention). Despite these advances, it is the argument of this chapter that people with disabilities still lack visibility and comprehension when it comes to discussions of connection, participation, and engagement in the information age. Accordingly, this chapter discusses disability as a key part of understanding the "unconnected."

The broad approach taken here is to regard disability as a socio-cultural and political phenomenon that is dynamic and variable, and takes on different forms, meanings, and identities across cultures. Thus I draw upon the literature and theoretical frameworks developed in critical disability studies (Goggin & Newell, 2005; Meekosha & Shuttleworth, 2009; Shakespeare, 2006; Shildrick, 2012). In tandem with this, my approach is informed by the concept of social shaping of technology, and other allied ideas, developed through social studies of science and technology (Goggin & Newell, 2003; Johnson & Wetmore,

2009; Latour, 2005; McKenzie & Wajcman, 1999). Actually, it turns out that disability is an excellent, thought-provoking case in point of the value of critical theories of technology and society—so this will hopefully be a useful thread running through this chapter, which adds something significant to our understanding of theories of social exclusion, inclusion, and disconnection in information technologies.

In what follows, firstly, I sketch the context for understanding disability and information and communication technologies. While access has improved, many problems still remain, due to affordability, training, cultural capital, and literacy but also inaccessibility of applications, interfaces, programs, and equipment. At the heart of the issues regarding the unconnectedness of people with disabilities are profound issues concerning design. The affordances of the various layers of technology, not least the conduits that are the infrastructure, are not systematically reflected upon and interrogated for how they enable or constrain users with disabilities. Secondly, to better understand the processes of unconnecting users with disability, we need to look at the new forms of communication being practised by various groups of people with disabilities through digital cultures and technologies. Here, we find an intriguing interaction between flourishing experimentation and everyday user innovation and the information "have-less" that many people with disabilities structurally become in the contemporary digital environment. Having established the context for grasping people with disabilities as a group that forms part of the "unconnected," I look at the prospects for new, just, better-designed digital technologies. I consider how the UN Disability Convention provides a strong international framework, featuring many provisions specifically regarding better accessibility, design, media content, and cultural participation for this group. Finally, I consider how connection is being reshaped in light of this, not least in the new kinds of crucial media and urban environments, the new media cities (McQuire, 2008; Sundaram, 2010) in which new connections for people with disabilities could either unfold or be stymied.

Disability and the Information Society

What kind of access to communication and information technologies do people with disabilities enjoy? It is difficult to specify with any precision the state of play of connection of people with disabilities to the information society. While the international community, especially through the International Telecommunications Union, has redoubled its efforts to build a detailed picture of access to, and use of, information and communications technologies by all in the world—especially those poorer citizens—there is a lack of reliable statistics on people with disabilities. Commenting on a 2008 report on the Global Information Society, Waddell observed

> that most reporting countries are able to disaggregate Internet use data by individual characteristics, such as age, level of education and gender. In this case the country statistics demonstrate a lack of metadata and ICT indicators for ICT accessibility and its use by persons with disabilities. (Waddell, 2009)

Waddell suggested examples of useful indicators, including:

> How many persons with disabilities use the Internet?

> How many cell phones are in use with navigation and menus that speak out loud for persons with visual disabilities?

> How many text telephones are in operation and how many people use them?

> How many Total Conversation services are in place and how many people use them?

> How many talking ATMS are in operation? (Waddell, 2009)

Article 31 of the UN Disability Convention requires countries to gather statistics in order to implement the treaty, and while this is doubtless underway, progress is slow. For instance, the annual World Telecommunication/ICT Development Report 2010 contains only two mentions of disability, let alone any indicators or targets (ITU, 2010b). The welter of other ITU data, with a strong focus on "digital divide" issues (for instance, see the ITU's ICT Eye Web site, http://www.itu. int/ITU-D/icteye/, ITU, 2010a), especially in the wake of the World Summit on the Information Society, does not yet include disability and accessibility.

Europe has perhaps undertaken the most comprehensive work mapping disability and ICTs statistically through its eAccessibility program, which forms part of its Information Society initiatives. Its 2007 study, and the 2008 follow-up report, found that "there was only limited progress towards eAccessibility detected in Europe" (EU, 2010). In particular the European Commission (EC) highlighted:

> The eAccessibility"deficit." People with disabilities in Europe continue to be confronted with many barriers to usage of the everyday ICT products and services that are now essential elements of social and economic life. Such eAccessibility deficits can be found across the spectrum of ICT products and services, for example, telephony, TV, web and self-service terminals.
>
> The eAccessibility "gap." From a comparative perspective, the eAccessibility situation for people with disabilities across Europe as a whole, in terms of both eAccessibility status and eAccessibility policy, compares very unfavourably withcomparison countries examined in the MeAC study [Australia, Canada, and the US].
>
> The eAccessibility "patchwork." ...both eAccessibility status and eAccessibility policy is very much a patchwork at present. The overall picture shows many important gaps, uneven attention across the spectrum of eAccessibility themes, and wide disparities across the Member States. (EU, 2010)

In 2008, the EC expressed its dismay and declared:

> As our society is evolving to an "information society," we are becoming intrinsically more dependent on technology-based products and services in our daily lives. Yet poor e-accessibility means many Europeans with a disability are still unable to access the benefits of the information society. ...Web accessibility, especially the accessibility of public administration websites, has emerged as a high priority due to the growing importance of the Internet in everyday life. The Commission considers it is now urgent to achieve a more coherent, common and effective approach to e-accessibility, in particular web accessibility, to hasten the advent of an accessible information society. (EC, 2008)

Even when it comes to the "low-hanging fruit" of basic accessibility of government Web sites, people with disabilities remain firmly among those poorly connected or unconnected, as a 2009 report revealed:

> Levels of full compliance with existing web accessibility guidelines...remain very low and, at current rates of progress, the web accessibility situation across the EU seems set to fall far short of the targets set for 2010 in the Riga Declaration. (Cullen & Kubitschke, 2009)

There is even less information about how well people with disabilities are connected in developing countries and in what way. However, there is good reason to suspect that the situation for people with disabilities in relation to the information society is even more parlous in those countries. The UN's Global Alliance for Inclusive Information and Communication Technologies notes that: "two thirds of [people with disabilities in the world] are in developing countries...these demographic circumstances present considerable challenges on the one hand, and enormous opportunities on the other, for the increasingly important role of ICTs" (G3ict, 2010).

Something that particularly affects developing countries is the state of play of the availability and affordability of appropriately designed technologies, as the Global Alliance further suggests that

> similar to many emerging technology markets, accessible and assistive ICT solutions and products can proliferate only through standardization, economies of scale, and reduced production costs. While major ICT vendors realize that people with disabilities represent a significant market opportunity and understand the societal need, progress is slow when measured against current potential. (G3ict, 2010)

Thus far, I have sketched a very high-level, aggregate picture of access of people with disabilities to what are regarded by policymakers as the key services and technologies. The actual situation is far more complex. It is more complicated, for a reason that also applies to users in general, namely that what we term the information society, or similar, consists of layered, interdependent, iterable, complex ecologies of infrastructures, services, applications, and devices. Yet there is a particular additional reason why things are trickier still when it comes to disability. The "affordances" that arise as the sum of these contingent, global, yet localized ecologies have largely unrecognized consequences for people with disabilities that enable, constrain, channel, and modify use.

Because of the policies of deregulation and liberalization as well as the intermixed developments in technology, society, and cultures of users, the onus is increasingly placed on the user to integrate quite disparate technologies into a system each can use. For people with disabilities this requires even greater knowledge of options and how to modify technology, because accessibility is not often built into each infrastructure, service, or application; it certainly is rarely thought through from an end-to-end, interconnected, holistic perspective. This conundrum can be illustrated by an example of contemporary interest: mobile Internet. How does a user with a disability—say, a person who is blind—gain access to the various forms of mobile Internet? Depending on their vision impairment, user preferences, and literacy and expertise in the technology, they would at least need to put together a kit that comprised a mobile phone or media device, a suitable screenreader or other software, accessible apps, and an affordable mobile Internet connection. Each of these steps has pitfalls because the entire solution is not offered by many mainstream providers (the large or small businesses or shops that sell mobiles and Internet equipment and packages). I'll return to this example, but for the present let's explore the "user" picture—the ways in which various groups of people with disabilities have domesticated information technologies.

Do-It-Yourself Connections: Disabled User Innovation

In the interstices of the information society that has taken shape over the past four decades there has been a great, yet unnoticed, efflorescence of innovative use of technology by people with disabilities. That there exists such a dialectic at the heart of the symbiotic relationship between disability and technology that contributes hundreds of millions of people to the pool of those unconnected is a thesis that would require a much more elaborate argument (for instance, see Goggin & Newell, 2003). However, a classic example is the introduction of the Microsoft Windows operating system. A certain amount of accessibility had been possible with the previous MS-DOS operating system, which could work satisfactorily with screenreaders used by people who are blind and those with vision impairments. With the advent of graphical user interfaces (GIUs), Microsoft introduced its Windows OS in the second half of the 1990s, and suddenly the personal computer once more become inaccessible to those using screenreaders. It took a battle royale to persuade Microsoft to redesign Windows to once again become accessible (Goggin & Newell, 2003). With the advent of the personal computer, we see millions of users with disabilities finding uses for the technology—though they were not envisaged as users of the technology in any full sense. This occurs more fitfully than it might, notably with the supplementation of assistive technology or specialized software (such as screenreaders), but there is an increaseof the participation of people with disabilities in the public and private sphere through this.

The Internet has become an especially important site of the technology and media transformations, because it brings together (indeed underlies) the complex ecology of networks that underpins such developments. In overlapping waves, people with disabilities have developed new cultures of use centring on the Internet. This is clearly observable with email, both in interpersonal communication but also through collective forms such as email lists. For blind users who previously had to rely on intermediaries to write, post, and open letters, or to read documents or news items, email enabled new kinds of communication, media forms, and community creation and extension.

From the early 1990s onward, the World Wide Web brought with it new possibilities. With the development of the World Wide Web consortium (W3C) Web accessibility initiative (WAI) standards, those developing and offering Web sites were encouraged, and increasingly required, to code for accessibility. As we have seen, almost two decades after, basic Web accessibility standards are still not widely observed. Yet people with disabilities themselves were able to access a greater range of material through Web sites—despite barriers. They were also able to create their own Web sites. To generalize, the Internet afforded people with disabilities access to media, and thus the public sphere, in the same way it has done with many other minority and marginalized groups who historically have not been well served by existing commercial, public service, or community media (Goggin & Newell, 2007b; Goggin & McLelland, 2009).

The momentum accumulating around disabled-user innovation through the Internet gathered pace with the advent at the turn of the century of always-on broadband, and social media. With the rise of the blog we can witness the development of unique media forms coined by people with disabilities (Goggin & Noonan, 2006). Blind people took to audio blogs and Internet radio through blogging. Deaf communities developed video blogs that could use sign language, bandwidth permitting. Cross-disability concepts and practices emerged which saw blogs contribute to a kind of "disabled public sphere"—as well as broadening the diversity possible in other counter, and mainstream, public spheres. With the appearance of YouTube and do-it-yourself broadcasting, we see people able to make videos about a wide range of aspects of disability and make them available to both large and small audiences around the world.

There are many more examples of this user innovation by people with disabilities. Further research, analysis, and debate about the nature and significance of such practices and cultures are well overdue also. Ahead of this, there are real signs of how people with disabilities are inventively "making do" with the technology (cf. Daniels, 2010). Yet still, however, there is little recognition of the appropriation of technology and what it suggests about the need to radically broaden our ideas about the information society.

Social Justice, New Media, and the UN Disability Convention

The broad state of connectivity for people with disabilities is an uneven, lopsided affair, with inaccessibility improving only slowly (despite quite some effort) on the one hand and rich user innovation on the other hand. So wherein lies the path for social justice in this precinct of the real and imagined information society? A good place to look for the answer is in the UN Disability Convention.

The Disability Convention is an epochal development in the recognition of human rights for persons with disabilities—indeed for human rights in general. What is remarkable about the Disability Convention is the prominence accorded to recognizing the importance of new media technologies to the participation of people with disabilities in public and private life. In short, that something like an information society is not simply dawning, rather it is substantially here. The Disability Convention articulates the rights of persons with disabilities to such technologies. In doing so, it not only represents a long-overdue recognition of this aspect of citizenship and social inclusion for people with disabilities, it actually recasts and deepens our very understanding of the importance of connection, in all its senses, for social and cultural citizenship.

To provide some historical perspective, consider the 1948 Universal Declaration of Human Rights. The Declaration contains important reference to rights of expression, as stated in Article 19: "Everyone has the right to freedom of opinion and expression; this right includes freedom to hold opinions without interference and to seek, receive and impart information and ideas through any media and regardless of frontiers" (UN, 1948).

Sixty years on we would also link the right to impart ideas through media with the original articles regarding cultural rights and participation in cultural life set out in Articles 22 and 27:

Article 22.

Everyone, as a member of society...is entitled to realization, through national effort and international co-operation and in accordance with the organization and resources of each State, of the economic, social and cultural rights indispensable for his dignity and the free development of his personality.

Article 27.

(1) Everyone has the right freely to participate in the cultural life of the community, to enjoy the arts and to share in scientific advancement and its benefits. (UN, 1948)

Subsequently, the international community has built upon such principles with the efforts through UNESCO on the "New World Information and Communication Order" (MacBride, 1980), and the International Telecommunications Union's work on telecommunications and development, most recently in the World Summit on the Information Society (Raboy & Landry, 2005; Servaes & Carpentier, 2006). Communication and media scholars and activists have also theorized and debated the nature of communication and cultural citizenship rights (Dakroury, Eid, & Kamalipour, 2009), forming part of the wider conception and ensemble of human rights.

The existing international treaty framework, the domestic human rights and anti-discrimination law and policy arrangements as well as the existing norms and practice regarding technology have led to a very slow, indeed at times hostile and difficult, process for people with disabilities wishing to exercise their rights to social, economic, cultural, and other participation through digital technology (Goggin & Newell,

2003, 2007a, & 2007b). There are notable achievements worldwide in access, inclusion, and design of people with disabilities in technology, especially from the application of various national general anti-discrimination laws such as, in the Anglophone world, the 1990 US Americans with Disabilities Act, the Australian 1992 Disability Discrimination Act, and the 1995 UK Disability Discrimination Act, as well as other specific laws, regulations, and social policy, but puzzling gaps and most regrettable exclusions remain (Goggin & Newell, 2003 & 2007a). This is curious given that the 1990s was the period when the Internet's diffusion sharply increased around the world and mobile phones became commonplace, and yet, people with disabilities had to fight many battles for belated and poor access (Goggin & Newell, 2003 & 2006).

Against this history, it is noteworthy indeed that among the general obligations of the UN Disability Convention set out in Article 4 are unprecedented and powerful requirements for states to pursue research and development of universal design and for new technology (especially with reference to affordability) and to provide accessible information to people with disabilities concerning a range of mobility aids, devices, and technologies:

f) To undertake or promote research and development of universally designed goods, services, equipment and facilities...;

g) To undertake or promote research and development of, and to promote the availability and use of new technologies, including information and communications technologies, mobility aids, devices and assistive technologies, suitable for persons with disabilities, giving priority to technologies at an affordable cost;

h) To provide accessible information to persons with disabilities about mobility aids, devices and assistive technologies, including new technologies, as well as other forms of assistance, support services and facilities. (Article 4, CRPD)

Article 9 follows with specific obligations regarding accessibility, including that:

States Parties shall take appropriate measures to ensure to persons with disabilities access, on an equal basis with others, to the physical environment, to transportation, to information and communications, including information and communications technologies and systems, and to other facilities and services open or provided to the public, both in urban and in rural areas. (Article 9, clause 1, CRPD)

States Parties are also charged with taking "appropriate measures"

> g) To promote access for persons with disabilities to new information and communi-
> cations technologies and systems, including the Internet;
>
> h) To promote the design, development, production and distribution of accessible
> information and communications technologies and systems at an early stage, so that
> these technologies and systems become accessible at minimum cost. (Article 9, clause
> 2, CRPD)

In the declaration of the Disability Convention, these provisions concerning rights to technology appear quite early on in the document. When these statements regarding rights of people with disabilities to access to information and ideas do occur, the spirit and principles of the 1948 UN Declaration are suitably rendered to capture the realities of today's media environment:

> States Parties shall take all appropriate measures to ensure that persons with disabili-
> ties can exercise the right to freedom of expression and opinion, including the free-
> dom to seek, receive and impart information and ideas on an equal basis with others
> and through all forms of communication of their choice, as defined in article 2 of the
> present Convention, including by:
>
> a) Providing information intended for the general public to persons with disabilities
> in accessible formats and technologies appropriate to different kinds of disabilities in
> a timely manner and without additional cost...
>
> d) Encouraging the mass media, including providers of information through the In-
> ternet, to make their services accessible to persons with disabilities;
>
> e) Recognizing and promoting the use of sign languages. (Article 22, CRPD)

I have quoted the Convention declaration's provisions at some length because of their significance for greatly advancing the international understanding of what it means to connect people with disabilities to society through information and communication technologies. It really is a remarkable document. That said, much work is going on presently regarding the implementation of the Convention, and this will ultimately determine its success. Yet it is fair to say that the Convention is already enormously important for its endorsement and articulation of disability and human rights—but also for its recognition of the importance of technology to this end. Of course, there are significant shortcomings in the Convention document, and there are also critiques to be made of the technology provisions. For example, while it is heartening to see questions of design given such prominence, universal design is not a panacea (Goggin & Newell, 2007b). It can be argued that the Convention itself ushered in new power relations of disability in this embrace of universal design. Universal design is certainly an important approach when it comes to addressing issues of accessibility and disability, but it cannot sum up, and solve, all the issues of exclusion that will continue to be raised. This is evident when we tackle the question of how to move forward, with and beyond the UN Disability Convention—in the most profound sense, to re-imagine and re-design technology and its social relations for connecting all.

The scale of the challenge is evident if we consider the new direction in the information society that comes from the dynamic area of smartphones. Here there are considerable contradictions and tensions. For example, when introduced in mid-2007, Apple's iPhone was relatively inaccessible to blind users—because the menu was navigated by vision and touch. The user could neither rely upon the tactility of pressing buttons (previously the standard for mobile phones) nor upon screenreader software (easy to acquire, if expensive, for many brands of mobile phones, such as Nokia, with Symbian operating systems). Two years later, in 2009, Apple finally upgraded its operating system to include the quite good accessibility software that ships as standard on its Mac computers. And it was not just blind users who were satisfied with this; many others also acclaimed the iPhone as a break-through in accessibility.

In 2011, there are finally promising signs of accessibility and useful affordances emerging from different parts of the smartphone arena (both Apple's iPhone and iPad and Google's Android system). Moreover, the new phenomenon of mobile apps is an area attracting much interest too. The Apple iPhone galvanized user and developer interest in mobile data and applications. Of particular note was the possibility of apps bringing about a metamorphosis of the mobile, taking it well beyond both its identity as "phone" or, in Apple's case, as "computer" (or computing device) (Goggin, 2011). A workshop at the Internet Governance Forum in Vilnius, Lithuania, in September 2010, asked "Can mobile 'apps' create a new golden age of accessibility?"

Apps hold tremendous promise to help those with disabilities to connect and participate. Today applications such as voice control and others are available giving a new
meaning to accessibility. Is this the beginning of a new age of accessibility?...Will this
be a "need" transformed into an "affordable reality" for the community? (IGF, 2010)

As the case of the iPhone reveals, even companies such as Apple are
motivated to redesign their fashionable products in order to comply
with legislation on accessibility and design. Yet such action can be a
long time coming.

Conclusion: Designing for Disability Connections

There is clearly much work to be done if we are to embrace all in
our society, informationally or otherwise. The action to be taken needs
to happen on a number of inter-linked levels—urgently, comprehensive-
ly, and with great persistence.

To underpin and deepen governmental action at national and
international levels, we can develop much better statistics, data, research, and identification and mapping of use and consumption of
technologies by people with disabilities. For instance, we could bring
together the evolving discussion on human rights indicators for people
with disability (French, 2008) with the discussion on indicators for
access to information and communication technologies, developed by
the UN and ITU coming from the World Summit on Information
Society (ITU, 2009). There is very little reliable national, let alone cross-
national, data on disability and ICTs. Yet we have an excellent example
in the UN-ITU's data-gathering efforts on ICTs, which could be easily
extended to capture and report on disability and accessibility.

Such measures, if undertaken, are certainly promising, yet there is a
perhaps irreducible complexity to achieving human and communication rights regarding technology that goes to the heart of the creative
enterprise that is design and the trade-offs that are made when technologies are designed, implemented, and shaped by their inventors and fall
into the hands of their users. There is recognition now of the important
role that users as "everyday innovators" (Haddon et al., 2005) play in
the design of technology (Von Hippel, 2005), namely that quite often
they are co-creators, customizing or being "produsers" (Bruns, 2008). To
genuinely involve the users of the iPhone, for instance—whether the

dissenting users who are blind, cited above, or the various other users with disabilities not catered to in the iPhone decision—takes an opening up of design processes, to admit feedback and participation. It also takes resources and according of power and capacity to users and consumer groups as a counter-balance to the large corporate interests still dominant in technology.

Thus we need serious levels of resourcing for disability self-advocacy organisations and experts on disabilities in order to maintain and build capacity to participate in policy and standards development. The challenge in digital technologies and accessibility revolves around the welter of different technologies, interfaces, standards, and relationships between general and assistive technologies (Annable, Goggin, & Stienstra, 2007).

So there is much to be negotiated and worked out (indeed fought out) about how mobile phones and wireless technologies get developed, how online worlds evolve for the diverse needs and desires of people with disabilities, or the manner in which digital broadcasting ensures media access when it comprises things as diverse as digital television, audio and video blogging, YouTube, and Internet radio (Goggin, & Noonan, 2006). Real advances are made when people with disabilities can be integrally involved in research and development and in all stages of design and implementation. To make this possible, there must be dramatically greater resources available for such work, and we need to invest in capacity building, education, training, and career development for people with disabilities in the sphere of digital technology and other areas of technology.

As well as the importance of technologies to communication and cultural rights, as part of general human rights, there is a special significance to work in this area. Notably, digital technologies offer a fertile sphere for discussion, lobbying, and critique about disability and human rights. A number of commentators have noted that digital technologies were vitally important to the development of the Convention. They are also likely to grow in importance for achieving progress in disability and human rights. Education is crucial to making human rights a reality (Newell & Offord, 2008), and online, digital technologies are now a vital part of such a pedagogical project across all levels of society.

References

Annable, G., Goggin, G., & Stienstra, D. (2007). Accessibility and inclusion in information technologies. *The Information Society, 23*(3), 145–147.

Australian Communications Consumer Action Network (ACCAN) (2009). *Future consumer: Emerging consumer issues in telecommunications and convergent communication and media.* Sydney, Australia: ACCAN.

Braithwaite, J., & Mont, D. (2009). Disability and poverty: A survey of World Bank poverty assessments and implications. *ALTER: European Journal of Disability Research, 3*, 219–232.

Brewer, J. (2001). Access to the World Wide Web: Technical and policy perspectives. In W. F. E. Preiser & E. Ostroff (Eds.), *Universal design handbook* (pp. 66.1ff). New York, NY: McGraw-Hill.

Bricout, J. C., Baker, P. M. A., Ward, A. C., & Moon, N. W. (2009). Teleworking and the "disability divide." In E. Ferro, Y. Kumar Dwivedi, J. Ramon Gil-Garcia, & M. D. Williams (Eds.), *Handbook of research on overcoming digital divides: Constructing an equitable and competitive information society* (pp. 155–178). Hershey, PA: IGI.

Bruns, A. (2008). *Blogs, Wikipedia, Second Life, and beyond: From production to produsage.* New York, NY: Peter Lang.

Campbell, F. K. (2009). *Contours of ableism: The production of disability and abledness.* New York, NY: Palgrave Macmillan.

Clear, M. (Ed.). 2000. *Promises, promises: Disability and terms of inclusion.* Sydney, Australia: Federation Press.

Cornes, P. (1991). Impairment, disability, handicap and new technology. In M. Oliver (Ed.), *Social work: Disabled people and disabling environments.* London, England: Jessica Kingsley.

CRIS Campaign (2005) *Assessing communication rights: A handbook.* Retrieved from http://centreforcommunicationrights.org/images/stories/database/tools/cris-manual-en.pdf

Cullen, K., & Kubitschke, L. (2009). *Web accessibility in European countries: Level of compliance with latest international accessibility specifications, notably WCAG 2.0, and approaches or plans to implement those specifications.* Bonn, Germany: European Commission.

Dakroury, A., Eid, M., & Kamalipour, Y. R. (Eds.). (2009). *The right to communicate: Historical hopes, global debates and future premises.* Dubuque, IA: Kendall Hunt.

Daniels, S. (2010). *Making do: Innovation in Kenya's informal economy.* Analogue Digital. Retrieved from http://analoguedigital.com/makingdo/

Dobranksy, K., & Hargittai, E. (2006). The disability divide in Internet access and use. *Information, Communication and Society*, 9, 313-334.

Ellis, J. B., Abreu-Ellis, C., & Ricker, A. (2009). The digital divide in disability and education. In C. Vrasidas, M. Zembylas, & G. V. Glass (Eds.), *ICT for education, development, and social justice* (pp. 147-167). Charlotte, NC: Information Age.

Ellis, K., & Kent, M. (2011). *Disability and new media*. London, England and New York, NY: Routledge.

Empirica and Work Research Centre (WRC). (2007). *Assessment of the status of eAccessibility in Europe*. Bonn, Germany: European Commission.

Empirica and Work Research Centre (WRC). (2008). *eAccessibility status follow-up*. Bonn, Germany: European Commission.

European Commission (EC). (2008). *Towards an accessible information society*. Retrieved from http://ec.europa.eu/information_society/activities/einclusion/policy/accessibility/com_2008/index_en.htm

European Commission (EC). (2010). *Assessment of the status of eAccessibility in Europe*. Bonn, Germany: European Commission.

French, P. (2008). *Human rights indicators for people with disability*. Brisbane, Australia: QAI.

Gill, J., & Shipley T. (1997). *The impact of telecommunications deregulation on people with disabilities: A review for COST 219bis by the UK Group*. London, England: Royal National Institute of the Blind. Retrieved from http://www.snapi.org.uk/info/reports/disaster.htm

Goggin, G. (2008). Innovation & disability. *M/C: Media and Culture*, 11(3). Retrieved from http://journal.media-culture.org.au/index.php/mcjournal/article/view/56

Goggin, G. (2011). *Global mobile media*. London, England and New York, NY: Routledge.

Goggin, G., & McLelland, M. (Eds.). (2009). *Internationalizing Internet studies: Beyond anglophone paradigms*. New York, NY: Routledge.

Goggin, G., & Newell, C. (2003). *Digital disability: The social construction of disability in new media*. Lanham, MD: Rowman & Littlefield.

Goggin, G., & Newell, C. (2005). *Disability in Australia: Exposing a social apartheid*. Sidney: UNSW Press.

Goggin, G., & Newell, C. (2006). Disabling cell phones: Mobilizing and regulating the body. In A. P. Kavoori & N. Arceneaux (Eds.), *The Cell Phone Reader* (pp. 155-172). New York, NY: Peter Lang.

Goggin, G., & Newell, C. (2007a). The business of digital disability. *The Information Society*, 24(2), 159-168.

Goggin, G., & Newell, C. (2007b). Disability and online culture. In V. Nightingale & T. Dwyer (Eds.), *New media worlds* (pp. 103–117). Melbourne, Australia: Oxford University Press.

Goggin, G., & Noonan, T. (2006). Blogging disability: The interface between new cultural movements and Internet technology. In A. Bruns & J. Jacobs (Eds.), *Uses of blogs* (pp. 161–172). New York, NY: Peter Lang.

Global Alliance for Inclusive Information and Communication Technologies (G3ict). (2010). *Background: Economic and social development challenges related to disabilities*. Retrieved from http://www.un-gaid.org/tabid/879/Default.aspx

Guo, B., Bricout, J. C., & Huang, J. (2005). A common open space or a digital divide? A social model perspective on the online disability community in China. *Disability & Society, 20*(1), 49–66.

Haddon, L., Mante, E., Sapio, B., Kommonen, K.-H., Fortunati, L., & Kant, A. (Eds.). (2005). *Everyday innovators: Researching the role of users in shaping ICTs*. London, England: Springer.

Harper, P. (2002). Networking the deaf nation. *Australian Journal of Communication, 30*(3), 153–66.

Hollier, S. E. (2007). *The disability divide: A study into the impact of computing and Internet-related technologies on people who are blind or vision impaired* (PhD thesis, Curtin University, Perth). Retrieved from http://www.sigaccess.org/community/theses_repository/phd/scott_hollier.php

Ingstad, B., & Whyte, S. R. (Eds.). (2007). *Disability in local and global worlds*. Berkeley, CA: University of California Press.

International Commission for the Study of Communication Problems (MacBride report). (1980). *Many voices, one world: Towards a new, more just and more efficient world information and communication order*. London, England: Kogan Page; Paris, France: UNESCO.

International Telecommunications Union (ITU). (2009). *Measuring the information society: The ICT development index 2009*. Geneva, Switzerland: ITU. Retrieved from http://www.itu.int/md/D06-DAP2B.1.3.7-C-0027/en

International Telecommunications Union (ITU). (2010a). ITU ICT Eye. Retrieved from http://www.itu.int/ITU-D/ICTEYE/Default.aspx

ITU. (2010b). *World telecommunication/ICT development report 2010: Monitoring the WSIS targets: A mid-term review*. Geneva, Switzerland: ITU.

Internet Governance Forum (IGF). (2010, September). *Can mobile "apps" create a new golden age of accessibility?* Workshop 182 conducted at the meeting of the Internet Governance Forum, Vilnius, Lithuania. Retrieved from

http://www.intgovforum.org/cms/component/chronocontact/?chronofor
mname=WSProposals2010View&wspid=182

Jaeger, P. T., & Bowman, C. A. (2005). *Understanding disability: Inclusion, access, diversity, and civil rights.* Westport, CT: Praeger.

Johnson, D. G., & Wetmore, J. M. (Eds.). (2009) *Technology and society: Building our sociotechnical future.* Cambridge, MA: MIT Press.

Katz, J. E., & Rice, R. E. (2002). *Social consequences of Internet use: Access, involvement and interaction.* Cambridge, MA: MIT Press.

Kennedy, H., & Leung, L. (2008). Lessons from web accessibility and intellectual disability. In L. Leung (Ed.), *Digital experience design: Ideas, industries, interaction* (pp. 69–80). Bristol, England and Chicago, IL: Intellect.

Kuzma, J. M. (2010). Accessibility design issues with UK e-government sites. *Government Information Quarterly, 27*(2), 141–146.

Latour, B. (2005). *Reassembling the social: An introduction to actor-network theory.* Oxford, England: Clarendon Press.

Lax, S. (Ed.). (2000). *Access denied in the information age.* Basingstoke, England: Macmillan.

Lord, J., Posarac, A., Nicoli, M., Peffley, K., Mcclain-Nhlapo, C., & Keog, M. (2010). *Disability and international cooperation and development: A review of policies and practices.* SP discussion paper, No. 1003.Washington, DC: World Bank.

McKenzie, D., & Wajcman, J. (Eds.). (1999). *The social shaping of technology* (2nd ed.). Buckingham, England: Open University Press.

McQuire, S. (2008). *The media city: Media, architecture and urban space.* Thousand Oaks, CA: Sage.

MacLachlan, M., & Swartz, L. (Eds.). (2009). *Disability & international development: Towards inclusive global health.* Dordrecht, The Netherlands: Springer.

Manley, S. (2001). Creating an accessible public realm. In W. F. E. Preiser & E. Ostroff (Eds.), *Universal design handbook* (pp. 58.1–58.22). New York, NY: McGraw-Hill.

Meekosha, H. & Shuttleworth, R. (2009). What's so "critical" about critical disability studies? *Australian Journal of Human Rights, 15,* 47-75.

Mont, D. (2007). *Measuring disability prevalence.* SP discussion paper, No. 0706. Washington, DC: World Bank.

Mont, D., & Loeb, M. (2008). *Beyond DALYs: Developing indicators to assess the impact of public health interventions on the lives of people with disabilities.* SP discussion paper, No. 0815. Washington, DC: World Bank.

National Council on Disability (NCD). (2004). *Design for inclusion: Creating a new marketplace.* Washington, DC: NCD.

Nelson, J. A. (1994). *The disabled, the media, and the information age.* Westport, CT: Greenwood Press.

Newell, C., & Offord, B. (Eds.). (2008). *Activating human rights in education.* Canberra, Australia: Australian College of Educators.

Parker, J. C., & Thorson, E. (Eds.). (2009). *Health communication in the new media landscape.* New York, NY: Springer.

Raboy, M., & Landry, N. (2005). *Civil society, communication, and global governance: Issues from the World Summit on the Information Society.* New York, NY: Peter Lang, New York.

Roulstone, A. (1998). *Enabling technology: Disabled people, work and new technology.* Buckingham, England, Philadelphia, PA: Open University Press.

Rubaii-Barrett, N., & Wise, L. R. (2008). Disability access and e-government: An empirical analysis of state practices. *Journal of Disability Policy Studies, 19*(1), 52–64.

Sapey, B. (2000). Disablement in the informational age. *Disability and Society, 15,* 619–36.

Schillmeier, M. (2010). *Rethinking disability: Bodies, senses and things.* New York, NY: Routledge.

Seelman, K. D. (2001). Science and technology policy: Is disability a missing factor? In G. L. Albrecht, K. D. Seelman, & M. Bury (Eds.), *Handbook of disability studies* (pp. 663–692). London, England and Thousand Oaks, CA: Sage.

Servaes, J., & Carpentier, N. (Eds.). (2006). *Towards a sustainable information society: Deconstructing WSIS.* Bristol, England: Intellect.

Shakespeare, T. (2006). *Disability rights and wrongs.* London: Routledge.

Shildrick, M. (2012). Critical disability studies: Rethinking the conventions for the age of postmodernity. In T. Thomas, A. Roulstone, & N. Watson (Eds.), *Routledge Handbook of Disability Studies,* NY: Routledge, 30-41.

Sundaram, R. (2010). *Pirate modernity: Delhi's media urbanism.* London, England, New York, NY: Routledge.

Von Hippel, E. (2005). *Democratizing innovation.* Cambridge, MA: MIT Press.

Waddell, C. D. (2009). Introduction to developing policy. Retrieved from http://www.eaccessibilitytoolkit.org/toolkit/developing_policy/Introductio n_to_developing-policy

Warschauer, M. (2004). *Technology and social inclusion: Rethinking the digital divide.* Cambridge, MA: MIT Press.

Webster, F. (2006). The information society revisited. In L. A. Lievrouw & S. Livingstone (Eds.), *The handbook of new media: Updated student edition* (pp. 443–457). London, England, Thousand Oaks, CA: Sage.

World Bank. (2009). How many disabled people are there world-wide? Retrieved from http://web.worldbank.org/

Section 2

Conduit

Chapter 4:

Systematic Considerations for Addressing "Online Dead Zones" Impeding the Social Engagement of Persons with a Disability: Policy and Practice Implications

John C. Bricout, Abiy Agiro, and Alex Casiano

Introduction

The sea change that is represented by the proliferation of information and communication technologies (ICT), the Internet, telecommunications, and mobile and "smart" devices and systems, while penetrating every aspect of social life, has not been universally available, accessible, or usable, creating a "*digital* divide" for those who are unable to access the full benefits of ICT. Commonly identified barriers on the user side include skill, competence, knowledge, money, or some combination thereof. On the technology side they include design process shortcomings, inadequate evaluation and feedback mechanisms, and misplaced priorities. The so-called "disability divide" points to the ways that people with disabilities have lagged behind the general population in ICT use (Bricout, Baker, Ward, & Moon, 2010). Similarly, the "disability digital divide" signals the complex factors that have led to lower ICT use by people with disabilities, due to socioeconomic status, employment status, affordability, attitudes, usage patterns, age, digital skills, use and usability differences by disability type, and perhaps most prominently, technical accessibility barriers, including adaptive technology lags vis-à-vis ICT development (Vicente & Lopez, 2010). At the heart of this divide is a profound gap, not only in communication, information, and knowledge but also in civic participation and social engagement, situating people with disabilities in a virtual-world "dead zone," cut off from social learning critical to accessing social goods, such as education, employment, public services, health care, businesses, and recreation, all of which are increasingly online.

Mediating the divide requires not only closing the gap but also building the habits and capacity of participation and engagement. This demands more of a transformation than a "patch," altering the relative influence of trends towards rebuilding the offline world as we know it in the virtual space and trends towards using the virtual space as a canvass for new types of exchanges, communities, and even social norms and contracts. For people with disabilities specifically, eliminating the online dead zone implies first a shift in the role they play in generating the knowledge that informs virtual space development (technical and social) founded in participating in critical social learning exchanges and networks and predicated upon revised power relations through social innovation processes. How this agenda of enhanced social learning participation and social innovation can be advanced is the focus of this chapter, addressing the question of how to overcome what is now a debilitating online dead zone. First establishing the parameters of the participation challenges is critical to redressing the issue of online dead zones for people with disabilities.

Accessibility Challenges

In a study of 9,807 individuals using the European Commission's Information Society (IST) program's eUser survey conducted in 2005, affordability and accessibility emerged as the key barriers to ICT use by the 20 percent of the sample with self-reported disabilities, for whom the rate of Internet use was only 35 percent, compared to 61 percent for the rest of the sample (Vicente & Lopez, 2010). Policies to improve accessibility could leverage the (relatively) low cost of mobile phones and increase consumer/user inputs into design and resources for enhancing adaptive technology interfaces or interoperability with ICT (Vicente & Lopez, 2010). However, the deeper social roots of the divide cannot be addressed without substantial attention to the political and economic spheres, for which public discourse is a critical medium for advocacy, innovation, and collaboration aimed at addressing disparities.

Perhaps the most profound change resulting from the emergence of ICT as the portal to services, communication, education, and information has been its impact on public discourse, simultaneously bonding far-flung communities while isolating population segments lacking key Internet skills and knowledge, such as people with disabilities, in islets of silence (van Duersen & van Dijk, 2009). The online dialogues of public life are not only inaccessible for those isolated on the far side of the digital divide, they are also largely unintelligible, separated by divergent ideas, experiences, and contexts that government can only bridge with clear usability benchmarks for design and performance (Jaeger, 2006). Usability poses a higher bar for compliance than accessibility, focusing on ease of use, simplicity, and practicality for particular users (Jaeger, 2006). A Website or Web-based application (including social media) may be accessible, inasmuch as the information is made available, and yet fail the test of usability for a particular user; for example, an accessible blog site that is blocked by an employer because of concerns about the workplace relevance of participation. In the United States the federal government has devoted resources towards developing accessible social media for people with disabilities, aimed at increasing the flow of information and exchange. The Disability.gov platform supports a Twitter feed, Really Simple Syndication feeds (RSS), blogs, and information on federal resources. The platform also supports learning, communication, personalized news, updates, and online discussions.

Information sharing and discourse are important pre-conditions for information dissemination and, predicated upon information literacy (Williamson & Asia, 2009), a reminder that citizen's attributes as users are also key considerations in closing the gap in public discourse online. Yet the digital divide is not simply a problematic gap to be bridged on the road to civic engagement, it can also be a space suitable for forging a new discourse built around emergent understandings and dialogue.

As access to public goods, services, and participation has moved online, much of what constitutes the 21st century "polis" has taken on a virtual guise, beginning and, increasingly, ending with a Web-based interaction using ICT. The relevant scope of online interaction exceeds e-government, or online government resources, exchanges, and services, to encompass e-governance, or the connective tissue of electronic networks that link government and civil society in service of the procurement and delivery of public goods and services (Helbig, Gil-Garcia, & Ferro, 2009; Jho, 2005). E-governance is a nexus of which government and the political sphere are but two nodes, together with non-profit organizations, neighborhood associations, businesses, educational institutions, and other entities operating in the public sphere (Odendaal, 2003; Torres et al., 2006). Online civic engagement takes place in the midst of this Internet-based nexus, sometimes referred to as a virtual "Agora" or marketplace in the classical Athenian sense, where transactions critical to social life and survival take place (Hatzakis, 1999). In this virtual marketplace, as in physical marketplaces, social and economic forces shape the network architecture and design; they reciprocally shape social forces in kind (Meneklis & Douligeris, 2010). The digital divide manifests the power-based imbalance in the interactions between marketplace actors and their relative centrality or marginality in key transactions influencing social opportunities, goods, and well-being. Despite strong efforts by the federal government, such as the Disability.gov Website, the marginal position of people with disabilities in the online marketplace is reflected in the poor accessibility and receptivity of e-governance, and low Internet participation vis-à-vis the general population (Bricout & Baker, 2010; Dobransky & Hargittai (2006). These factors situate people with disabilities on the disenfranchised side of the digital divide (Bricout et al., 2010).

People with disabilities constitute an economically, politically, and socially marginalized minority throughout the world (Garcia, 2002), and the social exclusion that they all too often endure is reflected in communities whether formal political entities—the so-called polis—or covenant-bound entities such as neighborhood associations, that are not responsive to their needs and aspirations. The most obvious manifestations of social exclusion in the built environment are inaccessible spaces, or perhaps, somewhat more subtly, spaces that are transiently accessible, such as when a ramp is periodically blocked. Civic engagement in the context of contemporary societies is constrained directly by individual capacity for decision-making and access to transportation, supports, and services but also indirectly by social forces, such as government policies and regulations governing the design of constructed spaces, societal beliefs and prejudices, and inadequate education or income, which may need collective action (Carling, 1990; Imrie, 1996; Wehmeyer & Bolding, 1999). There are striking parallels between the physical and virtual world, as evidenced by the lower participation of people with disabilities in the Internet vis-à-vis the general population

(Bricout et al., 2010). These disparities underscore the importance of framing the online participation gap in terms of a space where discourse does not take place due to underlying inequalities.

In the virtual realm, people with disabilities encounter systematic barriers to Internet connectivity, usability (end-user fit), and accessibility. Web literacy, as well as content barriers, varies with the functional impairments of the user and the adaptability of the interface technology (Goggin & Newell, 2007; Stienstra & Troschuk, 2005). Because of the heterogeneity of impairment, functionality, and independent living goals of people with disabilities, it is sometimes described in terms of "multiple accessibility audiences," rather than a monolithic group facing common online accessibility barriers (Anderson, Bohman, Burmeister, & Sampson-Wild, 2004). The ICT accessibility and usability barriers for people vary with type and severity of impairment, financial resources, and adaptive technology costs. For some groups, such as people who are blind, lags in adaptive technology may be most problematic, for other groups, such as individuals with neurological disabilities, adaptations may be prohibitively costly, while for others, such as individuals with intellectual disabilities, appropriate content may not have been developed (Dobransky & Hargittai, 2006).

One consequence of the lack of accessibility, compounded by cost barriers, is the comparatively low home Internet use by people with disabilities (Dobransky & Hargittai, 2006). However, the picture is not uniform across subgroups; the U.S. Census Bureau's 2003 Current Population Survey Supplement results speak to the heterogeneity within the population of people with disabilities; the lowest percentage of Internet use was by adults over 65 years of age with multiple disabilities (8.3 percent), 5.9 percent of whom lived in a broadband household, compared to 72.1 percent of employed persons in the 25–60-year-old age bracket who are deaf or who have a severe hearing impairment, 25.6 percent of whom lived in a broadband household (US Department of Commerce, 2004). These patterns reflect larger societal trends, with younger and more affluent individuals participating more in Internet use. Clearly, the Internet does not level the effects of economic disparities and social exclusion, suggesting the removal of cost- and knowledge- (Web literacy) barriers to online participation.

In this vein, an alternate approach to costly end-user-tailored adaptations to ICT interfaces is to promote universal design principles— "design for all"—for Internet architecture and content that eliminate barriers altogether (Brophy & Craven, 2007). There is movement in that direction, abetted by Section 508 legislation here in the United States, mandating accessible electronic and information technologies, and by World Wide Web Consortium's (W3C) Web Content Accessibility Guidelines (WCAG) 2.0, (Brophy & Craven, 2007; Brys & Vanderbauwhede, 2006). Thus, while interface barriers to online civic engagement exist and pose a significant challenge, there is progress along that dimension. Perhaps more daunting are the resource barriers to participation in the public sphere, which are tied to less tractable complexities of social learning, informed decision making, and action in modern life.

Participation

There is no single agreed-upon definition of participation in the context of the lived experience of people with disabilities, but the World Health Organization's International Classification of Functioning, Disability and Health (ICF) is perhaps the most pervasive and thoroughly researched. The ICF defines participation in terms of the individual's involvement in life situations: complex activities that encompass roles, rather than discrete tasks (Jette, Haley, & Kooyoomijian, 2003). It is assessed by his or her current or usual environment "performance" with environment inclusive of the physical, social, and technological surround. Personal factors, such as background, endowment, and adaptation have yet to be specified in a clear taxonomy. Although the ICF embraces an ecological perspective on participation, its stance on participation can be described as "value neutral" inasmuch as the goal of participation is not citizenship or full engagement in the polity. Although the ICF view of participation is not exclusive of political considerations, it is fairly agnostic about the relationship between power and participation. As such, the ICF notion of participation puts less emphasis on the place where participation is enacted, overlooking the embedded nature of power and place. Similarly, the role of network position or status in shaping the nature of participation is given scant attention. Status and network position are confounded with physical location as, for a variety of reasons, people of similar means tend to live and work in proximity to each other. Co-location has consequences for the decisions people make as captured by the theory of focused choice. The theory of focused choice, which has been validated empirically, states that by engaging in joint activities individuals' opportunities for differentiated outside connections are diminished (Yuan, Gay, & Hembrooke, 2006), implying that for people with disabilities, engagement with the mainstream, online or offline, is impeded. The social context of participation thus takes on more importance.

An alternative model to the ICF, the Disability Creation Process model, adds an explicit socio-cultural context to social participation, which is defined in terms of the effective performance of valued daily activities and social roles or so-called "life habits" (Dumont, Gervais, Fougeyrollas, & Bettrand, 2004). Situating social participation squarely in a socio-cultural context through life habits valued by the target person adds a helpful dimension to understanding participation that is amenable to research aimed at understanding the role of personal factors in adapting to social life (Brown et al., 2004). It does not, however, advance our understanding of particular socio-cultural contexts from multiple points of view.

Perhaps most fundamentally, what is lacking in extant frameworks of participation is the notion of social learning that informs the character and quality of participation. When the focus is on community participation this shortcoming becomes more visible, particularly when the goal is to assess and compare community participation across localities. Individuals' participation in the unique configuration of relationships, resources, and places that constitutes a given community can be conceptualized in terms of the overall tenor of the transactions between the individual and his or her environment as he or she learns how to collaborate with others in creating a context that is responsive to civic participation.

Social Learning

Social learning points to the transpersonal properties of learning; that is, the sense in which learning takes place in a social context in the course of participating in groups, collaboratively, through a distributed network (Cho, Lee, Stefanone, & Gay, 2005; Hemetsberger & Reihardt, 2006). Such learning communities may be online, as in the case of computer-mediated teams (Yuan, Gay & Hembrooke, 2006), or offline (Flores, 2007), or both (Matzat, 2010). Online learning communities are made more robust when linked with offline social exchanges of knowledge (Matzat, 2010).

Social learning that leverages social capital is an important means for promoting positive outcomes in key social and economic domains as people benefit from the collective and distributive properties of information that surpass the capacity of individuals (Fang, Tsai, & Lin, 2010). Participation in social learning networks is a function of several factors: individual access to such networks, closely related to social capital, or accumulated value-bearing relationships, social competence, or capacity to engage in sustained social relations, and cognitive capacity (Fang et al., 2010). In large measure, having access to the "right" social networks is pivotal because of the capabilities of networks to compensate for individual deficits (Fang et al., 2010).

For people with disabilities, learning takes place in a socio-cultural context in which experiences and exposure taken for granted by the general populations may be lacking (Ross-Gordon, 2002). Specifically, people with disabilities may lack educational and social experiences that are critical to learning (Ross-Gordon, 2002). When placed in the context of social learning, the absence of such experiences may negatively impact tacit learning, or learning "how" in contrast to learning "what," that is explicit learning (Duguid, 2005). Thus, by virtue of not participating in the mainstream learning community, people with disabilities may be disadvantaged, finding even accessible explicit knowledge unintelligible at least insofar as knowledge for action is concerned. People with disabilities tend to have smaller, more circumscribed social networks compared to the general population, with individuals who have intellectual disabilities having significantly attenuated social networks compared to those with physical disabilities (Bigby,

2008; Lippold & Burns, 2009). So-called "weak ties" or distant network ties outside one's habitual circle are important to the diffusion of knowledge and innovation (Hauser, Tappeiner, & Walde, 2007). Weak ties are less readily available to people with disabilities, with those with intellectual disabilities having the least access (Bigby, 2008; Lippold & Burns, 2009). Thus for people with disabilities, social learning may be attenuated at least in part by barriers to distributed social networks that online resources, but most especially those related to social media, may help mitigate.

Inclusive Participation and Social Media

Social media constitute a medium that may address some of the current limitations on inclusive social learning, informed decision making, and action. Increasingly prevalent and interactive, social media encompass social networking services and blogs, both of which can be either incorporated directly into public services, or linked to such services, if government is willing to collaborate with civil society and the private sector in the pursuit of public goals (Jaeger et al., 2007). The interactive architecture of Web-based social networking sites is especially well suited to coordinating not only government-citizen transactions but also non-governmental or private exchanges disseminating public information and linking to public services (Heller et al., 2007; Makinen & Kuira, 2008).

In one high-profile case, the parents of a six-year-old girl with developmental disabilities published a blog with their daughter to communicate their daughter's treatment choices, quality of life, and aspirations (Kirschner, Brashler, & Savage, 2007). The focus on ethics, medical services, and treatments, while not directly related to e-governance, points to the use of social media as a platform for discourse of import to the public good. Nonetheless, there remains a dearth of studies examining the role of social media, in particular blogs, used by people with disabilities (McClimens & Gordon, 2008). Lived experience, information, ethical, and identity issues appear to be the focus of such inquiry (i.e., Kirschner et al., 2007; McClimens & Gordon, 2008) rather than issues pertaining directly to public policy and public services or e-governance. There is a substantial gap in our knowledge of social media use by people with disabilities in relation to social learning, which must be addressed. In particular, studies are needed that examine how the use of social media by people with disabilities has altered their opportunities for social learning and discourse online, especially those exchanges that redress the power imbalance between people with disabilities and the general population. For social media to redress the power imbalance and the negative participation skew they will need to take on the guise of a social innovation. That is, social media must be more than channels for communication, learning, informed decision making, and action, they must also be levers for change. The role of social media as tools for social innovation must be articulated if social media are to overcome the online dead zones of today.

Social Innovation

The concept of social innovation has many connotations for different authors. But before going through the definitions and critical reflections, it would be interesting to note a few things about innovation. Bryson (1988) defined innovation as something that takes place when truly important discussions take place across organizational levels and functions. Innovations introduce new methods, ideas, processes, or products to strategically change an already existing situation. Because innovation is something new, whether in form, application, or nature, the success of innovation is only known after implementation. Consequently, innovations often fail initially before succeeding later (Bryson, 1988). Bryson goes so far as to suggest that every innovation is a failure in the middle of another innovation. Hence innovations are parts of strategic changes where, in accordance with Karl Marx's adage, change in degree will lead to change in kind.

For Friedmann (1992), the definition mainly focuses on the "social and political empowerment of the individual and the household through social movements and actions" (p. 33). In parallel reasoning extended to the virtual realm, Restler and Woolis (2007) postulated that community engagement within online Communities of Practice (CoP) fosters the development of knowledge for action and is transformative within the online community. Citing Max Weber, Moulaert and Delladetsima (2001) defined social innovation "as innovation in the relations between individuals and groups, different from other modes of innovation like that of technical" (p. 71). In other words, finding new forms of unveiling needs and concocting democratic ways of managing them is the crucial issue.

The above definitions share two chief similarities. First, they focus on the external relations of an individual or aggregates of individuals (groups) with the rest of society. Second, they emphasize informal, spontaneous, bottom-up creative bonding. However, Mumford (2002) argued that social innovation is not simply the creation of new social relations, it is also generative of new social organizations to implement practical measures to solve problems. Thus, not only social relations, but also organized, formally structured relations are taken into account. Social innovation, then, becomes the generation and implementation of new ideas, processes, and methods that transform social relationships and social organizations.

We propose *social innovation for civic engagement* as an approach and process that seamlessly engages all elements of the public in a sustainable and robust dialogue and exchange one that facilitates participation in and contribution to the development of public goods, services, and policies. This objective, perhaps complicated in the context of severe competition for resources and competing notions of the role of online civic engagement vis-à-vis the democratic process, is achievable, and ultimately cost-effective. Additional challenges are posed by the emergent nature of e-governance itself as it expands with the "cyber-sphere" into domains such as social networking media and virtual worlds. However, for all the systemic constraints and unknowns, developing inclusive social media must remain a fundamental value proposition for technologically advanced democracies, equally as critical as technological innovations, and a vital source for social innovations from the bottom up. People with disabilities are at the vanguard of the public in defining what inclusive social media ought to look like, and what resources, including policy tools, must be brought to bear. It is still early days from the perspective of empirical research on which to base policy tools, but there are certain principles that stand out with some clarity: universal access to content, and processes that promote and sustain relevant and robust discourse. Most of all, it is essential to acknowledge that inclusive social media, like the public processes they are meant to shape, are a moving target and thus will require an ongoing commit-ment on the part of policy makers to evaluate, assess, and modify the conditions and environments on which inclusive social media rely.

Conclusion

It has been recognized for some time now that connecting people with disabilities to the numerous benefits of access to ICT-mediated content and applications is more than a technical problem, more specifically, that problem-solving social participation and knowledge barriers is equally important. Prescriptions for overcoming these social barriers have largely focused on adaptations to the medium and its interfaces; issues of "fit" rather than issues of reciprocal change and influence. That is, the person with a disability was posited to primarily be a "user" rather than a member of a community with shared social knowledge. From this perspective, the online dead zone for people with disabilities is framed as a design problem, responding to known constraints in the system, rather than as a feature of online and offline social and power relationships in which social innovation promises to redress an imbal-ance of social knowledge by evolving the nature of online exchanges and thus the context in which the communication system exists. Only by altering this fundamental social dynamic can the digital divide, and the online dead zone that defines its boundaries, be eliminated for people with disabilities.

References

Anderson, S., Bohman, P.R., Burmeister, O. K., & Sampson-Wild, G. (2004). User needs and e-government accessibility: The future impact of WCAG 2.0. In C. Stary & C. Stephanidis (Eds.), *Web accessibility* (pp. 289–304). Berlin, Germany: Springer Verlag.

Bigby, C. (2008). Known well by no one: Trends in informal social networks of middle-aged people with intellectual disability five years after moving to the community. *Journal of Intellectual and Developmental Disabilities, 33*(2), 148–157.

Bricout, J. C., & Baker, P. M. A. (2010). Leveraging online social networks for people with disabilities in emergency communications and recovery. *International Journal of Emergency Management, 7*(1), 59–74.

Bricout, J., Baker, P., Ward, A., & Moon, N. (2010). Teleworking and the "disability divide." In E. Ferro, Y. K. Dwivedi, J. R. Gil-Garcia, & M. D. Williams (Eds.), *Handbook of research on overcoming digital divides: Constructing an equitable and competitive information society* (pp. 155–178). Hershey, PA: IGI Global.

Brophy, P., & Craven, J. (2007). Web accessibility. *Library Trends, 55*(4), 950–972.

Brown, M., Dijkers, M. P. J. M., Gordon, W. A., Ashman, T., Charatz, H., & Cheng, Z. (2004). Participation objective, participation subjective: A measure of participation combining outsider and insider perspectives. *Journal of Head Trauma Rehabilitation, 19*, 459–481.

Brys, C. M., & Vanderbauwhede, W. (2006). Communication challenges in the W3C's web content accessibility guidelines. *Technical Communications, 53*(1), 60–78.

Bryson, J. M. (1988). A strategic planning process for public and non-profit organizations. *Long Range Planning, 21*(1), 73–81.

Carling, P. J. (1990). Major mental illness, housing and supports: The promise of community integration. *American Psychologist, 45*(8), 969–975.

Cho, J.S., Lee, J.S., Stephanone, M. & Gay, G. (2005). Development of computer-supported collaborative social networks in a distributed learning community. *Behavior & Information Technology, 24*(6), 435–441.

Dobransky, K., & Hargittai, E. (2006). The disability divide in internet access and use. *Information, Communication and Society, 9*(3), 313–334.

Duguid, P. (2005). The art of knowing: Social and tacit dimensions of knowledge and the limits of community of practice. *The Information Society: An International Journal, 21*(2), 109–118.

Dumont, C., Gervais, M., Fougeyrollas, P., & Bettrand, R. (2004). Toward an explanatory model of social participation for adults with traumatic brain injury. *The Journal of Head Trauma Rehabilitation, 19*(6), 431–444.

Fang, S.C., Tsai, F.S, & Lin, J.L. (2010). Leveraging tenant-incubator social capital for organizational learning and performance in incubator programme. *International Small Business Journal, 28*(1), 90–113.

Flores, M.T. (2007). Navigating contradictory communities of practice in learning to teach social justice. *Anthropology & Education Quarterly, 38*(4), 380–404.

Friedmann, J. (1992). *Empowerment: The politics of alternative development.* Oxford, England: Wiley-Blackwell.

García, S. B. (2002). Parent-professional collaboration in culturally-sensitive assessment. In A. J. Artiles & A. A. Ortiz (Eds.), *English language learners with* special needs: Identification, placement and instruction (pp. 87-103). Washington, DC: Center for Applied Linguistics.

Goggin, G., & Newell, C. (2007). The business of digital disability. *The Information Society: An International Journal, 23*(3), 159-168.

Hatzakis M. (1999). The new agora on the Internet. *JAMA, 281*(8).

Hauser, C., Tappeiner, G., & Walde, J. (2007). The impact of social capital and weak ties on innovation. *Regional Studies, 41*(1), 75-88.

Helbig, N., Gil-Garcia, J., & Ferro, E. (2009). Understanding the complexity of electronic government: Implications from the digital divide literature. *Government Information Quarterly, 26,* 89-97.

Heller, R. F., Chongsuviatwong, V., Haliegeorgios, S., Dada, J., Torun, P., Madhok, R., & Sanders, J. (2007). Capacity-building for public health. *Bulletin of WHO, 85,* 930-934.

Hemetsberger, A., & Reinhardt, C. (2006). Learning and knowledge building in open-source communities: A social experimental approach. *Management Learning, 37* (2), 187-214.

Imrie, R. (1996) Equity, social justice, and planning for access and disabled people: An international perspective. *International Planning Studies, 1*(1), 17-34.

Jaeger, P.T. (2006) Assessing section 508 compliance on federal e-government websites: A multi-method, user-centered evaluation of accessibility for persons with disabilities. *Government Information Quarterly, 23*(2), 169-190.

Jaeger, P.T., Shneiderman, B., Fleischmann, K. R., Preece, J., Qu, Y., & Wu, P. F. (2007). Community response grids: E-government, social networks, and effective emergency management. *Telecommunications Policy, 3* (10-11), 592-604.

Jette, A. M., Haley, S. M., & Kooyoomijian, J. T. (2003). Are the ICF activity and participation dimensions distinct? *Journal of Rehabilitation Medicine, 35*(3), 145-149.

Jho, W. (2005). Challenges for e-governance: Protests from civil society on the protection of privacy in e-government in Korea. *International Review of Administrative Sciences, 71*(1), 151-166.

Kirschner, K. L., Brashler, R., & Savage, T. A. (2007). Ashley x. *American Journal of Physical Medicine & Rehabilitation, 6*(12), 1023-1029.

Lippold, T., & Burns, J. (2009). Social supports and intellectual disabilities: A comparison between social networks of adults with intellectual disabilities and those with physical disability. *Journal of Intellectual Disability Research, 53*(5), 463-473.

Makinen, M., & Kuira, M.W. (2008). Social media and postelection crisis in Kenya. *International Journal of Press/Politics, 13*(3), 328-335.

Matzat, U. (2010). Reducing problems of sociability in online communities: Integrating online communities with offline interaction. *American Behavioral Scientist, 53*(8), 1170-1193.

McClimens , A., & Gordon, F. (2008). Presentation of self in everyday life: How people labeled with intellectual disability manage identity as they engage the blogosphere. *Sociological Research Online, 13*(4), Retrieved at http://www.socresonline.org.uk/13/4/14.htm

Meneklis, V., & Douligeris, C. (2010). Bridging theory and practice in e-government: A set of guidelines for architectural design. *Government Information Quarterly, 27*(1), 70-81.

Moulaert, F., & Delladetsima, P. (2001). *Globalization and integration area development in European cities.* Oxford, England: Oxford University Press.

Mumford, M. D. (2002). Social innovation: Ten cases from Benjamin Franklin. *Creativity Research Journal, 14*(2), 253-266.

Odendaal, N. (2003) Information and Communication Technologies (ICTs) and locagovernance: Understanding the differences between cities in developed and emerging economies. *Computers, Environment and Urban Systems, 27*, 585-607.

Restler, S. G., & Woolis, D. D. (2007). Actors and factors: Virtual communities for social innovation. *The Electronic Journal of Knowledge Management, 5*(1), 89-95.

Ross-Gordon, J.M. (2002). Sociocultural contexts of learning among adults with intellectual disabilities. *New Directions for Adult and Continuing Education, 96*, 47-58.

Stienstra, D., & Troschuk, L. (2005) Engaging citizens with disabilities in edemocracy. *Disability Studies Quarterly, 25*(2), Retrieved at http://dsg-sds.org/issue/view/29

Torres, L., Pina, V., & Acerate, B. (2006). E-governance developments in European Union cities: Reshaping government's relationship with citizens. *Governance: An International Journal of Policy, Administration, and Institutions, 19*(2), 277-302.

U.S. Department of Commerce. (2004). *A nation online: Entering the broadband age.* U.S. Department of Commerce, Economics and Statistics Administration, National Telecommunications and Information Administration. Retrieved at http://www.ntia.doc.gov/files/ntia/editor_uploads/Nation OnlineBroadband04_files/NationOnlineBroadband.pdfc

Van Duersen, A. J. A. M., & Van Dijk, J. A. G. M. (2009). Improving digital skills for the use of online public information and services. *Government Information Quarterly, 6*, 333–340.

Vicente, M. R., & Lopez, A. J. (2010). Multidimensional analysis of the disability digital divide: Some evidence of internet use. *The Information Society, 26*, 48–64.

Wehmeyer, M. L., & Bolding, N. (1999). Self-determination across living and working environments: A matched-samples study of adults with mental retardation. *Mental Retardation, 37*, 353–363.

Williamson, K., & Asia, T. (2009). Information behavior of people in the fourth age: Implications for the conceptualization of information literacy. *Library & Information Science Research, 31*(2), 76–83.

Yuan, Y. C., Gay, G., & Hembrooke, H. (2006). Focused activities and the development of social capital as a distributed learning community. *The Information Society, 22*, 26–39.

David Jensen and James W. Harrington Jr.

Introduction: Access to Access

Information and interaction over the Internet are increasingly important for poor and homeless people as well as middle class people. However, the virtual space of the Internet is not the starting point for this access. Janelle and Hodge argued that although accessibility is multidimensional, including the cognitive as well as the physical, "physical proximity to resources" (Janelle & Hodge, 2000, p. 4) remains important. For many, a device capable of using the Internet and a means of connecting to the Internet are not always immediately at hand. For them, the issue is "access to access"—the movement in space and time necessary to get to a device capable of accessing the Internet.

This chapter frames the case for research into the actual effects of geography—distance, time, and travel—on access to access. This case centers on a general lack of information about poor and homeless Internet users in light of the increasing requirements imposed upon them if they are to use the Internet,[1] as well as the opportunities for social participation that Internet use opens up for them. This gap, from preliminary research, seems to be under-recognized and even ignored. We will also consider the effect upon users who are nominally middle class, and not homeless or considered poor, as there is reason to believe that they are also subject to similar problems and that is also under-recognized.

---

[1] This raises topics that are beyond the immediate scope of this chapter but deserve further attention. The increasing presence of the Internet in all aspects of life can be approached in light of the processes of neoliberalism, governmentality, and welfare state retrenchment.

Throughout this chapter we refer to ICTs (Information and Communication Technologies) and the Internet. A subset of ICTs,[2] taken together, comprises the various elements that come under the umbrella of the Internet, "which more than any other digital technology symbolizes the power of the digital age" (Couclelis, 2004, p. 8), including a suite of tools such as email, the World Wide Web, and, increasingly for younger users, chat applications and Twitter.[3] The 2004 City of Seattle Information Technology Residential Survey, a report prepared for the Gates Foundation's U.S. Library Program (Moore, Gordon, Gordon, & Heuertz, 2002), as well as a survey for the Pew Internet & American Life Project (Fox, 2005), both show that sending and receiving email are by far the most common and valued uses of ICTs by the public. These and other online activities almost always involve a Web browser.

Thus, when we speak of Internet access, we generally refer to the opportunity or resources to engage in email and Web browsing to whatever ends a person may desire. In that sense, almost any reference to computers going forward should be understood in the context of their use in terms of the Internet. It should also be understood from the term that information and communication are intimately connected. Communicating *is* information sharing; information seeking necessarily involves the means to communicate. Therefore, access to those means of access, and corresponding questions of distance and location, should be of fundamental interest.

Physical Distance and Digital Divides

In 1997, Frances Cairncross of *The Economist* proclaimed *The Death of Distance*. A corollary prediction is often made concerning the nature and even the very existence of cities. Graham (2004, p. 5), for example, provided a timeline from McLuhan in 1964, and no doubt it would be possible to go back even further. Predictions of this nature, from

---

[2] ICTs include telephone, fax, cable, and many other services and technologies (Graham & Marvin, 1996, 2001).

[3] Technically speaking, these three uses are all based on different protocols that interact as subsets of the Internet, which is home to many other protocols. A good explanation can be found at: http://netforbeginners.about.com/cs/technoglossary/f/Faq1.htm

futurists, philosophers, architects, and geographers, can be as sweeping as, for example, saying that "time...becomes instantaneous," or asserting that distance relationships will replace those of proximity. Taken together, these predictions envision nothing less than the physical end of cities, with all their "physical proximity...unpredictability, and social and cultural diversity" (Graham, 2004, p. 5). Graham noted their "implicitly anti-urban assertions" where city and new media networks exist apart, the latter antithetical to new media's "geographical concentration in cities and urban regions" (Graham, 2004, p. 16-17).

Dertouzos (1997), an engaging and thoroughgoing techno-optimist, took a similarly bold and broad approach to a book title, proclaiming *What Will Be* (Dertouzos, 1997). His view of an emergent technologically mediated "information marketplace" is expansive and largely unproblematized. To his credit, he does acknowledge that such a marketplace should not "be left to its own devices" (Dertouzos, 1997, p. 242), else the distance between rich and poor will only grow. Yet here, as is often the case, the scale of comparison is no finer than between first- and third-world nations. The effects of geography, and on geography, simply never enter into his discussion. Cities are only considered in that the Information Marketplace will make of us "urban villagers," ranging the world digitally while staying in place at home with family and friends, attending to personal relationships (Dertouzos, 1997, p. 305). The possibility that class, economic, and other structural differences have an effect on ICTs never really enters into the discussion.

Digital Requirements

Access matters. To participate in civic life, to make use of city services and other social services, it is increasingly necessary, or easier, to use the Internet. Washington is one of 25 states that allow and enable applications for food stamps online, although all 50 states provide downloadable application forms via the Internet.[4] E-government enables citizens to gain information, consult with specialists, apply for licenses, and pay bills and fines online. University students are expected to mediate their academic careers online from day one, from the

---

[4] http://www.fns.usda.gov/fns/forms.htm

procedural to the scholarly. There is an ever-increasing emphasis on the use of ICTs in the classroom and in the research required to meet course requirements. These are just some examples of the extent to which ICTs and the corresponding necessary access to them are interwoven into the everyday lives of citizens.

For many people, use of the Internet is a routine job requirement. "The Internet has been a big boon to the homeless," according to Michael Stoops, acting director of the National Coalition for the Homeless (www.nationalhomeless.org), as quoted in a wired.com article on the homeless and laptops (Ogles, 2006). Stoops also made the claim that more homeless people have email addresses than have post office boxes. This latter claim makes sense insofar as a Web-based email address is generally free and not locationally bound. While there may be many factors that limit the mobility options of the poor and homeless, their communications options may be increasing. The 2002 report to the Gates Foundation's U.S. Library Program (Moore et al.) reported that 52% of low income people who used the library for Internet access used it for keeping in touch with family and friends much more than for any other use. In a nod to geography, it notes that communications technologies can re-connect what transportation technologies have served to separate (p. 12).

Travel and movement to access ICTs is not solely a problem for the poor or homeless. David Jensen queried university students and acquaintances about their non-school access arrangements. These are all people who are very Internet aware and dependent. They have been using the Internet as a default in the course of their academic research and daily lives. High- speed Internet connections at school are a given in their experience. This is the expectation portrayed in so many ways in various media. Away from school, it is a different story. Their expectations and experience of access are anything but seamless. Travel and distance re-assert themselves as factors. These people rely upon a hodgepodge of connection strategies, often depending on the kindness or carelessness of strangers, or upon public resources such as the library. Here is a sample of their responses:

- KR only has dial-up service at home, which he considers inadequate to his needs. He walks several blocks to the Greenwood branch of the library to use the Wi-Fi on a laptop, where he is not subject to the one-hour usage limit.

- M was usually able to pick up one of a half-dozen anonymous Wi-Fi signals in her apartment building. Sometimes she would have to leave the building and find a Wi-Fi café.
- SI needed to borrow a laptop with wireless capability for use at home, where she too was relying upon anonymous Wi-Fi connections that could come and go, forcing her to find alternatives.
- J is entirely dependent upon school. Away, he needs to take his laptop to a Wi-Fi café.
- SP had a roommate who had the connection. The roommate moved, and now SP has to come to school or find a free Wi-Fi Hotspot.
- KE wishes he could find an unshielded Wi-Fi connection in his apartment building because maintaining his own connection on a graduate student income is problematic.
- VB responded that, yes, she does have broadband at home because she dislikes having to come into school to access the Internet.

These are all people for whom Internet access is the normal expectation, yet the spatial availability of a connection is uneven and cannot be taken for granted. Such ad hoc connection searches and travels are not necessarily reported or taken into account when answering survey questions. That is, people are not asked about, or are not considering, the travel time involved in getting to school, work, or wherever they have their access. These journeys are internalized and invisible parts of their Internet use.

These are also the people, generally already established Internet users, who are the target audience for the various projects to spread free or low-cost Wi-Fi-based Internet access to selected city neighborhoods. These are not spatially neutral approaches to access. Such projects would remove barriers to access for some while leaving them in place for others.

I believe that these examples demonstrate a hidden dimension to Internet access. Experienced, regular users of the Internet do not always have the totally un-problematic connectivity that might be expected. At the same time, the strategies they use to acquire access rely on means that are closed to others in need of access.

Digital Divides

Although its scope or even existence may be subject to debate, the term digital divide has a number of similar and widely used definitions. Kellerman (2002) used a basic 2001 definition by Paltridge as the difference between those with and without the "access to information and communications technologies," and glossed access as "the very existence of proper infrastructure, as well as economic abilities to pay..." (p. 176). Castells (2001) used a similarly basic but more specific definition of "...inequality of access to the Internet" (p. 248).

At its most common denominator, access is considered from a very instrumentalist perspective of physical possession of a computer (Parayil, 2005, p. 41). Although this is an extremely simplistic view, it helps to explain the digital-divide skeptics' contention that ever falling prices for the hardware will bring about widespread, if not universal, computer ownership, thus ending any divide.

Van Dijk and Hacker (2003) offered several interpretations of an evolving digital divide. These interpretations are assessments of what they see as the four broad positions on digital divide. The first two of these positions, denial and a rapidly disappearing divide due to market forces, reflect the conclusion of Compaine (2001), and may be thought of as generally politically conservative stances. Van Dijk and Hacker contended that both these positions fail to see "*relative* differences" and ignore facts such as rapid obsolescence of hardware and software. This same relative divide expresses itself when the divide around computer possession is replaced by broadband vs. narrowband connections (van Dijk & Hacker, 2003, p. 321-322). In fact, this difference in connection speeds is considered a very legitimate indicator of a new phase of digital divide (Fox, 2005; Davison & Cotten, 2003).

A third broad position, that a divide will probably grow, is built on pre-existing divides of "income, education, age, gender, ethnicity, and geographical location" (van Dijk & Hacker, 2003, p. 321). This is a politically left position, which, despite expressing a modicum of agreement with, the authors criticize as underestimating the possibility of entirely new inequalities growing out of the relative skill and usage differentials of the new technologies. They note the very real consumer and citizen participation opportunities that can emerge from Internet access treated as a public service (van Dijk & Hacker, 2003, p. 322–323).

The final broad position that van Dijk and Hacker (2003) developed on the digital divide is that it is shrinking in some respects and increasing in others (p. 321). This is essentially their authorial position; that any divide is a complex, far-from-static phenomenon, mirroring the ever-evolving technology. In the same vein as Van Dijk and Hacker focused on skills and usage access, and the dynamic nature of the digital divide, Davison and Cotten (2003) considered the divide not just as between users and non-users, but also as existing between users. This is a bandwidth argument, whereby users with broadband access accomplish significantly more online than narrowband users and find the Internet to be of much greater utility (p. 7). While they noted that differences between narrow and broadband users often involve the access of entertainment-related content and activities, this should not count against the importance of broadband. As the Internet is used increasingly for daily activities, service provision, and routine governmental affairs, Davis and Cotten contended that a person "limited to dial-up access will become [a] second-class citizen" (p. 6).

Compaine (2001), coming from the perspective of resource allocation, noted the long-standing preference for addressing information gap issues via libraries (p. 329). He suggested that resources allocated to digital information provision will necessarily have to replace some of those devoted to traditional "analog" resources. However, he went on to suggest that such a substitution could do away with the necessity for physical libraries (p. 331). This entirely ignores the reality of the library being for many the material point of access to those same digital information sources that supposedly make the library expendable. This is just muddled thinking.

A Motivating Example

I (Jensen) had stopped in Seattle's Central Library to take advantage of the free wireless access with my laptop. I found myself sitting across from a young woman who appeared to be anything but homeless and who was also using a laptop. I engaged her in conversation and discovered that she, too, was taking advantage of wireless access. In her case, however, it involved more than a quick check of email. She was using the Web for serious job research, so the one-hour-a-day limit on using library computers imposed a serious constraint on her ability to research.

Further conversation elicited more interesting details. Although she had her own computer, she apparently did not have home Internet access. She lived in the Columbia City neighborhood, which the City of Seattle had chosen for a pilot project to provide free wireless access in the core business district (Figure 5.1). According to her, this service is at best completely unreliable, a state of affairs that had been reported nearly nine months earlier in *The Stranger* (Fischer, 2005), when the service was first announced. Later that day, I checked a list of library branch locations. Sure enough, Columbia City has a library branch, but not one that as yet offered wireless access for those with the means. Thus, this woman, nominally middle class and educated, found herself having to drive or take the bus to the downtown branch, with all the attendant issues of time and distance involved.

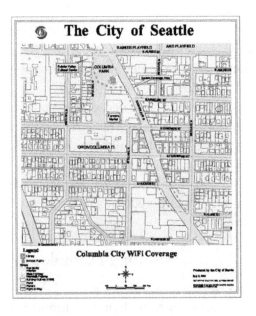

Figure 5.1: Publicly provided Wi-Fi in the Columbia City neighborhood.

My encounter with this woman, in this space, brought home several things. First, the library as a place of access to the Internet is an important resource for a broad range of people, not just homeless or low-income people. Second, that geography, with its traditional concerns with location and transportation, continues to be involved with peoples' everyday use of the Internet. Third, an unintended consequence of providing wireless access to those with the means to use it is the differential privileging of space within the library itself. I will address this in a discussion of my findings.

This raises our first question: how do local library systems, particularly the Seattle Public Library, and to a lesser extent, the UW library and other city initiatives, meet and address the modern information access needs of users? In addition, who *are* those users? Although our initial focus was on poor, low-income users, through a series of anecdotal encounters we have come to see this issue as increasingly affecting middle class users as well.

This leads to our second question. If Internet users are depending upon the library systems and a hodgepodge of spatially variable Wi-Fi resources for Internet access, what are some of the spatial landscapes involved in this dependency? What constraints of distance and time are involved? What spatial choices are created and foreclosed by such access?

Case Study: Seattle's Points of Public Access

In Seattle the major avenue of access to Internet resources with a public presence is the Seattle Public Library (SPL) system. We will also consider the special case of the University of Washington library.

Seattle Public Libraries

Public library branches are often the best, or only, place for many people to gain access to computers linked to broadband Internet services. The "Guiding Principles" for the Seattle Public Library mission statement (n.d)[5] include: "We celebrate Seattle's diversity and strive to

---

[5] http://www.spl.org/about-the-library/mission-statement

ensure that all people feel welcome in the Library. We strive to meet the needs and expectations of every Library patron....We are a learning organization and invest in our staff, technology, and infrastructure to improve service." Although the Internet and World Wide Web (WWW) may transcend information boundaries of space and time, geographically these libraries are discrete locations in space. There has been little discussion of how access to access differs across neighborhoods and in the daily lives of users.

The Seattle Public Library provides Internet access in each of its 28 branches (Figure 5.2). Each location has a number of computers, totaling approximately 600 throughout the system, which are available to patrons to use for access to the Internet. This is in addition to computers devoted solely to catalogs, databases, and other uses, including computers designated as Express terminals and limited to 15 minutes of use at a time, and computers associated with the children's books area, which have filtered Internet access.

One significant fact about the library provision of Internet access is the 90-minute daily limit in a 24-hour period. This is an absolute, inflexible limit. Put starkly, if a user has finished his or her quota and still needs more time, he or she is out of luck and cannot even leave that library branch and travel to another branch where there might be available computers. The barrier of time has been added to the barrier of distance.

In order to use any of these computers it is necessary to have a library card, although, with proper identification a visitor may acquire a one-day (one-time-only) pass good for 90 minutes of use. The number of library cards issued by the SPL has been hard to determine with any exactitude. A series of email exchanges with SPL and King County librarians (a reciprocal agreement between the two systems allows borrowing between them) gave figures ranging from approximately 396,000 to 456,000 cards. The higher figure would imply almost a one-to-one ratio with the population of Seattle. According to the library, their IT department indicates that every card has been used within the last two years, which would indicate that the number of cards extant is not distorted by legacy cards that have long since lapsed. In this light, the library has one Internet computer available for approximately every 800 card holders.

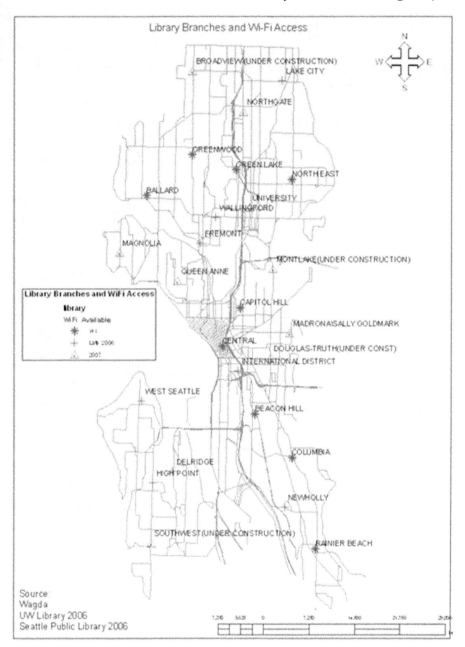

Figure 5.2: Map of library branches in Seattle.

The most basic requirements for a library card are identification and an address. A fixed, stable address is also a hallmark of the various forms of acceptable ID, such as a passport, driver's license, bank or credit card, or alien registration card. The necessity for a fixed, stable address may represent a further impediment to access in this case. Ironically, laptop users may use the library access without a library card and thus eschew the need for proper ID and fixed address, which would anyway be less likely to present a problem for someone with these resources.

We identified the number of computers with Internet access at each of the 28 SPL branches, and ascertained whether Wi-Fi access was available at the branches. The addition of Wi-Fi, especially in neighborhoods whose residents may be more able to afford laptops, should help to free up fixed computers for use by others. We also identified the population and poverty rate in the city-designated neighborhoods closest to each library branch. In most cases, there is an obvious correspondence between a neighborhood[6] and a branch of the same name. It should be clear that a given branch probably serves several neighborhoods and that a patron may use any branch of their choice.

Perhaps surprisingly, there was no particular relationship between population or population in poverty and the number of publicly accessible Internet-linked computers in the branches. Several relationships did stand out, however. The Central Library, serving an area with a high percentage of people in poverty, had the highest ratio of computers to population due to the large number of computers in the branch. The Queen Anne branch, one of the oldest in the system, and serving a middle-class neighborhood, had an exceptionally low computer-to-population ratio. The overall impression is one of lumpiness in distribution.

Dropping down to the scale of the Seattle Central Library building, we see a similar instance of disconnected spaces of proximity. Users without the resource of a personal laptop are primarily crowded together in one common space, while those with the means have free range of

---

[6] We combined two or more neighborhoods for the Central, Ballard, Lake City, and Lake Forest Park branches.

the library space. With the advent of Wi-Fi within the library most laptop users are not only freed of the time limit on Internet access associated with use of a library computer but are also free to roam about the building while using the Internet. All other users are limited to fixed locations. The most prominent of these locations, The Mixing Chamber, is on Level 5 of the SPL Central Library and contains nearly 150 Internet computers. This space is described as "a trading floor for information" where library patrons (sometimes referred to as customers) can expect to have all of their reference needs met in one place. Descriptions such as high-tech, seamless, and proactive are used in conjunction with this space.

Even "higher tech" are users with their wireless-enabled laptops, who can escape, avoid, or supplement this space. Thus, the space(s) of the library involved with Internet access may be seen as both inclusionary and exclusionary. They offer more opportunity to some than to others. Fifteen years ago, all library patrons interacted with the space in pretty much the same way. The evolving range of library services, particularly the embrace of ICTs, and class and economic differences has changed that. Insofar as The Mixing Chamber may enable people from all walks of life to work in close proximity, it is inclusionary; insofar as wireless laptops enable some users to work in areas separate and untethered from the fixed computers of The Mixing Chamber, these spaces are exclusionary.

We interpret the preceding to show that the SPL clearly plays a significant public role in the provision of Internet access and that access is uneven both geographically and within the spaces of the library branches themselves. The placement of neighborhood branches is largely determined by previous historical contexts. Indeed, the SPL regards the current number of branches as a fixed asset with no plans for additional branches. Neighborhoods have grown and shifted around branches that may have been in place for many years and served much different populations. Insofar as the SPL branches are providing this service, which appears to be in great demand, there is no understanding of travel factors that are involved in peoples' use of the resource.

The Special Case of the UW

We are including the University of Washington's Seattle campus libraries and wireless access resources in our discussion. This is justified for several reasons. First, the university is a major public institution, funded by the state and federal governments. The UW libraries are, by any measure, a significant library system within the Seattle urban area. In addition, the UW's designation as a Federal Repository library carries with it a certain acknowledgment of broader public access.

The degree of public, non-privileged access to UW library resources has changed markedly in the last four years. Where once it was possible for anyone to walk onto campus, enter the library, and use a computer to access the Internet, perhaps to check a Webmail account, this is no longer the case. The few computers that allow use without a logon identity are configured in a highly constrictive manner. This represents a new impediment to access for some and forces new choices upon them. The UW campus has a geographical footprint that is equal in size to several of the formally recognized Seattle neighborhoods. There is a continual material flow of people between the two neighborhoods, yet they represent two very different realms of access.

Finally, the evolving UW Wi-Fi network is a closed system that, while it can be "seen" by many, grants actual privileges of use to a set population. At the same time, it is being put in place within the context of a city neighborhood within a neighborhood. This all speaks to differentiated spaces of access and access to access.

Anyone using a library as their primary or sole venue for Internet access faces time and space constraints. Some degree of travel, regardless the method, and planning will be involved in getting to the library. In the case of the UW Library, the actual Internet access itself embodies constraints. Internet-accessible computers in the UW library complex fall into two categories. Unless a user has a UW NetID, he or she may only use a computer limited to .gov, .edu, .org, .mil, or .museum domains. Updated signage specifically notes that common email services such as Gmail and Hotmail are not accessible. There are 32 such computers in the main library.

The great majority of Internet computers in the Suzzallo/Allen library (116 in total) are not limited. The entirety of the Web is open to them, provided one is a member of the proper population—a holder of a UW NetID. These computers are even designated as Access+ computers, with all the attendant connotations of privilege. A further privileging and differentiating of the space of the library are created by the extension of wireless service throughout the library. Users with laptops— again, only holders of a UW NetID, others need not apply—may find quiet, less-crowded spots in which to work. Local space is reconfigured for these users, with placards placed throughout the library informing the user that a librarian is now just "a click away."

There are a few exceptions to the exclusion of .com domains. The major search engines are allowed as are some newspaper sites. However, these limited exceptions to the access restrictions are not at all obvious; the prominent signage on each computer indicates only the broad, blanket restrictions.

The policy also embodies, however unintentionally, the dubious distinction between use of the Internet as a tool for information gathering and for communication. The use policy in effect for the truly publicly available computers explicitly rules out the use of all the most widely used Web-based email systems, such as Hotmail, Gmail, and Yahoo. For many people, especially those without ISPs, such services are their only connection to email and all its attendant uses and benefits. It should be manifestly clear that research often involves two-way communication, to both acquire and convey information. Although the nature of that information may be subject to value judgments, it is information nevertheless. The ability and opportunity to communicate are access for many people.

The mobility of Internet access that is enabled by the UW Wireless Initiative, in conjunction with the changes in library policy, is effectively serving to create an invisible gated community bounded by the geographic confines of the University campus, which is a neighborhood in its own right adjacent to the University District neighborhood. A member of this neighborhood is free to cross the street to the University neighborhood but cannot cross and enter the wireless gateway. This comes within the context of a developing discourse around the presentation of Wi-Fi as the answer to Internet access issues.

Conclusions

The effects of distance and time on access to access remain understudied in Seattle, at the scales of neighborhoods and of individuals. This is probably the case in other cities as well. This chapter has attempted to point that out, to look at some of the reasons why, and propose a method for addressing the lack of information.

Since the initial research for this chapter, libraries have further embraced digital technologies. Libraries are no longer physical locations of Internet access but are increasingly accessible from the Internet in more ways than just a catalogue. An actual library branch is a proximate location, and a library's collection that is accessible via the Internet for download is a virtual location. The two states of connectedness are not the same. This is a net positive for the housebound and disabled who otherwise do not need a library as a point of Internet connection.

A case in point is the significant increase in offerings from the SPL (SPL.org) that can be "digitally checked out" and downloaded to wherever the user happens to be. These resources are considerably less, if at all, available to someone whose point of connection is an actual library.

We realize that, somewhat in common with the cyber-utopians, we are granting the Internet and ICTs a normative status. Unlike many of them, however, we see an ICT-mediated world as much more variable and contingent, a world that raises as many questions as it may answer. We believe that a highly ICT-mediated world is our future, one in which an emerging state of ambient connectivity, wherein a person with the right device is almost always able to access Internet-mediated or based resources regardless of location or activity. For these people it is increasingly becoming an expectation, whether for entertainment, socializing, on the spot information, or work.

We leave the reader with this picture:

> In Seattle, you could hypothetically find yourself riding on the 48 bus route, sitting next to a young woman who is taking advantage of the Wi-Fi service offered on that route. She is using her laptop or smart phone to check email. Or perhaps she is Web surfing. She might be engaged in as routine an activity as shopping, looking up movie reviews, or checking sports scores, or she might be involved in academic information-seeking. Perhaps she is downloading a PDF of a journal article, using her UW Library privileges, which she will be using in her master's thesis.

Elsewhere on that same bus, a young man is on the way to one of the library branches within a few blocks of the 48 route. He is taking the bus to a library to check email. Maybe he will be checking sports scores or doing some shopping, or applying for food stamps or other social assistance via the Web. When he arrives at the library, he takes a chance that a computer will be available for his use. Or perhaps he was able to reserve one in advance. If he has planned carefully, the library will be open long enough for him to use his full 90 minutes of access.

In these examples, we can see two major urban networks, the bus route and the Internet (themselves composed of multiple networks) in use by two people with two different experiences. One network is a traditional transportation network, whose purpose is to negotiate distance. The other, a network based upon ICTs (and itself connected to networks connected to yet other networks, their physical components extending from Seattle throughout the world), serves the purpose of rendering distance irrelevant.

For the young woman, these two networks complement one another, merging almost seamlessly. For the other rider, there is a disjuncture between the two networks, yet they form a necessary linkage at the same time. They are complementary but do not merge. There is a necessary order of precedence involved. The older physical network—the bus—is a precursor for even getting to the new virtual network—the Internet. Two people, in the same "place" at the same time, are involved with the same two networks. Her experience of these two networks is simultaneous; his experience is serial. Graham and Marvin (2001) compared the fixity and embeddedness and the frictional effects of distance and scales of operation of urban networks (p. 193). For the second rider, the "very high" frictional effects of distance involved in a transport network effectively attenuate the "very low" effects involved with the telecom network.

Upon a closer look we might find that the young woman's experience of access is actually more complicated than it first appears; that, while more flexible and less constrained than the man's, it too is subject to frictions of distance. It is contingent and contextual. It may be that outside of school or work she does not have ready Internet access or access at sufficient bandwidth. If she is not in school and is between jobs, she might not have any ready access other than a café offering Wi-Fi or her neighborhood library branch.

If her nearest branch option is closed that day due to budget cuts (15 of the 27 branches are now closed two days a week), she must walk, drive, bike, bus, or otherwise make her way to a branch that does. It should be immediately obvious that distance and time are very much back in play in this case. Her access to access, to information, even though she is in nominal possession of superior resources, is now subject to many of the same constraints as the other bus passenger. Weather may be an issue. The time of day may be a significant factor, in a much more traditional sense than Cairncross' (1997) contention that only relations across three time zones matter. Distance is not yet dead, despite the readiness of those who may pronounce it so. It should be clear that its effects continue to be pronounced and that the continuing implications for some members of society make it an important topic of geographic inquiry.

References

Cairncross, F. (1997). *The death of distance: How the communications revolution will change our lives.* Boston, MA: Harvard Business School Press.

Calhoun, C. (1998). Community without propinquity revisited: Communications technology and the transformation of the urban public sphere. *Sociological Inquiry, 68*(3), 373-97.

Castells, M. (1989). *The informational city.* Oxford, England: Blackwell.

Castells, M. (2001). *The Internet galaxy.* Oxford, England: Oxford University Press.

City of Seattle Information Technology Residential Survey final report. (2004). Retrieved from http://seattle.gov/tech/indicators/ITIndicatorsResSurveyReport2004Full.pdf

Compaine, B. M. (2001). Information gaps: Myth or reality? In B. M. Compaine (Ed.), *The digital divide: Facing a crisis or creating a myth?* Cambridge, MA: MIT Sourcebooks.

Couclelis, H. (2000). From sustainable transportation to sustainable accessibility: Can we avoid a new tragedy of the commons? In D. Janelle & D. Hodge (Eds.), *Information, place and cyberspace* (pp. 341-56). Berlin, Germany: Springer.

Couclelis, H. (2004). The construction of the digital city. *Environment and Planning B: Planning and Design, 31*(1), 5-19.

Davison, E., & Cotten, S. R. (2003, March). Connection discrepancies: Unmasking further layers of the digital divide. *First Monday, 8*(3). Retrieved from http://firstmonday.org/issues/issue8_3/davison/index.html

Dertouzos, M. (1997). *What will be: How the new world of information will change our lives.* New York, NY: HarperCollins.

Van Dijk, J. van, & Hacker, K. (2003).The digital divide as a complex and dynamic phenomenon. *The Information Society, 19*(4), 315-26.

Fischer, S. D. (2005, October). No-fi: City internet project crashes. *The Stranger*. Retrieved from http://www.thestranger.com/seattle/no-fi/Content?oid=23555

Fox, S. (2005). Digital divisions. Retrieved from http://www.pewinternet.org/Reports/2005/Digital-Divisions.aspx

Goulding, A. (2001). Editorial information: Commodity or social good? *Journal of Librarianship and Information Science, 33*(1), 1-4.

Graham, S. (2004). Beyond the "Dazzling Light": From dreams of transcendence to the "Remediation" of urban life. *New Media & Society, 6*(1), 16-25.

Graham, S. (Ed.). (2004). *The cybercities reader.* London, England: Routledge.

Graham, S. & Marvin, S. (1996). *Telecommunications and the city: Electronic spaces, urban places.* London, England: Routledge.

Graham, S., & Marvin, S. (2001). *Splintering urbanism: Networked infrastructures, technological mobilities and the urban condition.* London, England: Routledge.

Janelle, D., & Hodge, D. (Ed.). (2000). *Information, place and cyberspace.* Berlin, Germany: Springer.

Kellerman, A. (2002). *The Internet on earth: A geography of information.* Chichester, England: John Wiley.

Moore, E. J., Gordon, A. C., Gordon, M. T., & Heuertz, L. M. L. S. (2002). It's working: People from low-income families disproportionately use library computers. Retrieved from http://www.gatesfoundation.org/learning/Documents/Summary-ItsWorkingLowIncome.pdf

National Coalition for the Homeless. June, 22 2006. www.nationalhomeless.org

Ogles, J. (2006, June). Laptops give hope to the homeless. Retrieved from http://www.wired.com/news/technology/1,71153-0.html

Parayil, G. (2005). The digital divide and increasing returns: Contradictions of informational capitalism. *The Information Society, 21*, 41-51.

The Seattle Public Library. (n.d.). About the library. Mission statement. Retrieved from http://www.spl.org/about-the-library/mission-statement

Wi-Fi and the cities. (2006). *The New York Times*, pp. A22.

Wilson, M. (2001). Location, location, location: The geography of the dot com problem. *Environment and Planning B: Planning and Design, 28*, 59-71.

Douglas Noonan

Introduction

The social reach of information technology—connecting to the masses—poses some interesting empirical questions. The depth and breadth of information technology's reach into societies are moderated, in large part at least, by software. The common perception is that conventional, proprietary software has serious constraints on IT's reach. These include economic and technical constraints, where some segments of society may be underserved, overlooked, or not otherwise reached by the software industry. If the segment is too small to warrant developing customized software, if the segment is too poor to afford the software, or if the segment's needs are too difficult to meet, the link between IT and some groups in society may be severed. Perhaps alternative modes of software production can expand IT's reach. This chapter examines the empirical evidence on the reach of a prominent alternative to conventional software—open source software (OSS)—into certain "unconnected" segments of society. The results show that conventional wisdom and faith in alternatives may be poor substitutes for systematic empirical analysis. The promise of OSS is not yet matched by practice.

Open source software has an abundance of advocates and users. The OSS "movement" has no shortage of rhetoric, with evocative imagery of David vs. Goliath, evangelists and Luddites, cathedrals and bazaars, hackers and cyberpunks, furtive and monopolizing corporations, and heroes and villains. Hang out among the OSS boosters long enough and the stark imagery leaves an indelible impression. Even the scholarly literature succumbs to the grand and polarizing rhetoric; dwell long enough in it and you get the impression that OSS is more about religion and sociology than it is about software.

The legal scholars (e.g., Evans & Reddy, 2003; Determann, 2007) and a few other exceptions (Weber, 2005; Lerner & Schankerman, 2010) have portrayed OSS in a more nuanced and moderate light by emphasizing the technical distinctions between OSS and the alternatives (proprietary software). These distinctions ultimately boil down to legal frameworks and intellectual property regimes. Despite the advocates painting stark contrasts between OSS and proprietary software, in practice many of these distinctions are idealized or idiosyncratic. The idealized differences often involve claims such as: OSS is more democratic or communitarian; OSS is cheaper; OSS is more customizable; OSS is more inclusive; OSS is more creative and innovative; and OSS is free to all. Read enough peer-reviewed literature or spend enough time with those involved in producing OSS, however, and these all-or-nothing comparisons give way to shades of gray. In practice, OSS development is not necessarily cheaper, more democratic, more inclusive, more innovative, or functionally any better. It *might* be, but many OSS projects fail, and few outcomes or processes are written in stone. It is, after all, a highly open-ended production mode full of considerable variety. Few simple and universal "truths" are likely to hold.

Thus, despite the bold and unswerving claims of advocates, this muddied reality of OSS emphasizes the need for empirical analysis. Even if some theories or advocates predict that OSS will extend the depth and breadth of software's reach into society, this promise may not be matched by the data. This chapter explores the empirical evidence of OSS activity among some potentially under-served communities.

Examples of the Promise of Connectivity

A handful of quotes from some published OSS commentary depict the kind of promise that OSS holds for some:

- "For example, an open source software developer who writes just a few useful lines of code...has also enabled thousands of people using Linux to connect cell phones, PDAs and other devices to their computers for the first time" (Rushkoff, 2003, p. 60).
- Open source development helps gives the perspective "required of us if we are to move into a more networked and emergent understanding of our world" (Rushkoff, 2003, p. 61).

- OSS "provides a new forum for democratic action" (Working Group on Libre Software, 2000).
- "Open source provides a way for Africans to help themselves, not to wait for the first world, but to get up and do it themselves....The open source philosophy lends itself to making technology available to the masses" (Chonia, 2003, p. 1).
- "Control of technology may be democratized, its advantages spread more broadly than ever before" (Chopra & Dexter, 2007, p. xiii).
- Free and open software embodies radical change. (Chopra & Dexter, 2007, p. xiv)
- "FOSS may be the only viable source of software in developing nations, where programming talent is abundant but prices for proprietary-software licenses are prohibitive" (Chopra & Dexter, 2007, p. xv).
- The "promise" of the OSS economy depends on the removal of "the fundamental source of alienation"—the failure to recognize programmer's knowledge as the source of value. (Chopra & Dexter, 2007, p. 35)
- "The FOSS mode of open communication could become a model for political discourse: the populace could actively intervene by "developing," "bug-fixing," and "iterating" true participatory government" (Chopra & Dexter, 2007, p. 167).
- "The OSS projects are written, developed, and debugged largely by worldwide volunteers, who in most cases are connected and collaborate solely through the Internet" (Xu, Christley, & Madey, 2006, p. 206).
- "The promise of the digital networks as an open distribution medium is that anyone can now publish their work, bypassing gatekeepers and reaching the audience directly. Worldwide distribution is now within the reach of anyone, and there is a new opportunity for artists to be heard and to have their works broadcast. They can effectively build up a reputation within a social network" (Hanappe, 2005, pp. 213-214).

There are some contrasting views of OSS out there, even outside of advocates for proprietary approaches. For example, Yeats (2006) observed in his dissertation:

The rhetoric of Open Source, then, represents a false reality of a free and open society where individuals have control over the technology in their lives—a society where everyone is equally empowered to participate in active communities and where the ideas of others are valued and influential in development processes. Open Source fails to live up to this utopian promise. Instead, open-source software communities are closed to outsiders, especially ones who lack a high level of technological skill. Non-developer users are routinely ignored and wield considerably less influence than their developer-user counterparts. A technological development process that promises the democratization of technology thus simply upholds the status quo. (p. 189)[1]

Empirical Evidence on OSS

Data on Open Source software are hard to come by. State agencies generally do not collect data on OSS production or use (von Hippel, 2006; Noonan, Baker, Seavey, & Moon, 2011). Much of the rest of the scholarly literature is dominated by theoretical work or anecdotal evidence, case studies, and historical accounts. Collecting original data on the OSS industry and movement is very expensive and (in part due to the very nature of OSS) difficult.[2] Ghosh, in Feller, Fitzgerald, Hissam, & Lakhani (2007) wrote about why little empirical evidence exists for explaining why or how the open source model works. Hard data on the monetary value of OSS collaborative development are almost non-existent. The surveys that have been conducted tend to emphasize issues of programmer motivations for participating in the OSS development. (Of course, numerous surveys have been conducted by OSS consulting and marketing firms, although their methods and findings are not subject to peer review and perhaps may serve other ends as well.) In short, reliable data on OSS are notoriously scarce.

This scarcity of evidence is not absolute, so evidence is out there. The scarcity of evidence has also not deterred voluminous scholarly literature from developing. Some of the literature offers formal empiri-

---

[1] He (Yeats, 2006) goes on further to note: "It is not enough for open-source advocates to espouse inclusivity in their rhetoric without making genuine efforts to recruit the excluded. By recognizing that the open-source movement is based on the false view that participation is open to all, open-source community members can begin taking steps toward a truly democratic development process in which all are encouraged to participate (and offered the resources and training to participate), especially among the traditionally excluded groups of female, non-white, and older users." (pp. 200-201)

[2] The diffuse and decentralized nature of OSS development, coupled with a strong "hacker culture" and zealotry among its participants, complicates surveys eliciting behavioral information. With a global, volunteer workforce lacking a formal and identifiable population that can be sampled, obtaining a generalizable survey sample presents formidable challenges that few have been able to overcome. Examples include Lerner and Schankerman (2010) and David and Shapiro (2008).

cal tests of hypotheses about OSS, although much of it is historical or more dialectic. This has given rise to a host of grand claims about OSS (see above) and not much in the way of evidence to substantiate them. And this is where this chapter makes its modest contribution.

Some of the claims and conjectures about the impact and reach of OSS are ultimately empirically testable—if only a measure of OSS penetration or activity were available. Fortunately, one such empirical measure is now available in the form of an OSS Index (Noonan et al., 2011). After briefly reviewing the OSS Index construction in the section that follows, the hypotheses about the relationship between OSS and reaching "the unconnected" in society that are testable using the OSS Index are outlined. The results of a statistical analysis show mixed findings for these hypotheses. This leads to a concluding discussion that speculates that the implications of OSS for more inclusivity in the Digital Age are likely overstated, a mix of strengths and weaknesses, and not predetermined.

The OSS Index

In 2008, a prominent open-source software development firm, Red Hat, Inc., sponsored a project to develop a global index of OSS. To some fanfare on the Internet and in the blogosphere, Red Hat released the initial results on its Web site in April 2009.[3] These initial results were further refined and formalized in the form of the invited paper (Noonan, Baker, Seavey & Moon, 2010) at the Politics of Open Source conference held by the *Journal of Information Technology & Politics* in May 2010. That paper details the construction and robustness checks for the suite of indices produced by their Open Source Index project. While readers are referred to that source for the details, the complexity of the indices merits some additional brief explanation here before proceeding.

Noonan et al. (2011) constructed two primary indices: one for OSS *activity* (OSAI) and one for OSS *potential* (OSPI). The former aims to measure the amount of actual OSS development and usage activity in a particular nation. The latter aims to measure the contextual factors in a

---

[3] http://www.listman.redhat.com/about/where-is-open-source/activity/

nation that are expected to give rise to a fertile environment for OSS activity–regardless of how much activity is actually present. Taken together, these two index values (OSAI, OSPI) indicate which nations are over- or under-achieving with respect to their OSS potential.

Although actual OSS activity is key to much of the discussion of the social implications of the OSS movement, any empirical analysis of OSS activity ought to take into account that contextual factors may make comparing OSS activity in two disparate parts of the world fraught with difficulty. Comparing Haitian and French OSS activity may really be telling us much more about the dissimilarity of their IT infrastructure, more broadly, than anything about OSS itself. In a sense, controlling for OSS potential lets us "normalize" the OSS activity by the nation's underlying conditions. This helps with an "apples-to-apples" sort of comparison.

The indices themselves (OSAI, OSPI), as presented in Noonan et al. (2011), are really more *frameworks* for OSS indices than they are specific and final indices. The authors emphasize that different weights for the various components, different ways to combine the components, and even different constituent variables, might reasonably be used. Their analysis shows remarkable insensitivity for their "preferred" OSAI and OSPI measures across those different (arbitrary) construction choices. Thus, while the rank-orderings do not vary wildly across different versions of their indices, their indices do differ substantially in other ways; some indices have more comprehensive coverage of the nations of the world, while other indices use better variables. Some indices have better statistical robustness properties, while other indices give values that are more easily interpretable. Because this chapter is interested primarily in inclusivity and relative rank, the indices selected from Noonan et al. (2011) will be based on simple arithmetic means using the "best" variables for the "long" list of nations (i.e., $A_{aa, BL}$, $P_{aa, BL}$).

The following world maps depict the distribution of activity and potential values. Both Figure 6.1 (for the OSAI) and Figure 6.2 (for the OSPI) show the gradations from high to low index values. Light gray indicates the lowest index values, black indicates the highest index values, and white indicates that no index value is available for that country.

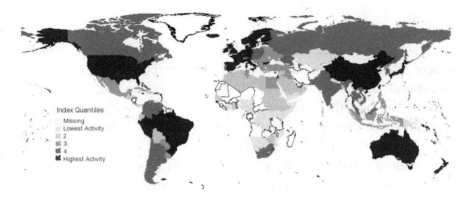

Figure 6.1: OSAI World Map

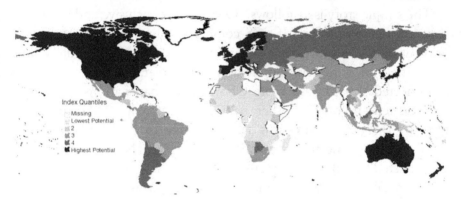

Figure 6.2: OSPI World Map

Like Noonan et al. (2011), the ratio of the activity and potential indices can be constructed to measure the OSS activity relative to its potential. This is a sort of "achievement" index. Because the original OSAI and OSPI values can be positive or negative, the *Ratio* variable is created after rescaling the OSAI and the OSPI values so that they range from 1 to 100.[4] The resulting *Ratio* value can, in principle, range from 0.01 to 100. In fact, it ranges from 0.03 to 1.88 for these OSS indices.

---

[4] Technically, let OSAI' = ([OSAI − min(OSAI)]/max(OSAI))*99+1. Define OSPI' similarly. Ratio = OSAI'/OSPI'.

Hypotheses

The extent to which OSS is able to connect to certain segments of society is an empirical question. This chapter seeks to test several hypotheses based on some of the common claims about OSS. In general, the hypothesis to test is that there is a positive relationship between OSS activity or diffusion and the size of certain subpopulations. This positive relationship may be conditional on other potentially confounding variables, such as aggregate wealth, or the maturity of the IT sector, more broadly. The hypotheses of greatest interest here are the *conditional* relationships—where the underlying contextual factors are controlled for—between OSS activity and subpopulation size.

The simple story is as follows: OSS is more inclusive and accessible than proprietary software. If OSS competes against (i.e., is a substitute for) proprietary software, then it should grow faster (in absolute terms) where the "unconnected" populations are larger. Nations with more unconnected should have more OSS activity than nations with fewer unconnected. If, on the other hand, OSS complements proprietary software, then it should grow faster relative to proprietary software where the unconnected populations are larger. Nations with more unconnected should have a greater OSS with greater market share (although OSS activity may be less in absolute terms than in the nation with fewer unconnected).

In particular, this chapter explores the relationship between OSS activity and the following subpopulations:

- the young—the population aged 14 and under.
- the elderly—the population aged 65 and over.
- the poor—the poorer populations, especially in light of the oft-argued price and cost advantage of OSS.
- the rural—the more remote populations outside of urban centers.
- the illiterate—the share of adults (over age 15) who are illiterate.
- those lacking access to mass information sources—inversely related to the number of radio sets per capita.
- those without phones—inversely related to the number of cellular phones per capita and the number of telephone mainlines per worker.

- those without Internet connections—inversely related to share of the population using the Internet or the number of computers connected to the Internet per capita.
- those without an open economy—inversely related to how connected the economy is to international trade (i.e., value of imports and exports divided by GDP).
- those without e-Government—better connectivity of the public with government via e-Government initiatives, as measured by a United Nations e-Government survey.

These groups are selected because of their frequent mention in discussions of IT accessibility and due to data limitations. The first few groups (age, income, rural-ness, illiteracy) are of primary concern in this chapter. Of course, other subpopulations (e.g., women, persons with disabilities) merit similar investigation when the data permit.

Some of the lofty claims of OSS advocates can be easily tested using the OSS Index if OSS is primarily a substitute for proprietary software (rather than a complement). Larger subpopulations should predict more OSS activity. So, a positive correlation between the subpopulation size and the OSAI supports the promise of the OSS movement. Alternatively, if OSS is primarily a complement to proprietary software, then larger subpopulations need not predict more OSS activity—rather they predict greater OSS activity *relative to proprietary software activity*. Thus, to observe the hypothesized relationship between subpopulation size and OSS activity when OSS complements proprietary software, the size of the proprietary software industry must be controlled for as well. Because the OSPI is based in large part on contextual factors that predict greater proprietary software activity, the following analysis will control for OSPI when testing the hypotheses under the null hypothesis of complementarity between OSS and proprietary software.

Whether OSS complements are competitors is an open question beyond the scope of this chapter. For now, it suffices to recognize that arguments can be made on either side. Much of the OSS movement—with its contrasting cathedrals and bazaars, and its talk of radical revolution and paradigm shifts—clearly casts the models as substitutes or competing alternatives. It may be, however, that OSS can enhance proprietary software development and vice versa. Where different production modes find fertile niches in the software ecosystem and diversity flourishes, a complementary system may yet prevail. The following analysis remains agnostic about the complementarity question, presenting and discussing results from both vantages.

To test these hypotheses, two approaches are taken. First, some simple pairwise correlations are reported. This offers an initial glimpse into the empirical relationship between OSS activity and the size of the subpopulation of interest. A significant correlation between OSAI and the subpopulation size is expected under the null hypothesis of OSS substituting for proprietary software. Under the null that they complement each other, a significant correlation between *Ratio* and the subpopulation size might be expected. The use of *Ratio* here (imperfectly) controls for the overall size of the software industry in testing whether OSS's relative "overachievement" correlates with subpopulation size. Both of these simple pairwise correlations overlook the possibility that other factors that may be associated with subpopulation size may be driving the correlation.

The second approach addresses this possibility by using a multivariate regression. Regressing the subpopulation measures on OSAI allows for testing of these hypotheses jointly. Moreover, controlling for OSPI in the regression further enables the testing of the relationships between the subpopulation size and the extent of OSS activity while controlling for the latent potential for OSS. Not only is the OSPI expected to be positively related to OSAI, the subpopulation size is expected to be positively related to OSAI even after controlling for OSS potential in a nation. It should be emphasized that these results are entirely descriptive. They offer no test of a causal relationship. Thus, it would be inappropriate, based on this evidence, to conclude that subpopulations can "cause" OSS activity or vice versa. Although not causal, the results do offer the first glimpse into how these measures actually do (or do not) vary systematically. Such descriptive evidence is an important next step in advancing our understanding of software and reaching the unconnected.

Results

First, it should be noted that there is a stark contrast between the sort of nations that have a lot of OSS activity, or a high *Ratio,* and those that do not. The bottom of both lists is dominated by impoverished and embattled countries in Africa and Eurasia. Mozambique, Kazakhstan, Moldova, Botswana, Azerbaijan, and Laos make the bottom 10 in both lists. (Note that OSAI and *Ratio* have different ranks for their bottom 10 because the *Ratio* value is available for only 107 nations whereas the OSAI is available for 132.) The top countries typically have much wealthier or emerging economies than those at the bottom of the lists. Interestingly, the wealthy and predominantly Western European nations listed in the top 10 of the OSAI are not necessarily those that are "overachieving" or that have the highest *Ratio* values. After all, those wealthy countries typically have the greatest potential for OSS activity due to their well-developed IT and educational infrastructure. The top 10 for the *Ratio* reflect the dominant position of Brazil and India in much of the popular discussions of OSS activity as well as some of the other high-profile nations with prominent pro-OSS government policies (e.g., China, Venezuela, Peru). In terms of the unconnected, a cursory glance at Table 6.1 suggests that the societies that are often thought of as the most connected and possessing the strongest IT are also those leading in OSS activity. The developing countries that appear to be losing touch with the rest of the developed and developing world are also those with the worst OSS index scores.

Table 6.1: *Top 10 and Bottom 10 Nations in OSAI and Ratio*

OSAI			Ratio		
Rank	Country	OSAI	Rank	Country	Ratio
1	Spain	1.78	1S	Haiti	1.88
2	France	1.76	2	Brazil	1.72
3	Belgium	1.71	3	Peru	1.52
4	Iceland	1.59	4	China (People's Republic of)	1.37
5	Brazil	1.58	5	Pakistan	1.35
6	Norway	1.44	6	Vietnam	1.32
7	United Kingdom	1.41	7	Venezuela	1.22

8	Qatar	1.29	8	Spain	1.16
9	Denmark	1.27	9	India	1.10
10	Finland	1.26	10	Belgium	1.06
...			...		
123	Cambodia	-0.51	98	Nepal	0.20
124	Mozambique	-0.53	99	Latvia	0.16
125	Kazakhstan	-0.53	100	Namibia	0.15
126	Tanzania	-0.53	101	Mozambique	0.15
127	Moldova	-0.54	102	Mauritius	0.13
128	Botswana	-0.55	103	Azerbaijan	0.08
129	Azerbaijan	-0.55	104	Kazakhstan	0.07
130	Tajikistan	-0.57	105	Botswana	0.04
131	Eritrea	-0.57	106	Moldova	0.04
132	Laos	-0.59	107	Laos	0.03

The pairwise correlations between the OSAI, OSPI, *Ratio*, and the measures of subpopulation sizes are presented in Table 6.2. Correlations that are significantly different than zero at the 5% level are indicated as such with an asterisk. The rows that are shaded are those that the simple hypotheses (under the assumption that OSS and proprietary software are substitutes) predict a *negative* correlation. As expected, there is a strong and significant correlation between OSS activity and potential. OSS activity is closely correlated with measures of subpopulations. The correlations with the subpopulations of primary interest (age, income, rural-ness, illiteracy) are generally inconsistent with the hypothesized relationships. Rather than be associated with large youth, senior, poor, rural, and illiterate populations, the OSAI is inversely correlated with these populations (except for the elderly subpopulations). Nations with more youth, more poverty, and more rural and illiterate populations tend to have much less OSS activity. The other subpopulation correlations also typically contrast with the promise of OSS to reach these unconnected subpopulations: higher OSS activity is associated with more widespread connections to various technologies (e.g., Internet, radios, phones).

The correlations in the OSAI column are merely pairwise correlations, not taking into account other confounding factors that might covary with OSAI. The rightmost column shows the pairwise correlations with *Ratio*, implicitly controlling for latent OSS potential. Interestingly, the *Ratio* variable is virtually uncorrelated with the other variables, except OSAI and Trade/GDP. How high a nation's OSS activity is in relation to its potential appears unrelated to the size of the subpopulations identified in Table 6.2. This suggests that if OSS and proprietary software were complements, the promise of OSS to better include these subpopulations is not being met generally. Economies that are more closed to international trade, however, do tend to have higher *Ratio* values, suggesting that OSS is better penetrating economies that are more disconnected from global markets.

Table 6.2: *Pairwise Correlations*

Variable[a]	OSAI	Ratio
OSPI	0.71*	0.01
Ratio	0.62*	1.00
% youth	-0.55*	-0.05
% elderly	0.08	-0.12
Income[b]	0.62*	0.01
% rural	-0.53*	-0.14
% literacy	0.41*	-0.05
Internet/person[c]	0.59*	0.13
Radios/person	0.59*	0.05
Phones/person	0.68*	0.06
Cells/person	0.69*	0.10
Trade/GDP	-0.06	-0.27*
eGov	0.68*	0.10

Note. [a] = all variables taken from Noonan et al. (2011), except *Ratio* which is calculated as above.
b = *in (GDP per capita).*
c = *computers with Internet connections per capita.*

The results of the multivariate regression are presented in Table 6.3. There are six different models estimated. The first three models estimate focus on only the major subpopulations of the potentially unconnected: youth, elderly, poor, rural, and illiterate. The second three models expand the analysis to look at access to media, IT, global markets, and e-Government. In each trio of models, the first simply predicts the OSAI using the subpopulation measures listed in Table 6.3. The second model predicts OSAI using the same covariates but also controlling for OSPI, effectively conditioning the analysis on the underlying potential for OSS development. The third model presents an alternative approach to this, replacing OSAI with *Ratio* to identify how the relative success of OSS depends on these subpopulations. All of the models are estimated using ordinary least squares with Huber-White robust standard errors.

As a broad overview, a few observations from Table 6.3 are apparent. First, the bulk of the variation in the OSAI can be explained by the variation in these subpopulation measures. Second, the variation in *Ratio* across nations is poorly explained by these subpopulation variables. Third, the additional explanatory power offered by OSPI in column 2 is largely captured by the additional variables (e.g., cell phones per capita) in column 5. This is unsurprising, considering that the OSS potential index is largely aiming to capture the same kinds of IT infrastructure that these additional variables capture. Fourth, throughout Table 6.3, the elderly population appears essentially unrelated to OSS activity or achievement.

Under the assumption that OSS and proprietary software are substitutes, the expectation that larger unconnected subpopulations lead to greater OSS activity is not well supported in Table 6.3. The first column of results shows that nations with more youthful, more impoverished, more rural, and less illiterate populations tend to have less OSS activity. Except for illiteracy, these results starkly contrast with the promise of the OSS movement to bring OSS to these marginalized subpopulations. Adding the additional controls for access to information and world markets dramatically alters these conclusions, however. Only the illiteracy variable retains any statistical significance. This points to the critical role of the broader IT and market infrastructure in moderating the relationship between OSS activity and these uncon-nected subpopulations. The fourth column of results shows that OSS activity tends to follow cell phone access, less open economies, and nations with higher e-Government scores. The presence of other unconnected subpopulations otherwise does little to attract more OSS activity—contrary to the promise of the OSS movement.

The remaining columns offer controls for the OSS potential of a nation. This can be seen as controlling for other differences in the country's propensity to adopt OSS that, if neglected, might bias the estimated relationship between the subpopulation measures and OSS activity. This can also be interpreted as testing the hypotheses about OSS's ability to reach these subpopulations when OSS complements (rather than competes with) proprietary software. Adding the control for OSPI (columns 2 and 5) changes the results modestly. More illitera-cy does seem to significantly advantage OSS. Similarly, more rural populations do seem to disadvantage OSS, although this appears to be at least partly driven by other connectivity in the economy and IT infrastructure. The failure to include youth and poor groups evident in the first column vanishes when OSPI is controlled for. While this indicates that youth and poverty do not disadvantage OSS, the insignif-icant results here offer no support that affordability and age are barriers that OSS excels at overcoming.

Table 6.3: OLS Regression Results for OSAI and Ratio

Dependent Variable: Variable	OSAI Coef.	OSAI Coef.	Ratio Coef.	OSAI Coef.	OSAI Coef.	Ratio Coef.
OSPI		0.667***			0.131	
		0.133			0.245	
% youth	-0.016**	-0.008	-0.010*	-0.009	-0.011*	-0.010*
	0.006	0.008	0.005	0.006	0.007	0.005
% elderly	0.128	-0.188	-0.259	-0.091	-0.093	-0.220
	0.335	0.281	0.284	0.234	0.248	0.281
Income	0.184**	-0.044	-0.058	-0.074	-0.087	-0.096*
	0.063	0.087	0.055	0.053	0.067	0.057

% rural	-0.005*	-0.006*	-0.005*	-0.002	-0.003	-0.003
	0.003	0.003	0.003	0.003	0.004	0.003
% literacy	-0.606**	-0.584**	-0.621*	-0.514*	-0.572*	-0.552
	0.254	0.283	0.349	0.288	0.302	0.328
Internet/1000 persons				0.648	0.602	0.262
				0.371	0.399	0.227
Radios/1000 persons				0.045	0.034	-0.081
				0.080	0.103	0.065
Phones/1000 persons				-0.326	-0.485	-0.498
				0.421	0.597	0.394
Cells/1000 persons				0.778**	0.781**	0.426**
				0.349	0.378	0.215
Trade/GDP				-0.003***	-0.003**	-0.002***
				0.001	0.001	0.001
eGov				1.638**	1.390*	0.648
				0.638	0.749	0.533
Constant	-0.431	1.451	2.106***	0.728	1.186	2.179***
	0.747	0.971	0.699	0.637	0.890	0.691
N	125	103	103	108	96	96
R^2	0.426	0.5316	0.0777	0.6388	0.6332	0.1732
F	19.99***	21.98***	1.82	22.84***	19.09***	2.88***

Note. Robust standard errors appear below the coefficients. *, **, *** indicate significance at the 10%, 5%, 1% levels, respectively.

The third and sixth columns of results, based on *Ratio* as the dependent variable, show that these subpopulations do a remarkably poor job of explaining which nations "overachieve" and which "underachieve" with regard to OSS. Cell phones and openness to international trade are strong predictors, but the other variables are not significant at the 5% level. A weak effect of youth populations appears, not supportive of the OSS promise here. Likewise, the negative effect of rural subpopulations in the third column suggests that OSS is not especially adept at reaching remote populations. A weak effect—certainly worthy of further investigation—can be detected for income and literacy. The nations that excel in OSS activity relative to their OSS potential tend to be somewhat poorer and less literate in the rightmost column, which is faint evidence in support of the OSS promise.

Conclusions

The empirical analysis offers mixed and, on the whole, unfavorable results for proponents of OSS's ability to reach certain subpopulations that have historically been underserved in the Digital Age. These findings stand in contrast to some of the casual impressions and outright hyperbole that permeates discussions of OSS. The OSS movement, full of rhetoric and passion, is often portrayed as having great promise for reaching the unconnected in ways in which proprietary and conventional software has failed. This promise is based in part on theory and in part on high hopes. Not much is based on systematic, quantitative data and formal hypothesis testing.

How does the promise of the OSS movement for reaching certain subpopulations hold up to empirical analysis? Not too well. Yet. While the OSS index and other data employed in this cross-sectional analysis of 100-plus nations are admittedly both crude and not ideally designed for these hypotheses tests,[5] the dearth of evidence to support claims associated with the OSS movement sets a very low bar for empirical analyses. The descriptive statistical approach undertaken here shows weak relationships between the size of subpopulations and OSS activity. When the relationships are statistically significant, they usually work in exactly opposite directions as predicted by the OSS promise. OSS does *not* appear better able to reach poor nations, or rural communities, or to connect to youth or elderly subpopulations. Perhaps the only exception is illiteracy, where the results of this analysis do suggest that OSS tends to relatively flourish where illiteracy rates are higher.

The IT infrastructure does play an important role in moderating the effectiveness of OSS in reaching these subpopulations. A common measure of the openness of a nation's economy to international mar-

---

[5] Ideally, an OSS index that measured OSS activity relative to proprietary software activity as a whole would be available. In addition, measures of OSS activity within or by each subpopulation would be preferred, thus avoiding the possible ecological fallacy associated with making inferences about subunits based on aggregate relationships.

kets also appears inversely related to OSS activity.[6] This finding may be the most surprising and novel positive result (unlike the predominantly null findings for the rest of the subpopulation variables). OSS flourishes in nations that are less connected to the global system. This result holds whether or not the nation's OSS potential is controlled for. OSS may be an effective way to circumvent global isolationism and protectionism. This result might not be too surprising considering the decentralized and online nature of much OSS development and distribution. None-theless, OSS appears to offer a strong connection to the global system.

Overall, some less-connected subpopulations may be well served by OSS, and others appear to remain relatively unconnected. The promise of OSS seems greatly overstated, although it may be too early to tell. Future efforts, with more and better data, may yield different results. The success of OSS in bringing the Digital Age to the masses and breaking down the high walls of "the cathedral" of proprietary software remains an unfinished story. If these results are any indication, the open-source movement is likely to improve connectedness for some subpopulations and possibly even worsen matters for others. Realizing the potential of OSS to reduce alienation and reach a broader audience is unlikely to occur simply because of faith in an OSS philosophy. Rather, it will likely also require deliberate effort to connect to them.

References

Chonia, G. H. (2003, October). Free and Open Source software in Africa. *Developing countries access to scientific knowledge: Quantifying the digital divide.* Open round table at the Abdus Salam ICTP, Trieste, Italy.

Chopra, S., & Dexter, S. D. (2007). *Decoding liberation: The promise of free and Open Source software.* New York, NY: Routledge.

---

[6] Note that this measure of openness, from the World Bank's World Development Indica-tors database, accounts for the gross flow of total value of goods and capital into and out of a country normalized by its GDP. Thus its value ranges from roughly 20% to almost 300% in the data. High values of Trade/GDP result from greater two-way economic flows to other countries or from smaller domestic economies. The most integrated countries in the dataset are Luxembourg and Malaysia. The least integrated countries per this measure are Japan and Argentina.

David, P. A., & Shapiro, J. S. (2008). Community-based production of Open-Source software: What do we know about the developers who participate? *Information Economics and Policy, 20*(4), 364–398.

Determann, L. (2007). Dangerous liaisons—Software combinations as derivative works? Distribution, installation and execution of linked programs under copyright law, commercial licenses and the GPL. *Berkeley Technology Law Journal, 21*(4), 1421–1498.

Evans, D. S., & Reddy, B. J. (2003). Government preferences for promoting Open Source software: A solution in search of a problem. *Michigan Telecommunications and Technology Law Review, 9*, 313–394. Retrieved from http://www.mttlr.org/volnine/evans.pdf

Feller, J., Fitzgerald, B., Hissam, S. A., & Lakhani, K. R. (Eds.). (2007). *Perspectives on free and Open Source software.* Cambridge, MA, London, England: MIT Press.

Ghosh, R. A. (2007). Understanding free software developers: Findings from the FLOSS study. In J. Feller, B. Fitzgerald, S. A. Hissam, & K. R. Lakhani (Eds.), *Perspectives on free and Open Source software* (pp. 23–45). Cambridge, MA, London, England: MIT Press.

Hanappe, P. (2005). Building open ecosystems for collaborative creativity. In M. Wynants & J. Cornelis (Eds.), *How open is the future?* (pp. 199–229). Brussels, Belgium: VUB Brussels University Press.

Lerner, J., & Schankerman, M. (2010). *Comingled code: Open Source and economic development.* Cambridge, MA: MIT Press.

Noonan, D. S., Baker, P. M. A., Seavey, A., & Moon, N. W. (2011). Where cathedrals and bazaars are: An index of Open Source software activity and potential. *Journal of Information Technology & Politics, 8*(3), 273–303.

Raymond, E. (1999). *The cathedral & the bazaar: Musings on Linux and Open Source by an accidental revolutionary.* Cambridge, MA: O'Reilly Media.

Rushkoff, D. (2003). *Open Source democracy: How online communication is changing online politics.* London, England: Demos.

Von Hippel, E. (2007). *Open Source software projects as user innovation networks,* In Feller, J. et al., (Eds.), *Perspectives on free an Open Source software.* Cambridge, MA: MIT Press.

Weber, S. (2005). *The success of Open Source.* Cambridge, MA: Harvard University Press.

Working Group on Libre Software. (2000). *Free Software / Open Source: Information Society Opportunities for Europe?* Retrieved from http://eu.conecta.it/paper.pdf

World Bank (2002). *World development indicators*, Retrieved from http://www-wds.worldbank.org/external/default/WDSContentServer/IW3P/IB/2002/10/12/000094946_0210120412542/Rendered/PDF/multi0page.pdf

Wynants, M., & Cornelis, J. (Eds.). (2005). *How open is the future?* Brussels, Belgium: VUB Brussels University Press.

Xu, J., Christley, S., & Madey, G. (2006). Application of social network analysis to the study of Open Source software. In J. Bitzer & P. J. H. Schröder (Eds.), *The economics of Open Source software development*. Amsterdam, Holland, Boston, MA: Elsevier B.V.

Yeats, D. (2006). *Open-source software and user-centered design: A study of Open-Source practices and participants* (Dissertation, Texas Tech University). Retrieved from http://thinktech.lib.ttu.edu/ttu-ir/handle/2346/20898?show=full

Section 3

Content

Jeremy Hunsinger

Introduction

How do virtual worlds govern the unconnected? It seems a simple question, but the unconnected are willfully not inside participating in virtual worlds. The unconnected are necessarily knowledgeable and related to people who are part of virtual worlds. This group of people outside of the virtual world is seemingly ungovernable, but their subjectivities extend through their assembled relations into the virtual world. The capacity of the unconnected's subjectivities to act through these assemblages and the knowledges in virtual worlds is not constrained by the liminal constructs of the virtual world itself but extends through those liminalities from their everyday life into the virtual worlds and eventually through those virtual worlds' other liminal boundaries into the infrastructures, designs, and related assemblages of the world-builders. The unconnected, through their assemblages, become an identifiable set of people whose subjectivities need to be addressed and governed in relation to the virtual world. But, they are also a group that can only be partly addressed, and to some extent they will always be ungoverned. To help engage with the question of governing the unconnected of virtual worlds, I develop the distinction between the in and the within of virtual worlds, as the modes through which the unconnected operate vary through these distinguishable groups.

The distinction between what it means to be in a virtual world as opposed to be within a virtual world seems to be a minor operant within an assemblage of knowledge around virtual worlds. But when contemplating the virtual world, we need to consider our own reflexive situatedness in relation to virtual worlds (Hunsinger, 2008). To be in a virtual world is to be in a relation to that world where one operates subjectively in the co-created spaces and agencies in relation to those virtual worlds; whereas to be within or of a virtual world is to actually have the working knowledges of the infrastructures of the virtual worlds. The insider knowledges of the person who is within the world require knowing the intimate and intricate facts of the interior, and, most importantly, the liminalities of that interior. The insider knowledges possessed by those within are not better knowledges than those of those who are in; these knowledges are simply a different set of knowledges than possessed by a person who primarily exists in, and passing through, virtual worlds. The groups build their knowledges on different sets of experiences with the world, and we should not collapse these categories into consumer/producer/prosumer in this case either, as the idea is less that those within the world do not produce and consume the world, rather more that they do it differently than those that are merely in the world. What differentiates the two is the extant territory that their knowledges map in the world; the number, and varieties of their commonplaces differ. This distinction is important, because access to different commonplaces generates different operant conditions of modulation; that is, when governing, when people know different things, they act differently. In the case of the in versus the within, the differences in knowledges and thus commonplaces construct two different appreciations of being governed while governing. The within group has more awareness of their situation in that regard, whereas the in group has less awareness but more significance for the unconnected.

Virtual worlds are defined by their worldliness, much like game/worlds (Klastrup, 2010). For my purposes, they are defined by their construction of space and therefore the communities that create and sustain that place. The communities' interactions in and through these places, both independently and collaboratively, construct and reify the existences of both the community and the space. The communities co-construct a plurality of mutual knowledges and shared experiences through which they create a plurality of commonplaces. These commonplaces are constructed from the assemblages of the communities in the virtual world and then inscribed not just into the software and its memories but also into the combined memories of the inhabitants (Carruthers et al., 1992). The memories are both the back story and the referential infrastructures to the commonplaces that the connected and unconnected of virtual worlds inhabit. Each inhabitant occupies different parts and shares different territories with the different communities in which it participates. This plurality of knowledges about our subjective commonplaces creates problems both in governing the lives of the connected of virtual worlds, and in governing the unconnected of virtual worlds in relation to those virtual worlds.

Much like our textual commonplaces that we construct from textual memories represented as snippets of text and memories, the commonplaces of virtual worlds are co-constructed from the memories and interactions with the environment and its communities; the commonplaces of virtual worlds function as a platform for neotribalism, and the specific forms of legitimation found in the partial and alternative narratives in those groups (Maffesoli, 1996; Lyotard, 1984). Neotribalisms need the commonplace in order to structure their narratives, legitimize their power relations, and justify their systems of internal governance and their relations to external governance. The nature of these virtual-world neotribes depends on those narratives and their interpretations of the communities, the people, and their mutually constructed contexts within the virtual world. The interpretations and operations are those that are re/encoded in the world by the creators of the world, but also those that are re/encoded into the memory systems of the communities both within and without the world. The tensions between the memory systems of the creators and the communities that inhabit the virtual world create the space for the communities to develop, giving the users something to operate against and the creators something to create; thus the creators partly govern the virtual worlds and the neotribes through the creation of content in those worlds.

Not all creators or developers of virtual worlds are necessarily inside the world, though they are likely within it, and because of their relation to the virtual world those creators may be members of the unconnected. This class of creators that govern but are separate causes significant challenges for the development of commonplaces between the developers and the other subjects in the virtual world. Without the common understandings and shared memories of some of the perspectives of the communities in the world gained through participating with these groups, creators create governance abstractly and out of context, which causes tension across all populations in the world.

This idea of governing by creating brings us back to the question of who are the unconnected in virtual worlds. Who are those that are not experiencing the virtual world directly but are being partly governed by the virtual world because of their relations and their assemblages? The unconnected are people who are related to the virtual world in some manner, usually through relations to someone in or within the world. Their virtual world is mediated through a variety of assemblages through which they experience it. Beyond their mediation, they might have been in or within the world themselves formerly but have left the world and are no longer connected in any direct sense to the virtual world. When we think about the unconnected, we should not assume that they do not know what the virtual world is, nor should we assume they should know a great deal, all we can assume is that they know a person or people involved in the world but that they choose not to participate in the virtual world. There is a larger set of unconnected that has no relation to the virtual world at all, but they are not unconnected as they were never connected. When we conceive of the unconnected of virtual worlds, we think of a person who shares part of their reality with the virtual world, even if they do not directly interface with that virtual world themselves. The relationship between the person outside and the person inside is another relationship with plural subjectivities and plural commonplaces. It is through the relationship that knowledge of the virtual world and thus governance flows. There is a system of representations surrounding that virtual world and its participants that the unconnected participates in and incorporates into their own assemblages and commonplaces. Without the relationship to the person/s in the world, the unconnected are really just never connected, and without the connection there are no commonplaces to operational-ize and therefore no space for governance to function.

On Governance of Communities in Virtual Worlds

All inhabited spaces are spaces of governance. When addressing governing and governance we are not speaking of the laws or policies, nor are we talking about the politics of those laws and policies (Bevir, 2010; Hajer & Wagenaar, 2003). Governance is only partly the opera-tionalization of those laws and policies, but most of governance is the operationalization of what modulates our everyday lives and worlds. Governance is the key concept for how our lives are managed by governments and non-governmental bodies today. The modulation of behavior is part of what Deleuze (1990b; 1990a) termed the control society (Hunsinger, 2009b). In the control society, you are not told what you should do, but the environment that you inhabit is constructed in such a way as to encourage you to choose paths that serve the needs of the governor, and the governor is frequently as much you and your acceptance/rejection of certain norms, practices, and ways of being than it is any external entity. Governance is less a system of rules than a system of designs, norms, conventions, and methods of constructing your subjectivity in which you are encouraged to pay more attention to certain parts of reality; while you follow your own desires and goals, the only paths that seem to be before you are the ones that you are being encouraged to follow (Thévenot, 1984; 2001; 2002). This governance of signs and codes interoperates through our everyday life in order to structure the distribution of those designs, norms, goals, and conventions. However, while governance is internalized to the subjectivities of the population and the population itself constructs it through our daily activities, it is also mediated by us individually, through our communities/neotribal relations, and through the media that we use to understand our world. Governance is not alienated from our subjectivities, but it is intrinsic, and usually feels more natural than constructed because we are so deeply uncultured within its systems (Bevir, 2010; Hajer & Wagenaar, 2003).

Virtual worlds, as designed spaces meant to encourage certain behaviors in them, are systems of governance of the communities within and in them. They might allow us to be free, but virtual worlds also have constraints on that freedom built into them at all levels, as well as modes of making you capable of acting in certain ways and less capable of acting in other ways. These tools built into the code provide the infrastructures of governance for the virtual world. The specifics of the infrastructures of governance are part of the knowledge that only people with deep knowledge of the virtual world have. You may gain those knowledges either through what Geoffrey Bowker et al. (2009) and Susan Leigh Star and K. Ruhleder (1994) called "infrastructural inversion," which is when you are directly exposed to the inside of the machine and you can see how the metaphorical "black box" operates from within, or you learn it through the process of experimentation and experience, which is a process of testing the black box to see what happens when you act in certain ways in the virtual world, which might be termed "hacking" the black box (Bowker, Baker, Millerand, & Ribes, 2009; Star & Ruhleder, 1994; Hunsinger, 2009a). These processes develop different sets of knowledge because they are based on different sorts of experiences; neither is better, but the experimental method tends to take more time and is possibly incomplete, whereas infrastructural inversion may take less time but is more taxing on the capacity to understand, and the expertise necessary to understand might not be present without the experimentation. In either case, coming to know the way in which a virtual world is governed is never only about the actual operations of the mechanisms and symbols of governance but is also about understanding the population and the way that they self-govern.

The ability to know this type of infrastructural and operational knowledge in virtual worlds is what differentiates the commonplaces of the in and the within. The within have knowledge and take care to know how those systems operate and how they are used in relation to them, whereas the in merely take those knowledges as part of the environment. They are both aware of the existence of infrastructure because it is implied by the virtual world in which they exist, but only the within are taking care to note the infrastructure and its changes.

Access to this knowledge, and to what extent the knowledge is accessible, is a question of governance and the modulation of the population within the world. For many who care deeply about knowing how things work, there is a right to this knowledge, and the inability to access it is a matter of social justice. However, sometimes access to knowledge creates problems for governing virtual worlds, and the interests of those seeking knowledge must be balanced against other interests. For instance, certain forms of experimental access to infrastructural knowledge of virtual worlds might impinge upon other people's user experiences or cause damage to the systems. This occasionally happens with some forms of experimental action in virtual worlds, though not always. Knowledge of infrastructures and the mechanics of governance they imply is central to being able to engage reflexively with the virtual world. One of the modes of governance operates around the management of information and informational power (Hunsinger, 2006). The limiting and directing of information to audiences controls the audience and modulates its behaviors.

Governing virtual worlds is not merely informational, it is also semiotic and programmatic. The signs in virtual worlds are designed to have certain meanings, and the world is designed to have certain affordances. In a virtual world, you might have the capability to do certain things and not other things, and rarely do these capacities designed in the world come without signs of their presence. The ability to read these signs and interpret the affordances present is possessed to a greater or lesser degree by all participants in the virtual world, and various groups in and within the world promote various interpretations and operations above others in order to pursue their own objectives. The commonplaces provide for part of the operationalization of the semiotics of governance of virtual worlds.

The commonplaces also accord you a circumspection of the programmatic systems that control and direct your behavior in virtual worlds. There are real programs in virtual worlds in which you have to perform certain activities in order to be able to do others. These are commonplaces too, shared cultural references that operate much like rites of passage do in our everyday lives. They modulate our behavior and make us pass through certain norming processes that may help us understand the virtual world, or in some cases they might also confuse our understanding. The programs of virtual worlds all have their enforcement regimes. However, the commonplaces and their creation do not necessarily relate to those enforcement regimes; they might instead relate to the communities or neotribes that inhabit the spaces of virtual worlds.

Neotribalism of the In and the Within

Virtual-world communities enact their own contemporary neotribalisms and the related micropolitics of identity formation around their subjectivities and knowledges. As a neotribalism, they enact openness to their own kinds but also a closeness toward differences (Maffesoli, 1996; Bauman, 1990; Fox & Miller, 1996). Within their neotribal relations they create militaristic or other authoritarian structures sometimes called clans and other times called guilds, which structure their community. I will not explore guilds and clans in depth in this chapter, though others have done so extensively, and their work provides background to considerations regarding the tribality of these groups (Adams & Smith, 2008; Chen, 2011). While clans and guilds are interesting constructions of neotribalism, they are not alone; there are also art groups, pop culture groups, groups that pursue a myriad of fetishes, and groups that seem to exist solely to create trouble or to antagonize other groups (Boellstorff, 2010; Ludlow & Wallace, 2007; Pearce, 2009). Any of these groups may inhabit many different virtual worlds at any given time yet still may be composed of the same people performing or enacting analogous, occasionally divergent roles within the group. We can think of some of these neotribal groups as based upon affinities that have over time been reified into their tribal identities.

Though their neotribal identities are always in the process of becoming reified through their communal activities, I would not say that they are necessarily becoming fixed in any way other than memory, which may then be forgotten. The identities are fluid as are the members that act within them. Governance structures of the tribe, while rarely democratic and usually authoritarian, do sometimes operate on consensus and, through that consensus, distribute the authority to enact changes and plan activities for the group. These governance activities are performed both with consent and dissent. It is the dissent from which we derive some of the most interesting interactions from the within communities versus the inside communities. When the governance of the virtual world fails to achieve consent on some trajectories that are important to one of their neotribes, then that neotribe may seek to leave the virtual world. It may fragment or otherwise dissolve also, but in those cases, usually the members of the neotribal system will seek out other tribes within the world, or in other worlds, in which to participate.

When dissent is universal across a neotribal community, these tribes migrate in whole or in part from virtual world to virtual world. The history of Second Life®, a prominent virtual world developed by Linden Lab®, shows how neotribal groups with strong affinity relations might migrate from virtual world to virtual world and how the networked media that they use might change with them (Au, 2008; Boellstorff, 2010; Ludlow & Wallace, 2007). The canonical example of this is the transition of the Alphaville Herald into the Second Life Herald. The migration of this minor media outlet is the sign of another movement in which players of the Sims Online® migrated to Second Life®. Some of these players that had a strong affinity to a certain understanding of what might be thought of as libertarian politics and its property relations migrated to a virtual world, Second Life®, and lobbied its creators to change policies to better meet their ideals. However, there were already communities within Second Life® with their own ideals who were pursuing their own interests within the current models of governance. These groups were popular and well known among the developer community of the virtual world, and eventually their capacity to be within the virtual world was questioned by those who were outside of the within and merely in the world. The tensions in this broader community caused the conflict between two loosely orchestrated neotribal identities within the mediated arena surrounding the virtual world and, through their actions, may have driven the insiders to eventually reject both communities in order to open up the system of governance to broader community involvement.

The migration of Sims Online® players into Second Life® is not the only community that joined the world en masse. Art groups who were performing large-scale/multiple actor theatrical-type performances in Star Wars Galaxies® were forced to leave the world when the developers changed the settings that prevented the large groups from occupying the same places in the world. In this case, it was the developers reacting to performance issues in the game that had effects on the community. The community unable to do as they wished in the virtual world went to join a world that was more open to their artistic endeavors. However, even prior to their migration the group set up artistic protests in which they attempted to communicate their concerns to the developers.

The question might be posed as to whether these affinity groups around art and politics actually were neotribal formations. In that the two groups acted together in both worlds, that members of the group surrendered elements of their own identity in one virtual world in order to migrate to another, and co-constructed a group subjectivity that acted along an ideological construct to symbolically construct their own counter-identity to the groups within the virtual world, they certainly seem like neotribal activities. The extent to which one can identify their symbolic actions as forms of semiological violence and norm-breaking within the game are up for debate, but it is one possible interpretation of their actions. They acted in the interest of their group, even if that interest was counter to the investments of time and resources that any given member of the group had invested in the virtual world. Their actions once they migrated to the new virtual world also demonstrated that they were acting in a system of neotribal relation, as they attempted to establish the grounds and justification for their own communities' existences as part of, and occasionally separate from, though inside of, the larger Second Life® communities.

Some of the governance structures of Second Life® post-2006 are evidence of the effects of these migrations on the broader community. The changes in the Second Life® map tool, which once let you locate all your friends but later gave those friends the capacity to be invisible on the map to some or all of their friends. Similarly, once locating a friend being able to teleport directly to them instead of having to teleport to a standard teleportation location, enabled community-building and successful group development, encouraging people to find and meet other groups, and generally made the world very sociable; therefore the norms were socially policed. These changes were under-mined by interests supporting closedness and privacy that lobbied for changes that allowed people to close their networks. Linden Lab undermined their capacity to govern by transforming the communities in the interest of the people who were seeking privacy controls. Linden Lab created controls aimed at allowing people to have privacy, by blocking people from seeing them and from teleporting to them. This slowly transformed the world from an open world where everyone could see everyone, into one of cliques and tribes, where you were always going to be an outsider unless you were already an insider through other means. This construction of new possibilities of closed communi-ties increased the centralization of knowledge within groups. In turn, this centralization caused even more neotribalism to spread around those knowledge communities. Granted, some of the groups that supported privacy changes did profit from those changes, and their virtual-world experience was made slightly better. However, their increased experience was gained at the expense of a self-governing population.

These changes also occurred during a period of extreme growth for Second Life®. The population explosion caused tensions between older and newer communities, increasing the liminalities between old migrations that formed the earlier user base and the current user base, giving those with older privileges different understandings of the world, its management, and who benefited from that. These understandings were often debated in the blogs around Second Life® and can still be found in archives. What developed from those debates was less a common understanding between communities and more a mutual antagonism, which now had to be managed. These antagonisms, combined with the growth in population, increased the number of competent malcontents, which then took up the practice of griefing events, or otherwise acting out to get attention for themselves or to undermine others.

Griefers and griefing practices are one of the sets of behaviors that are more easily policed by smaller populations. Once you are governing a large enough population, people can hide in relative anonymity. That said, what really went on within and in virtual worlds during this period had significant effects on those who were unconnected to virtual worlds and led to significant numbers of people quitting virtual worlds, and likely many more never joining them.

These griefers could be thought of as one end of the neotribal spectrum of socialities, one that anchors a certain empiricist, nihilist, or radical reaction to the governance systems of the world. It may be that they are experimenting with the world itself in order to understand it, but their actions are not the central topic of this paper. Their existence, though, shows that there are groups that are acting in relation to governance in virtual worlds, and some of these groups are attempting to resist that governance. We have already discussed in this section the groups that migrated away from governance of a virtual world in order to join one that was more amenable to their ideological outlook or artistic practices. These groups, both griefers and migrants, might be thought of as the unconnected also, as they are either attempting to break the commonplaces and reconfigure them anew in their own service or are leaving old ones behind in order to partially reconstruct the commonplaces in a new environment.

Governing the Unconnected in Virtual Worlds

The direct tools of governance in virtual worlds—informational governance, semiotic governance, and programmatic governance—do not necessarily all extend outside of the virtual world in ways that could govern the unconnected. However, when developing knowledges and social relations in virtual worlds, the problems of governing the unconnected become clearer. The virtual world mediates governance through the assemblages and commonplaces in which the unconnected participate with the connected or its mediated representation.

Beyond this assemblage of governing structures reaching out and dragging the assemblages around the subjectivities of the unconnected into a governed relation to the virtual world, there are other governed relations that are enacted through the relationships between the connected and the unconnected. These come down to implications on what the subjects in those assemblages value and how those differences in values are negotiated. There is an indirect system of governance in place on the unconnected. The unconnected are governed by the commitments of the other subjects in the assemblage, but they are also governed by the mediations of the others' desires, both inside and outside the world. Their relationships with the virtual world and its mediations have an effect on what their relations desire, and, as such, that molds what they desire in relation to that. The translation of these desires into relationships with the virtual world is what will eventually partly govern the unconnected in relation to the virtual world, as those desires allow the unconnected and the connected to operate within a commonplace through which the desires can be interpreted as part of the whole of their everyday lives. This commonplace will frame their desires and form a governing modality through which they then renegotiate the situatedness of their subjectivity, transforming the norms of their relations in relation to the virtual world and revising their prior relationship to include their understandings around the relations around the world. This returns us to the question of mediation and knowledge, because those concepts are the central concepts that allow the indirect governance of the unconnected to be governed in the virtual world. The unconnected must have knowledge, and that knowledge will be in part influenced by the relations they have to the virtual world and those that mediate that knowledge. This knowledge will transform the sets of knowledges and the commonplaces that contextualize those knowledges. This transformation will necessarily include the signs, codes, and conventions of governance of the virtual world, and the meanings of these signs will bleed through the liminalities of the virtual world and into the spaces of meaning that the relationship between the unconnected and connected inhabit. That new tertiary commonplace conceptually becomes partly the virtual world because the necessary assemblages are part of that virtual world. The languages and meanings of the virtual world slowly enter the common points of interpretation in the everyday lives of the unconnected and the connected. Through this new tertiary commonplace, the unconnected are now governed by the conceptualizations and meanings, desires, codes, and conventions of the virtual world and its related subjectivities. In short, the unconnected who has a relation to the virtual world will be governed indirectly by the virtual world, through their relationships and the assemblages around them. While indirect, the level of knowledge that the unconnected have about the world is parallel to many of the neotribe's members. We can think of them as in the world without being connected to the virtual world, because they share commonplaces of the virtual world with the other subjectivities with whom they have relations.

That is not to say that governance through virtual worlds is the only outcome of the new negotiations; the unconnected can and frequently do become the ungoverned and the ungovernable, but this requires the radicalization of the unconnectedness, which is a rejection of the mutual assemblages and the relations around them. This radical unconnectedness in relation to virtual worlds is the basis for the success and failure of virtual worlds because it is the success or failure of meaningful everyday lives. The sociality of the everyday life is tied to the subjective assemblages through which we construct our meaningful lives. Without the shared memories of the group to rely on, the unconnected individuals must interpret the situation and actions of other people in light of the commonplaces they share, and without the construct of the virtual world and its mediations, the unconnected are now disconnected, ungoverned by the virtual world and completely outside of the system of governance.

Conclusions

This chapter has engaged the question of governing the unconnected in virtual worlds by proposing a model based on knowledge and relationships that create commonplaces based on shared memories and assemblages based on relationships. The model was divided into the connected and unconnected with the connected having subjects that are in and other subjects that are within, and the unconnected having subjects that are, in some respects, in the world as they have analogous knowledges to those that are in, and are indirectly governed by the relations and mediatizations of that world, at least partly. In that the model proposed is primarily a model of governance centered on three modes of governance—the informational, the semiotic, and the programmatic—the extension of those modes out of the virtual world and into the everyday lives of the subjectivities of the participants is to be expected, as the knowledges that sustain those modes of governance are present outside of virtual worlds.

The chapter relies upon a description of the communities of people that are either in or within the world as participating in neotribal systems surrounding the world that are based on shared commonplaces, shared systems of legitimation, and shared modes of governance as they exist in virtual worlds. It is clear that there are governable populations in virtual worlds, as it is clear that some people resist governance in virtual worlds, and through those resistances usually become complicit in the governance of virtual worlds.

In conclusion, this chapter argued that the unconnected, a population distinguished by not directly using the virtual world, but having relations to other subjectivities in the world and having knowledge of the virtual world, can be governed by the world through their participation in larger systems that include the virtual world. It is also clear that there may exist a group of people who are unconnected and within the virtual worlds; these might be developers who are both within the world, but not using the world or participating in the commonplaces inside the world. They too are unconnected yet governed by the virtual world, though in substantively different ways than the external unconnected. The other groups of unconnected are those that are trying to come to know and change the world in ways that willfully break or transform it, and who, if they do not manage to accomplish their goals, may just leave the world, becoming external and unconnected. However, even these becoming-unconnected neotribes are governed by the virtual world. The ungoverned of virtual worlds are not those that resist governance but those that are completely disconnected from the virtual world, and must have broken from the relation to the virtual world, or not have knowledge of the virtual world, which in either case destroys the locus communis of the virtual world, which is truly where the virtuality of it exists.

References

Adams, T. L., & Smith, S. A. (2008). *Electronic tribes: The virtual worlds of geeks, gamers, shamans, and scammers.* Austin, TX: University of Texas Press.

Au, W. J. (2008). *The making of Second Life®: Notes from the new world.* New York, NY: Collins.

Bauman, Z. (1990). Philosophical affinities of postmodern sociology. *The Sociological Review, 38*(3), 411–44.

Bevir, M. (2010). *Democratic governance.* Princeton, NJ: Princeton University Press.

Boellstorff, T. (2010). *Coming of age in Second Life®: An anthropologist explores the virtually human.* Princeton, NJ: Princeton University Press.

Bowker, G. C., Baker, K., Millerand, F., & Ribes, D. (2009). Toward information infrastructure studies: Ways of knowing in a networked environment. In J. Hunsinger, L. Klastrup, & M. Allen (Eds.), *International handbook of Internet research.* Dordrecht, Netherlands: Springer.

Carruthers, M. J., Minnis, A., Boyde, P., Burrow, J., Copeland, R., Deyermond, A., Wetherbee, W. (1992). *The book of memory: A study of memory in medieval culture.* Cambridge, England, New York, NY: Cambridge University Press.

Chen, M. (2011). *Leet Noobs: The life and death of an expert player group in World of Warcraft* (1st ed.). New York, NY: Peter Lang Publishing.

Deleuze, G. (1990a). Control and becoming. In G. Deleuze (Ed.), *Negotiations 1972–1990.* New York, NY: Columbia University Press.

Deleuze, G. (1990b). Postscript on control societies. In G. Deleuze (Ed.), *Negotiations 1972–1990*. New York, NY: Columbia University Press.

Fox, C. J., & Miller, H. T. (1996). *Postmodern public administration: Toward discourse*. Thousand Oaks, CA: Sage.

Hajer, M. A., & Wagenaar, H. (2003). *Deliberative policy analysis: Understanding governance in the network society*. Cambridge, England, New York, NY: Cambridge University Press.

Hunsinger, J. (2006). The political economy of the Internet: Contesting capitalism, the spirit of informationalism, and virtual learning environments. In J. Weiss, J. Nolan, J. Hunsinger, & P. Trifonas (Eds.), *International handbook of virtual learning environments* (pp. 189–206). Dordrecht, Netherlands: Springer.

Hunsinger, J. (2008). The virtual and virtuality: Toward dialogues of transdisciplinarity. In N. Panteli & M. Chiasson (Eds.), *Exploring virtuality within and beyond organizations: Social, global and local dimensions*. London, England: Palgrave Macmillan.

Hunsinger, J. (2009a). Introducing learning infrastructures: Invisibility, context, and governance. *Learning Inquiry, 3*(3), 111–14.

Hunsinger, J. (2009b). Toward nomadological cyberinfrastructures. In J. Hunsinger, L. Klastrup, & M. Allen (Eds.), *International handbook of Internet research*. Dordrecht, Netherlands: Springer.

Klastrup, L. (2010). Understanding online (game)worlds. In J. Hunsinger, L. Klastrup, & M. Allen (Eds.), *International handbook of Internet research*. Dordrecht, Netherlands: Springer.

Ludlow, P., & Wallace, M. (2007). *The Second Life Herald: The virtual tabloid that witnessed the dawn of the metaverse*. Cambridge, MA: The MIT Press.

Lyotard, J.-F. (1984). *The postmodern condition: A report on knowledge*. Minneapolis, MN: University of Minnesota Press.

Maffesoli, M. (1996). *The time of the tribes* (1st ed.). Thousand Oaks, CA: Sage.

Pearce, C. (2009). *Communities of play: Emergent cultures in multiplayer games and virtual worlds*. Cambridge, MA: The MIT Press.

Star, S. L., & Ruhleder, K. (1994). Steps towards an ecology of infrastructure: Complex problems in design and access for large-scale collaborative systems. *Proceedings of the 1994 ACM Conference on Computer Supported Cooperative Work*, USA, 253–264. doi: 10.1145/192844.193021

Thévenot, L. (1984). Rules and implements: Investment in forms. *Social Science Information, 23*(1), 1–45.

Thévenot, L. (2001). Pragmatic regimes governing the engagement with the world. In T. R. Schatzki, K. K. Cetina, & E. Von Savigny (Eds.), *The practice turn in contemporary theory*. New York, NY: Routledge.

Thévenot, L. (2002). Conventions of co-ordination and the framing of uncertainty. In E. Fullbrook (Ed.) *Intersubjectivity in economics*. New York, NY: Routledge.

Chapter 8:

The Study of Digital Connectedness: A Case for Public Informatics

Thomas Jacobson and Susan L. Jacobson

Introduction: The Challenge of Public Connectedness

The theme of connectedness in studies of the digital society usefully focuses attention on a range of important subjects. The lack of connectedness among individuals can be found in economic conditions or in terms of artistic taste. It can be seen in differential levels of awareness about, and access to, social services. In all these spheres where connectedness can and should be strengthened, the apt use of digital technologies can presumably help.

Progress in all these areas also requires the political will necessary to forge relevant policies to spread economic benefits, to support the arts, and to monitor the public agencies providing services. Whether through the application of digital technology or not, progress in all these specific areas depends on one prior particular form of connectedness. This is the connection among citizens over matters of common need, or the common good. The common good, whether in relation to economic well-being, promotion of the arts, or the responsive administration of social services, requires the formation of public will to advance widely shared interests. This kind of connection has historically been served most crucially by journalism, where news media serve to monitor citizen expressions of interest, circulate public information, act as a watchdog on public and corporate malfeasance, and, when necessary, help the public "throw the rascals out."

This essential medium for public connectedness faces a number of daunting challenges. One is the economic challenge of changing business models faced by print as well as broadcast media. Digital information services have radically altered both news consumption and also advertising practices. Revenue streams have diminished substantially and survival has become a serious problem, especially in the newspa-per business.

Another challenge can be found in the complicated state of affairs sometimes referred to as the digital divide. Internet access is high in the United States but not ubiquitous. And access to high bandwidth services through systems such as mobile technologies is even less widespread. Thus, not everybody has this access, and among those that do have access, some have more access than others. In addition, even where access is available, the ability to use new information technolo-gies fully depends in part on education levels, which vary widely.

The problem of the digital divide first gained currency during the Clinton Administration in the United States. The National Telecom-munication and Information Administration (NTIA) (1995, 1998) issued two studies related to the use of information technology in society: a first report calling attention to information "haves" and "have nots," and a second report identifying a problem termed the "digital divide. Since that time this divide has often been treated as one of access to, and use of, information technology. More recently, this definition of the digital divide as a binary, "haves" vs. "have-nots," has been criticized as being oversimplified (van Dijk & Hacker, 2003; Light, 2001; Warschauer, 2003). As Warschauer (2002) explained:

> ...meaningful access to ICT encompasses far more than merely providing computers and Internet connections. Rather, access to ICT is embedded in a complex array of factors encompassing physical, digital, human, and social resources and relationships. Content and language, literacy and education, and community and institutional structures must all be taken into account if meaningful access to new technologies is to be provided (p. 3).

Warschauer's definition of the problem goes beyond a binary and technologically oriented definition and merits further exploration. The problem is not one of technology access or even use, but what John Dewey (1927) addressed in *The Public and Its Problems*: the problem of the extent to which social institutions reflect the active involvement of citizens, particularly within, but not limited to, political institutions alone. Thus, new complexities attend the process of access to news through new technologies. Simple access to the Internet or other digital technologies does not in and of itself comprise the active involvement of citizens in public discussion and debate.

This is one of the relatively new challenges facing journalism. Journalism faces a challenging business environment, but digital information systems can make it difficult to get information to audiences in spite of the apparent ubiquity of information technologies. Literacy alone was the single requirement for access to low-cost newspapers of the past. Today, full participation in the great public discussion is a more complex affair.

The subject of this chapter is journalism's need to develop new ways of connecting to citizens within a new technological environment and the additional challenge of increasing societal complexity.

The social and political systems on which journalism have customarily reported have become much more complex. The density of economic, social, and political actors is increasing rapidly at municipal, county, and national levels, and the connections among them are increasing geometrically. In addition, contingencies affecting these economic, social, and political actors are increasingly global. What transpires in political, economic, and religious institutions around the world can quickly affect national and even local concerns. Given this increase in complexity, journalism is increasingly unable to keep up with the sheer number of stories citizens need to cover changing economic conditions, to attend to evolving policy needs, and to advance political processes.

We use the ideas of John Dewey and Walter Lippmann to reflect on responses American society has made to increases in social complexity. Both scholars recommended that American media should be employed precisely in response to complexity. Their ideas remain in play today as can be seen in the work of contemporary theorists such as Niklas Luhmann (1995) and Jurgen Habermas (1984, 2006). Habermas's work on the public sphere, in particular, updates Dewey's.

We argue that given both increases in social complexity and increases in the complexity of new information systems, the standard paradigm of what information citizens need for self-governance and how it should be provided to them is outdated. The standard model of the press-state relationship taught to students is the libertarian model of the press (see, for example, Siebert, Peterson, & Schramm, 1963). This model represents the news media as being free, to the extent that they are privately owned, and therefore free from government interference. It is posed in contrast to the communist, authoritarian, and social responsibility models. Free from government interference, journalism's publishers and editors should be able to print what they determine is fit to print, and this should inform the public in a manner sufficient to enable democratic self-governance.

We propose development of a research program in public informatics to update this paradigm, which would be both old and new. The need is as old as democratic politics—a Fourth Estate is required to serve as a non-official partner to the three main branches of democratic government. But the technologies are new; the social and economic environments are more complex. Contemporary conditions require a major rethinking of what is required to make possible the practice of free and democratic dialog.

Two Theoretical Divides:
Lippmann Versus Dewey on Intelligence

Walter Lippmann was a towering figure in American opinion journals and newspaper columns from the 1920s almost until his death in 1974. He wrote columns at the *New York Herald Tribune* and later at the *Washington Post*. Lippmann also addressed the problems of the day in his highly influential book, *Public Opinion* (1922), by taking in the sweep of history while assessing the significance of rapid changes in American society, such as urbanization, industrialization, and the increasing importance of communications media.

Given increasing social complexity and shortfalls in the press's information about the complex changes impacting American society, citizens were seen as rapidly losing competence to govern themselves. The knowledge and imagination needed to comprehend policy needs in modern society outstripped the resources of average citizens, who were in any case increasingly less interested in the problems of others. The citizenry was drifting away from collective participation in public life and becoming, for Lippmann, a "phantom public" (1925).

For Lippmann, the requirement to infuse additional "intelligence" into the political system was much needed but was no longer provided by the citizenry. He believed that a remedy could be found in the increasing pool of individuals trained in the skills of information processing, analysis, and decision-making. Although the social sciences had not yet attained the stature of the physical sciences, it was clear that their dispassionate attitude and systematic approach to social analysis was becoming more relevant and could be employed for the betterment of governance.

> I argue that representative government, either in what is ordinarily called politics, or in industry, cannot be worked successfully, no matter what the basis of election, unless there is an independent expert organization for making the unseen facts intelligible to those who have to make the decisions. (Lippmann, 1925, p. 31)

He proposed a permanent "intelligence section" for each department of the federal government (p. 386), where people would be well trained and independent from Congress. Their independence would be guaranteed by lifetime tenure, freeing them to employ their talents (pp. 379–397). This was a solution that tended to circumvent the public while trying to serve it.

This was a compelling argument for many, since it combined an astute description of the problem with the image of a competent, managerial solution. Due to Lippmann's adept prosecution of this viewpoint and the elements of truth it contained, this view of the bystander public became prevalent among mid-century political theorists including Harold Lasswell (Lasswell, 1927, pp. 4–5; 1930, p. 194). Given the concomitant creation of the public relations industry at this time, the need for government influence over public opinion regarding American participation in the World Wars and other factors, there emerged a near consensus on the importance of democracy's newest invention, the "manufacture of consent" (Lippmann, 1922, p. 248).

John Dewey was America's preeminent educator and philosopher. His book *The Public and Its Problems* (1927) was written largely in response to Lippmann's views as expressed in *Public Opinion* (1922) and *The Phantom Public* (1925)

Dewey (1927), too, was aware of the growth in complexity of American society and its changing demographics. He was aware of drops in public participation and interest in government. "The number of voters who take advantage of their majestic right is steadily decreasing in proportion to those who might use it. The ratio of actual to eligible voters is now about one-half" (p. 117). However, he interpreted the nature of the problem differently. Yes, the public was increasingly out of touch with the mechanisms of power, but Dewey's response was to improve the public rather than to circumvent it.

Like Lippmann, Dewey saw the solution in intelligence, but it was intelligence of a different sort. Lippmann's intelligence was a scientific intelligence possessed by the few and employed by them for benevolent purposes. Dewey's intelligence, alternatively, was scientific intelligence possessed by society at large and employed by ordinary citizens.

For Dewey (1927), the education of every individual was beneficial for democratic society as a whole—the democratic promise of universal education. Education provided a foundation, but society needed institutions capable of surveying the events of the day, processing them and circulating them widely on a timely basis. The information needed to be high quality, and it needed to be taken up in discussion among citizens at all levels of wealth and education. Only when combined with good information and opportunities to discuss issues of the day could individuals serve as citizens in democratic self-governance.

For Dewey (1927), the remedy did not lie in "intelligence services" attached to departments of the federal government. He talked instead of "embodied intelligence," a kind of intelligence combining the education of individuals with the knowledgeable practices of agencies and institutions whose specialized purposes included the processing and circulation of information for social and public good (p. 210). These knowledgeable practices might include newspapers, but the point was not so much the institutions as the quality of discussion that was needed. A combination of professional, amateur, educational, and social scientific skills would be required. For Dewey, "That is *the* problem of the public" (p. 208).

Dewey banked his hopes not so much on a new kind of institution as on a widely distributed set of social practices employing journalistic, social scientific, and even literary skills in presenting information addressing public need but not in the routinized and often sensational-ized manner journalism had come to assume.

> The highest and most difficult kind of inquiry and a subtle, delicate, vivid, and re-sponsive art of communication must take possession of the physical machinery of

transmission and circulation and breathe life into it. When the machine age has thus perfected its machinery it will be a means of life and not its despotic masters. Democracy will come into its own. (Dewey, 1927, p. 184)

In summary, we see a debate between two of America's most prominent social analysts of last century, who shared a number of key observations. Social complexity was increasing, while the public was not able to keep up with this complexity. The news media, rapidly evolving as they were at the time, were not filling the gap. Looking into the period a little closer one finds even more remarkable and detailed parallels. Access to information technologies was differential, but ability to use these technologies was also differential. Lippmann's ideas would place the locus of informational control and democratic power in the hands of the few specialists, while Dewey's would make as its first priority the placing of informational control, discussion, debates, and public opinion formation into the hands of citizens.

Luhmann and Habermas on Complexity

Today, social complexity is increasing at a more vigorous pace. In place of high-speed presses, telegraphy, and radio there is now cable television, high-bandwidth Internet access, and mobile networks. In place of a form of globalization represented by the threat of world war, there is now the increasingly interdependent global economy. Voter turnout remains low. As in the 1920s, these problems are widely recognized among social analysts, whose approaches to solutions remain varied. In contemporary discourse, Lippmann and Dewey are represented by the theorists Niklas Luhmann and Jurgen Habermas.

Luhmann (1995) is today's most prominent social theorist focusing on complexity, basing his ideas on autopoetic, or self-organizing, systems theory in which social systems comprise subsystems of individuals and institutions whose only concern can be for the continuity of their own complexity, their own needs and interests. There can be no such thing as a public because the idea of a public implies shared concern among private individuals and institutions for common interests, i.e. shared awareness, debate, and collectively developed public will. In Luhmann's thought, government is nothing but one system among many, perpetuating its self-organization as a response to immediately impinging inputs from its nearby environments. On this view, the digital divide, or any other divide is of marginal importance.

This view is like Lippmann's in only a few ways, though what they share is important. First, the two are alike in assigning the idea of a public to relative unimportance. The public for Lippmann was a phantom. For Luhmann the idea of a public is a reification, an invalid abstraction away from facts on the ground, which represents outdated sentiment rather than real social conditions. The viewpoints of these two are also alike in their implications for social policy. For Luhmann, as for Lippmann, the fact that the public is out of the loop diminishes the need for possible justifications for public investment in systems serving the public interest.

Jurgen Habermas (1975) professes a theory of society that vests modernity's future precisely in a Deweyan form of shared public interest. Like Luhmann, Habermas employs a version of systems theory, but for him, a standard autopoetic systems theoretic view of society provides an adequate account for only half of the processes society requires to reproduce itself. System processes, and the instrumental communication that sustains them, are suitable for the management of economic systems and administration. However, for matters concerning the transmission of social norms, the integration of social and political subsystems, and the formation of individual identity, another kind of communication is required. This kind of communication is prized by Dewey. It is communication based in the commonly shared language frameworks provided through education and the embodied intelligence contained in public discussion and debate (Habermas, 1984, 1987).

This viewpoint focuses attention on the idea of a shifting and socially contextualized analysis of information technologies and the ways these technologies might serve to connect citizens to one another and to government. New information technologies might be of crucial importance both for equalizing life opportunities across the citizenry and for the continued operation of economic and political systems. Dewey (1927) emphasized the importance of public "association and communication" that attends to public needs, fears, and hopes. Similarly, Habermas (1996) calls this communicative action in the public sphere.

From Mass Media to Digital Information Services

It is a simplification to say that the problem of the digital divide is a political one. As Dewey saw, politics are intertwined with education, embodied intelligence, and social values; no single social system provides a lever on the problem. Technology is neither the problem nor the solution; it is only one element of any possible attempt to improve the quality of, and opportunities for, democratic life. Given this the challenge of applying information technologies to politics can seem overwhelming.

The problem must be treated as a matter of public communication if it is to be made tractable. Communicative functions must be served in addressing public need; specific technologies themselves can then evolve as necessary. If Dewey's great community is to be served, and Habermas' public sphere is to be reinvigorated, and widespread public benefits of information technology are to be realized, then what kind of communication functions are required?

It is clear that the press cannot solve this problem. It didn't solve it in the 1920s, nor does it today. Industry trends make it increasingly less likely that anything other than profit will motivate coverage patterns, but given increases in social complexity, the market orientation of the press is not really the point. Social complexity has increased 100-fold over the last 100 years. The news-hole of a daily newspaper is now outmatched by the information needs of public life. Today, "newspapers" cannot and should not be expected to fully serve the public's information needs, even if they remain a vital player in democratic communication. Although the importance of freedom of expression in relation to democracy remains valid, the means for free expression and the circulation of information have changed dramatically. The best hope is that present need might be met by new information systems comprising old and new media, including these beyond forms imagined today.

Emerging Public Information and Communication Technologies

How can this be done? What might it look like? What follows is a categorization of new public information resources, and an analysis of how they might fulfill the paradigm of a new Fourth Estate, as a means of public discourse for democratic self-governance. Categories include online news organizations, information databases, collaborative databases, and social media networks. Some categories may overlap, and any given information resource may fall into more than one category.

It is important to note that while the democratic nature of publishing on the Internet may seem to advance Deweyan/Habermasian principles of empowering the public, access to publishing platforms is not sufficient to guarantee a free and fair and meaningful exchange of information for collective self-governance. Indeed, both Dewey and Lippmann might argue that without educating citizens on how to discern truth-telling from spin or how to weave a solid argument based on evidence, the much-vaunted democratic communication capabilities of the Internet may contribute to the situation we have today, where the more extreme and most sound-bite worthy perspectives often play most readily in mainstream news organizations. Still, the democratizing potential of new news and information services made possible by digital communication seems to promise increased public engagement with matters of public interest.

News Organizations

This category includes mainstream news organizations, such as most newspapers and TV news channels; "new" news venues, such as blogs; and grassroots news organizations, such as *IndyMedia*. Most of the mainstream media organizations and the blogs maintain the trappings of traditional newsrooms: they have identifiable writers, reporters, and editors, who create content, set the news agenda, and perform gatekeeping functions. Shirky (2002) would identify these organizations as institutions that "filter, then publish" material, meaning that editors carefully select and review material prior to publication. Some new information services, discussed below, publish first then rely on their audience to filter or weed out inaccurate or inferior material after publication.

Mainstream news organizations whose primary publication venue is not the Internet tend to repurpose most of the content for their Web sites from their print or broadcast vehicles, and supplement their republished content with online extras, such as video published by newspapers or text from wire services on TV news Web sites. The amount of original online content on these sites has increased in recent years, but the overwhelming majority of the material still comes from the news organizations' primary venue of publication.

While multimedia, interactive, and participatory content does appear on the Web sites of mainstream news organizations, and may be increasing in volume, most news organizations are still a long way from fully embracing the digital qualities of the Web (Deuze, 2004; Quandt, 2008; Jacobson, 2010). Studies show the level of audience interaction, discussion, and feedback is quite limited (Singer, 2006; Rosenberry, 2005). Mainstream media's decision to limit interaction with what Rosen (2006) has called "the people formerly known as the audience" may be moot, however, as Goode (2009) pointed out that news-rating sites such as Digg, and social networking recommendations, may override mainstream news organizations' decisions to limit comments on their articles. Goode further stated that the ability to share stories widely and quickly through social networking also upends the agenda-setting privileges of mainstream news organizations as audiences are quick to circulate stories that strike a responsive chord, an action that in turn feeds the news agendas of the mainstream media.

Most of the mainstream news media sites do not allow for unmoderated user contributions. They are more likely to use audience photos and comments only after they have been sifted and vetted by editors, reflecting Shirky's "filter then publish" model. CNN is one of the exceptions, as the CNN iReport accepts and publishes any material on the Web. CNN editors warn users of the iReport site that the material published there is neither edited nor fact-checked. CNN editors select which submissions to highlight on the site, and any material that CNN then uses on its Web site or cable news network is carefully vetted. While other mainstream news organizations have created opportunities for citizen contributions to their sites, arguably none has been as comprehensive or successful as iReport.

The most successful "new" news format ushered in by the Internet is the blog. While most mainstream news organizations at least claim some level of objectivity, many of the most popular news blogs openly promote a point of view. Based on February 2012's rankings of the most popular blogs by the blog portal Technorati, the liberal-leaning Huffington Post is the most popular blog on the Internet. The most popular genres in Technorati's top 25 blogs are technology, politics, and celebrity gossip, and eight of the top 10 political blogs have either a liberal or conservative perspective.[1]

The content of most blogs consists of material re-published from other sources, commentary on content from other sources, and original reporting. More specialized news blogs, such as the popular technology blogs Gizmodo and Mashable, are written for audiences with a higher-than-average knowledge of their subject matter. Gizmodo and Mashable are quick to publish bursts of new information on technology, and their readers are quick to pass on important stories to their friends through social networking. At their best, these specialized blogs may enable informed dialogue between blog editors and audiences, potentially creating the kind of word-of-mouth talk that can effect change in a specialized field such as technology.

Perhaps the most successful new grassroots news organization arose from public demand for stories that mainstream news organizations were not covering: IndyMedia grew out of protests against the World Trade Organization meeting in Seattle in 1999, which generated little mainstream news coverage about the issues that sparked the protests. *IndyMedia* is a collective of independent Web sites around the world. Any person may contribute stories to IndyMedia sites. Unlike mainstream news media and the blogosphere, IndyMedia exemplifies the publish, then filter, philosophy. While IndyMedia has had some impact on the coverage of issues that its audience members and contributors

---

[1] Based on information available from February 5, 2012 at http://technorati.com/blogs/top100/ and http://technorati.com/blogs/directory/politics/uspolitics/

are concerned with, it does not command the audience figures that the most popular blogs do.

There is reason to hope that the Web presence of major news organizations will be able to offer news in more depth than their traditional vehicles of print and broadcast have allowed. Such Web sites could significantly help improve the circulation of news and information, and hold some of the promise of fulfilling the role of a new Fourth Estate. The emergence of new voices on blogs and citizen news sites may also contribute to increased public discourse for collective self-governance, although the popularity of partisan perspectives may limit the effectiveness of the blogs. The audience's ability to participate in the news agenda-setting process via social media recommendations is also a promising development for the kind of embodied intelligence that could aid in collective self-governance, although it remains to be seen whether "important" information can break through the steady stream of videos about piano-playing cats.

Online Information Databases

One of the Web's strengths is that it provides a platform for the publication of potentially useful information to the public in a way that is more accessible than reports contained in a printed book at the public library or records locked away in government offices. Government records, policy research, and other data that could inform discussion in the public sphere are increasingly available online, but it costs money to convert records into a digital format and to make them available to the public in a meaningful way for the average citizen. Like the mainstream news media, the content available in these online databases is created by experts and vetted prior to publication, and this information may help inform public debate for collective self-governance.

U.S. Government documents are increasingly available online, as sunshine laws encourage the wide sharing of government information. The Census Bureau publishes much of its data on the census.gov Web site, widely used in news reports, academic research, and policy papers. Information on the Census Bureau's Web site is displayed in already processed modules that the Census Bureau thinks will be of most interest to most people. Although the online accessibility of census data has improved somewhat, before data for the 2010 census became available much of the information was in the format of spreadsheets, requiring users to know how spreadsheets work and to have access to software that would open them. As a result, Census data were inaccessible and opaque to most of the U.S. public, which made the Census Bureau vulnerable to those who wished to question the motives of Census data collection as a ploy to invade the privacy of ordinary citizens.[2] Information about individual citizens provided to the Census is strictly confidential (the Census Bureau uses only collective statistics), but the opacity of the census.gov Web site did nothing to encourage citizens to believe that the Census process was transparent and that individual information was private. Although published with the best of intentions, government records databases such as census.gov fall short of providing useful information because of their opaque formats.

Crick (2009) argued that Dewey recognized that to make information not just available but useful to the public required presenting the information in a format that was meaningful to the citizens it was designed to inform: "[Dewey] suggests that the limitations to public understanding of complex issues can be practically overcome through the techniques of art, with 'art' broadly construed to mean any productive act of giving expressive form to an impulse, idea, or representation" (pp. 492–493). In the realm of online databases we can perhaps interpret Dewey's notion of "art" to mean innovative Web software interfaces that would make it easy for citizens to access and view data. However, Crick also recognized that in emphasizing presentation, public information may be in danger of slipping towards propaganda. Information professionals such as journalists, academics, and policy researchers are just beginning to embrace the art of information design in their work. It will take some time for these professionals, and the public at large, to become aware of the solutions and pitfalls that interactive multimedia presentations may pose for public information databases.

---

[2] In 2009, some members of Congress encouraged their constituents to boycott the 2010 Census. See, for example: Stephen Dinan's "Census Protocol Challenged" in *The Washington Times* (2009). Calls to boycott the Census date back to at least 100 years earlier.

Public information is also increasingly available from private databases. Private sources tend to invest more in the accessibility of their data because they are motivated by profit, prestige, or vested interest. One of the best examples of public information from private sources is Google Maps. First introduced in 2005, Google Maps has become a ubiquitous tool that has migrated from the Web to cell phones and GPS systems and has won several awards for interface design. The core geographic data and interface are strictly controlled by Google, but the company has created an "API" that allows other software to interact with the geographic database so that companies may build applications to work with Google Maps. Individual users annotate maps for their own use. The combination of a strictly controlled information database with a customizable interface makes Google Maps a core component of many Web 2.0 "mashups" or new applications that are created by combining two or more existing applications. As a result, many cell phone users may find the location of nearby restaurants, post offices, or polling places with greater ease and convenience. Organizations are using the Google API to map neighborhood statistics that let average citizens examine everything from high-crime areas to block-by-block housing values. Sadly, few interfaces are as successful or accessible as Google Maps. While more information is available on the Internet, there is no guarantee of effective use. Librarians, cognitive scientists, and new media companies know that the effective design of information systems for specific users, and their specific purposes is absolutely crucial if high usage levels are to be expected. Public information databases must be designed with public purposes and citizen use in mind, providing the kind of information individuals need when and where they need it (Dervin, 1997; Dervin, Jacobson, & Nilan, 1982).

Unlike free-of-charge government information databases, publicly available databases created by non-governmental organizations run the gamut from free to paid services. A new class of information service is the "freemium" service, where some basic information is free, but users must pay to access more in-depth material. One common example of "freemium" information services are "people finder" sites that let the public access very basic information on individuals free of charge and then charge increasing amounts for more information. Arguably, the "freemium" model makes some information more accessible to the average citizen.

Freely available issue-centered information is often provided by policy think tanks ranging from the liberal-leaning Brookings Institute to the conservative Heritage Foundation. Both conservative and liberal policy organizations make their reports available for free on their Web sites, with headlines designed to entice individuals who share their perspective. Web sites such as Moveon.org and Freedomworks.org tease their audiences with soundbite-sized headlines ("Healthcare 4 All") and catchy graphics, while the language of their reports is often written in the jargon of policy or in soundbites that are so simplified that they fail to convey any useful information to the public. For example, Moveon.org touts "Democracy in Action," while Freedomworks is for "more freedom."

The content of most of these public information databases produced by non-governmental organizations is tightly controlled by the organizations themselves, but most of the content has ties into social networking sites that allow their readers to share stories or encourage their friends to vote on polls, providing at least some opportunity for the public to help shape the dialogue that surrounds this information.

Overall, online information databases most likely do improve the climate of public discourse for collective self-governance by simply making information more available and, in some cases, making it more accessible through the use of well-designed interfaces. Like reliance on any authoritative source, the public, when using these services, must pay attention to where the information comes from, whose agendas the information might serve, and whether an agenda shapes the form or quality of the information.

Collaborative Databases

Collaborative databases are online repositories of user-generated content. Almost all of these services embrace the philosophy of publish first, then filter. Filtering is usually done by other users who may edit, rate, or tag content. Services are often dedicated to a specific topic, idea, or medium, and include Wikipedia and other "Wikimedia"; user-generated content portals such as Flickr and YouTube; and news-rating

Web sites such as Digg. Collaborative databases represent the democratic nature of Internet publishing at its best, although some have questioned the quality and reliability of information that comes from these resources.

YouTube, Flickr, and other self-publishing multimedia databases are more likely to generate Internet memes and viral media, such as videos of cats playing pianos, than hard-hitting exposés on current events. YouTube has been the publishing platform of choice for citizen eyewitness videos that get attention from the mainstream media, such as "gotcha" videos of politicians making impolitic statements or celebrities acting badly in public. For example, *YouTube* popularized the "macaca moment," where a U.S. Senate candidate was caught on camera referring to a young man of Indian descent as "macaca." The video went viral, was replayed on TV news, analyzed in newspaper articles, e-mailed across the country, shared on social networking sites, and may have cost Republican George Allen the Senate race in Virginia.[3]

Videos flow from YouTube to the mainstream media through the "meta-journalism" process of rating, commenting, sharing, and tagging stories via social networking and news rating sites. Goode (2009) saw news-rating services such as Digg as one of the more successful examples of citizen journalism, noting that the rating of news articles makes it possible for the news audience to participate in the news agenda-setting process, if not the actual creation of content. News rating also lets the public act as gatekeepers after the fact of publication as interested parties are quick to point out falsehoods or inaccuracies in news coverage. However, Goode noted that the research shows that a small group of individuals do most of the rating of stories on Digg, and create most of the stories that appear on Digg's front page. In other words, a small band of self-appointed citizen experts have disproportionate influence on the news-rating site.

As the most famous collaborative database of user-generated content, Wikipedia has survived its critics, surpassing Encyclopedia Britannica in both scope and readership. Anyone may write or edit Wikipedia

---

[3] See "GeorgeAllenIntroducesMacaca":http://www.youtube.com/watch?v=r90z0PMn
KwI

entries. While not every article is carefully peer reviewed, the most frequently accessed ones almost certainly are. Media scholar Henry Jenkins (2007), historian Roy Rosenzweig (2006), and others saw Wikipedia as a potentially useful tool in scholarship, provided that those who use it understand its weaknesses and take advantage of its strengths.

WikiNews applies the Wikipedia model to current events. Thorsen (2008) and others have found that most WikiNews material is synthesized from other news sources, although some original reporting does exist. WikiNews, like WikiPedia, has a "neutral point of view" policy, stating that the language of WikiNews entries should be free from bias, and as many viewpoints on a particular issue as possible should be included in a WikiNews story. Thorsen found that WikiNews stories did, indeed, seem to embrace fewer subjective perspectives than news stories published on other new media formats, such as blogs, but that sometimes in striving for neutrality the self-appointed editors of WikiNews removed relevant information from the stories. Bruns (2006) found that WikiNews engendered very little discussion on the substance of the issues raised in the articles published on WikiNews, and much more discussion about editing decisions, and the extent to which specific articles conformed to WikiNews' principle of the neutral point of view. The public-imposed removal of all subjectivity in WikiNews seems to have the unintended consequence of diluting the power of WikiNews to enable public discussion and thereby effect social change.

These user-fueled Web sites give voice to people and points of view that might not otherwise be represented in the mainstream media. Collaborative databases may amplify some of the stories of the mainstream media, as news stories can be linked and shared and rated, but they may also raise issues with the accuracy and fairness of mainstream media reports. In turn, YouTube, Flickr, and similar sites may feed the news hole of mainstream media outlets when user-generated content captures something outside the realm of mainstream news. The process of peer review by the world seems to temper the content on these sites along a gamut that makes the information potentially more useful as a tool of public discourse for collective self-governance, such as the case of Wikipedia, to less useful, as with WikiNews.

Social Media Networks

Broadly defined, social media are communication tools that let people connect others for the purpose of sharing news, gossip, and information. There are two main categories of social media: microblogging sites, such as Twitter, and profile sites, such as Facebook or MySpace.[4]

Facebook is the largest online profile site, claiming more than 800 million active users as of December 2011.[5] Facebook was founded in 2004 as a way for people to create an online "presence" and share information about themselves and connect with friends. Facebook users publish "status updates" in the form of text messages, photos, videos, links to interesting Web sites, polls, quizzes, and more. Individual Facebook users' status updates are re-published on the "feeds" of their "friends" or fellow users who choose to "follow" them online. Status updates quickly ballooned beyond the scope of social chatter to include calls to action, product recommendations, requests for donations to charitable causes, commentary on news stories, and more. Popular causes on Facebook explode into public consciousness through an electronic version of six degrees of separation. Facebook has become so effective at drawing public awareness that Goode (2009) believed a new phenomenon of "social media optimization" has emerged where material is presented in such a way as to maximize its dissemination through social media networks. It is this phenomenon that is enabling the agenda-setting power of the Internet grassroots, or "netroots."

Beginning in 2009, the microblogging site Twitter started to generate interest as a social media platform. Twitter is a radically simplified variation of social media, limited to 140-character status updates. Hermida (2009) described Twitter as a form of "ambient" communication, where readers check in occasionally to read updates on their

---

[4] YouTube, Flickr, and other collaborative databases are often folded into discussions about social media, and they do incorporate some social media tools. However, unlike Twitter and Facebook, their primary focus is not just person-to-person communication, but multimedia publishing, perhaps combined with person-to-person communication. For this reason, YouTube and Flickr are discussed in the previous section.

[5] See: http://www.facebook.com/#!/press/info.php?statistics

Twitter feed but do not give any individual message, or "tweet," the same level of consideration as, say, an e-mail message. Instead, Hermida theorized, Twitter creates a kind of "awareness system," where users give low cognitive recognition to individual tweets until several tweets on a similar topic start to indicate a trend that may merit more attention. A classic example of the "awareness" nature of Twitter was the volume of tweets coming out of Iran in the wake of protests following the 2009 Iranian presidential election. The Iranian government banned journalists from covering the protests, but was unable to stem the flood of 140-character Twitter messages and cell phone videos uploaded to YouTube by ordinary citizens. News organizations around the world culled through thousands of tweets and videos from Iran and republished them. While news organizations acknowledged that the accuracy and reliability of the individual tweets or videos were nearly impossible to verify, the sheer number of them was an indication that the general sense of the messages was most likely true.

Both Twitter and Facebook are partly enabled by the ubiquity of the mobile phone, as users can easily update their status messages on most cell phones. The short status update is almost certainly an extension of what is likely the world's most popular form of personal electronic communication: the SMS text message. It is difficult to overstate the impact of the mobile phone on global communication. Most people in the world now have some access to mobile communications technology, making the mobile phone perhaps the single most important development to shift the discussion of a "digital divide" away from issues of technology access and towards questions of public empowerment. The story of the Iranian protests of 2009 was not the first event to be publicly disseminated via the mobile phone. Gordon (2007) found that Chinese citizens used text messaging to communicate with each other about the SARS outbreak in 2003 when the Chinese government was still denying the problem and censoring reports; and victims of the 2004 Indonesian tsunami were able to send and receive information about their situation more quickly and effectively with their mobile phones than through government information channels.

One note of caution here is that while Twitter and Facebook may represent the most democratic form of public communication, other forces, such as government policy or commercial decisions by the private companies that own these social networking sites, may render them less effective as agents of public information and social change.

All of the emerging public communication and information services discussed in this section, from collaborative databases to social media networks, have the potential to both empower and hinder public discourse for collective self-governance. But they offer no guarantee that political institutions will become more responsive. The forces of politics as usual are employing new information technologies as well. Virtually all members of Congress employ Web tools (Jones, 2004), not only to solicit information from their constituents but also to court journalists (Lipinski & Neddenriep, 2004). In addition, new information technologies make it possible to demographically segment political audiences and practice pandering in ways previously unimagined. As some analysts have observed, the forces arrayed against democratic provision of digital information systems are considerable (Froomkin, 1998; Lessig, 1999, 2001). Whatever the nature of the outcome, the Internet is becoming a significant source of public and political information.

In summary, these systems may comprise an increase in what Dewey referred to as embodied intelligence. The public is more complex and varied than in Dewey's day. But this is not all bad, for much of this public is better educated and better informed. Despite references in both Lippmann's and Dewey's writings to the "mass" of citizens and voters, American politics have never been defined by mass interests. Special interests have always called the shots in the form of commercial lobby groups, political action committees, voluntary non-governmental groups, single-issue lifestyle groups, and so on. It is these groups whose work the Internet will advance, or not. Web-based news sources, discussion systems, and public databases have the potential to serve these groups and their collective interests, along with those of the mass public.

Conclusion: A Case for Public Informatics

How much really is there to the promise that new information systems could serve public need? How effective might they be in making contemporary political institutions more responsive to public need? Exactly how would they do so? What would be their relationship to traditional media and to traditional political forces such as labor and the church? Dewey argued: "The highest and most difficult kind of inquiry and a subtle, delicate, vivid and responsive art of communication must take possession of the physical machinery of transmission and circulation and breathe life into it" (1927, p. 184). Is this not the promise of emerging digital media as surveyed above?

The true amount of promise that information technology might have for democracy is not so much a single question as a broad front of issues and possibilities. There is at least some evidence of improvement. Some observers find already existing examples of political discourse on the Internet, including Habermasian communicative action, to be highly participatory (Froomkin 2003). We would like to suggest here that the sensible current response is not to seek an answer but rather to seek the means for a broadly based response. This broadly based response would be to establish a discipline of research and practical activity into Dewey's hope, a field or subfield of public and social scientific activity. This broadly based response would be a study of the relationship between information technology and public need, a subfield called public informatics.

Informatics is an ill-defined field of study. Much or perhaps most of it comprises IT-based support for health services. A social dimension to the subject was added with the work of Rob Kling at Indiana University (1999). Kling and his associates defined social informatics as "the interdisciplinary study of the design, uses and consequences of information technologies that takes into account their interaction with institutional and cultural contexts" (Kling, 1999). A *Journal of Community Informatics* advances a new area of study and practice addressing, "the study and the practice of enabling communities with Information and Communications Technologies (ICTs)" (http://ci-journal.net/index.php/ciej). This body of work ranges across personal, social, and economic ICT applications as these can benefit communities (Rathswohl, 2003). The idea of a public informatics would be a specific subset of either social or community informatics, focusing on information technologies that may support public discourse for collective and democratic self-governance.

The vast majority of Internet impacts valorized in the media today reflect use of the Internet for the pursuit of private concerns. Whether Internet use is for games, distance education, job hunting, or shopping, this use is for the gain of individuals. Internet uses for public concern are largely absent from public awareness. Just as the explosive growth of non-governmental organizations in America has taken place off the public radar screen, so too has growth in public uses of the Internet. A study of public informatics could help to remedy this oversight.

There is little novelty in such an idea. The American study of communication for the past half century began as a response to new technologies. At the dawn of the 20th century, public speaking and rhetoric were a required part of every educated individual's training. But at mid-century the study of communication had changed dramatically in an attempt to explore the impact of broadcasting. A half a century later a wave of new communications and information technologies has emerged from the Internet. They require new forms of analysis and perhaps new combinations of theory and practice.

Opportunities to employ, and to enjoy, new information technologies are indeed stratified socially, but the concept of a divide does not accurately suggest this stratification in its complexity. And the troubles news media face today are more complex than can be solved by new revenue streams. Thus, the circulation of public information moving forward will require an almost infinite variety of information systems attending to ever-shifting sets of needs, resources, and expressly public interests.

But change is a challenge rather than a conclusion. Dewey argued that, "a subtle, delicate, vivid and responsive art of communication must take possession of the physical machinery of transmission." This, he hoped, would breathe life into what we now refer to as the public sphere. Public informatics would be a new subfield of study designed to investigate how new media might help citizens engage in public discourse in the public sphere, for democratic self-governance, given a complex and dynamic social environment.

References

Bruns, A. (2006). Wikinews: The next generation of alternative online news? *Scan*, *3*(1). Retrieved from http://scan.net.au/scan/journal/display.php? journal_id=69

Crick, N. (2009). The search for a purveyor of news: The Dewey/Lippmann debate in an Internet age. *Critical Studies in Media Communication*, *26*(5), 480–497.

Dervin, B. (1997). Given a context by any other name: Methodological tools for taming the unruly beast. In P. Vakkari, R. Savolainen & B. Dervin (Eds.), *Information seeking in context*. Cambridge, MA: Taylor Graham.

Dervin, B., Jacobson, T., & Nilan, M. (1982). Measuring aspects of information seeking: A test of a quantitative/qualitative methodology. In M. Burgoon (Ed.), *Communication Yearbook 5* (pp. 419–444). New Brunswick, NJ: Transaction Books.

Deuze, M. (2004). What is multimedia journalism? *Journalism Studies*, *5*(2), 139–152.

Dewey, J. (1927). *The public and its problems*. Athens, OH: Ohio University Press.

Dinan, S. (2009, June 18) Census protocol challenged. *The Washington Times*, p. A2.

Froomkin, M. (1998). The empire strikes back. *Chicago Kent Law Review*, *73*, 1101, 1114–1115.

Froomkin, M. (2003). Habermas@Discourse.Net: Towards a critical theory of cyberspace. *Harvard Law Review*, *116*(3), 751–873.

Goode, L. (2009). Social news, citizen journalism and democracy. *New Media and Society*, *11*(8), 1287–1305.

Gordon, J. (2007). The mobile phone and the public sphere: Mobile phone usage in three critical situations. *Convergence: The Journal of Research into New Media Technologies*, *13*(3), 307.

Habermas, J. (1975). *Legitimation crisis*. Boston, MA: Beacon Press.

Habermas, J. (1984). *The theory of communicative action: Reason and the rationalization of society* (Vol. 1). Boston, MA: Beacon Press.

Habermas, J. (1987). *The theory of communicative action: A critique of functionalist reason* (Vol. 2). Boston, MA: Beacon Press.

Habermas, J. (1991). *The structural transformation of the public sphere: An inquiry into a category of bourgeois society*. Boston, MA: MIT Press.

Habermas, J. (2006). Political communication in media society: Does democracy still enjoy an epistemic status? The impact of normative theory on empirical research. *Communication Theory, 16*(4), 411–426.

Hermida, A. (2009, September). Twittering the news: The emergence of ambient journalism. Presentation at the Future of Journalism Conference, Cardiff, Wales.

Jacobson, S. (2010). Emerging models of multimedia journalism: A case study of nytimes.com. *The Atlantic Journal of Communication, 18*(2), 63–78.

Jenkins, H. (2007, June). What Wikipedia can teach us about the new media literacies (part one). Retrieved from http://www.henryjenkins.org/2007/06/what_wikipedia_can_teach_us_ab.html

Jones, A. (2004). The internet and the evolving nature of congressional communication: An interview with Girish J. Gulati. *Press/Politics, 9*(1), 3–6.

Kling, R. (1999). What is social informatics and why does it matter? *D-Lib Magazine, 5*(1).

Lasswell, H. (1927). *Propaganda technique in the world war.* New York, NY: A. A. Knopf.

Lasswell, H. (1930). *Psychopathology and politics.* Chicago, IL: University of Chicago Press.

Lessig, L. (1999). *Code and other laws of cyberspace.* New York, NY: Basic Books.

Lessig, L. (2001). *The future of ideas: The fate of the common in a connected world.* New York, NY: Vintage Books.

Light, J. S. (2001). Rethinking the digital divide. *Harvard Educational Review, 71*(4), 709–733.

Lipinski, D., & Neddenriep, G. (2004). Using "new" media to get "old" media coverage: How members of congress utilize their web sites to court journalists. *Press/Politics, 9*(1), 7–21.

Lippmann, W. (1922). *Public opinion.* New York, NY: Macmillan.

Lippmann, W. (1925). *Phantom public.* New York, NY: Harcourt, Brace.

Luhmann, N. (1995). *Social systems.* Stanford, CT: Stanford University Press.

National Telecommunication and Information Administration. (1995). Falling through the net: A survey of the "have nots" in rural and urban America. Washington, DC: United States Department of Congress.

National Telecommunication and Information Administration. (1998). Fall through the net II: New data on the digital divide. Washington, DC: United States Department of Commerce.

Quandt, T. (2008). (No) news on the World Wide Web: A comparative content analysis of online news in Europe and the United States. *Journalism Studies, 9*(5), 717–738.

Rathswohl, E. (2003). Introduction to the special series on community informatics. *Informing Science Journal*, 6(101–102).

Rosen, J. (2006, June). The people formerly known as the audience. Retrieved from http://journalism.nyu.edu/pubzone/weblogs/pressthink/2006/06/27/ppl_frmr.html

Rosenberry, J. (2005). Few papers use online techniques to improve public communication. *Newspaper Research Journal*, 26(4), 61–73.

Rosenzweig, R. (2006). Can history be open source? Wikipedia and the future of the past. *The Journal of American History*, 93(1), 117–146.

Siebert, F., Peterson, T., & Schramm, W. (1963). *Four theories of the press: The authoritarian, libertarian, social responsibility and Soviet Communist concepts of what the press should be and do.* Champaign, IL: University of Illinois Press.

Shirky, C. (2002). Broadcast institutions, community values. Retrieved from http://shirky.com/writings/broadcast_and_community.html

Singer, J. (2006). Stepping back from the gate: Online newspaper editors and the co-production of content in campaign 2004. *Journalism & Mass Communication Quarterly*, 83(2), 265–280.

Taylor, B. (2005). Mapping your way. Retrieved from http://googleblog.blogspot.com/2005/02/mapping-your-way.html

Thorsen, E. (2008). Journalistic objectivity redefined? Wikinews and the neutral point of view. *New Media Society*, 10(6), 935–954.

van Dijk, J., & Hacker, K. (2003). The digital divide as a complex and dynamic phenomenon. *The Information Society*, 19, 315–326.

Warschauer, M. (2002). Reconceptualizing the digital divide. *First Monday*. Retrieved from http://firstmonday.org/issues/issue7_7/warschauer/index.html

Warschauer, M. (2003). Demystifying the digital divide. *Scientific American*, August, 42–47.

Paul M. A. Baker

Introduction

The near ubiquitous use of information-centric technologies, such as the Internet, offers important opportunities to revisit and re-conceptualize the operation of communities, especially those in which modes of communication substitute for geographic proximity. Looking specifically at virtual religious communities, the somewhat disappointing outcomes of some efforts to sustain virtual religious communities without an underlying recognized proximate connection seems to suggest that a core concept of community must exist, that the successful functioning of a virtual community results from some extant interconnection, and not the converse. However, building virtual spiritual communities simply because it is possible often results in an empty space, or, in the example of Second Life, in lifeless avatars, unless there is connection that supports "communion." Conventional wisdom on virtual spaces for persons of faith communities at one time assumed that "if you build it they will come," but it has become apparent this is only the case if people have some reason for going there. This chapter explores the connectivity- and community-related issues behind faith as a motivating factor for participation in online communities, using the case of Second Life.

The construct and interpretation of virtual communities as considered here concentrates on three constituent components of online (virtual) religious groups: Community, Proximity, and Practice, using as examples Buddhist communities and the de facto community (gamers) based entirely in a virtual communication construct, namely Second Life. These are particularly of interest in a virtual setting due to the meditative/mystical, praxis-oriented characteristics of the former case, and the self-organizing, substrate-dependent characteristics of the latter.

In terms of structure, the term virtual community refers to the aggregations of group interactions (hence "community") made possible by digital information and communication technologies (ICTs) (virtual), where the group cohesion or connection is based primarily on electronic, generally computer-mediated, interactions. This is in distinction to the more common usage of the term, community, in which communication is in-person and contextual, both temporally and proximately, or geographically linked. Yet as Ward (2001, p. 246) noted, virtual and "imaginary" communities have existed for some time before the contemporary cybernetic usage.

While communities are by definition grounded in a commonality of interest, most typical usages of the term suggest a neighborhood, interest, political, social, or proximate (geographic) orientation; increasingly, the communication component of community has been noted (Delanty, 2003). The character and functioning of spiritually based groups offer an interesting set of cases where the community is one of interest, in this case, religion and spirituality, or practice of spirituality, operating in a non-proximate, virtual realm made possible by the digital communication of information interlinking distributed computers.

Ward (2001, pp. 248–9) took a somewhat more restrictive approach, arguing that virtual communities are not really places, spaces, or states but rather a praxis, an artifact of telecommunications, and of participation in that medium, and lack the significant substance of which "real communities" are composed. However, if virtual communities can be understood as types of real communities that use new systems of communication or particular mediated modes of social interaction to sustain themselves (Burnett, 2002), then understanding the ways in which virtual communities function must focus on the mode of interaction, as well as on the conditions within which such interaction takes place rather than the locale in which such interactions take place. For these communities, the where is of less interest than the what, that is, the communication (or "text") is the focus of the analysis.

In either case, given the core component of communication in these groups, it is useful to consider not only structure/composition of virtual communities but also the content (text) of the interaction that lends itself appropriate to the tools of cultural hermeneutics. According to Aarseth (2001, p. 231), "the basic tenet of hermeneutics is that understanding is gradual, a circle alternating between the parts and the whole, and thus closing in on a better view of the world, but with the realization that there can never be a final, closed interpretation." The hermeneutic circle is a particularly useful model for the computer-based processes and virtual environments where simulation can be thought of as not necessarily creating new realitiesbut alternative interpretations and understandings of our extant realities. Burnett (2002) argued that a process much like the one described by Ricoeur as "the mode of 'as if'" is used by participants in virtual communities as a means of creating and sustaining those communities. This process unfolds in an ongoing public "performance" of writing texts, reading and interpreting those texts, and making those readings and interpretations explicit through the creation of further texts. Additionally, Ward (2001,p. 71-72) focused on cultural hermeneutics and cultural transformation in which there is no general hermeneutics or isolatable text but a situation practice specific to the cultural context in which it operates, providing alternative insight to community hermeneutics.

Exemplar Groups

This chapter explores the application of hermeneutic examination to two examples of virtual communities with varying degrees of objectively defined spiritual components. Buddhists, and "gamers"—in the latter case, individuals who participate in online immersive virtual worlds such as Second Life and who have an interest in spiritual activity. Buddhist groups represent an interesting case, in as much as one can generalize about Buddhist worldviews, with respect to concepts of community, transmission of knowledge, and technology. Can there be Sangha, or spiritual community, in an online or virtual space? This is a nontrivial question, as Buddhism can be thought of as a practice, or way of approaching life, as much as a philosophical/theological structure (see Gethin, 1998). It is best practiced corporately, with others traveling the same path, and with those who embody its goal. Traditionally, the Sangha was the community of monks and nuns who lived together and served to transmit the Buddha's teachings to the community (Gethin, 1998, p. 92), and which served as a "witness to Buddhism" (Abe, 1993, p. 109). However when considering the evolution of Buddhism as it expanded west, in the broadest sense, Sangha is often thought of as referring to all of the Buddhists in the world and all those of the past and of the future. This is especially a useful definition if one is referring to the aggregate interactions and transmission of teaching that occurs in cyberspace, or what Prebish (1994) referred to as the cybersangha. In general western usage, however, Sangha refers to other Buddhists with whom one is in a practice context.

In contrast, an alternative type of online community shifts the connection from an emphasis on content that is, the specific connection involved, to the substrate, which we could refer to in a sense as habitus, in a virtual, constructed world, or, in the sense of gamers, the platform. Here we are using the substrate, a specialized case of "online," in which the "space of social possibles" (Ward, 2001, p. 23) is the virtual gaming environment as well as the way individuals are represented as graphical avatars or representatives instead of by the literally textual content of communication (Grossman, 2007).

Technologies of Virtual Spaces

As used here, the term virtual communities refers to a self-defined construct, a "space of flows" (Castells, 1996), a "condition of co-presence": (Giddens, 1991), or a praxis or participation in a medium (Ward, 2001), generated by the aggregations of communication made possible by digital information and communication technologies (ICTs), and where the group communality is based primarily on electronic interactions. The operation of virtual communities, in general, and with respect to the translation of religious or spiritual practice to this virtual, online substrate, can be thought of variously, representing an extension of the use of communications technology by traditional spiritual communities (top down), or the use of communications technologies to allow the identification of, and organization of, individuals of like-minded interests (bottom up). While a number of observers have noted the increasing use of ICTs by religious-based groups (e.g. Brasher, 2001; Barzilai-Nahon & Barzilai, 2005; and Hoisgaard, 2005), particularly those with fundamentalist or evangelical orientation, this chapter focuses on communities that use the Internet as a primary venue and are non-proximate in composition. Interestingly enough, the use of ICTs has been linked, not without some irony, to both the decline, as well as facilitation, of community: depending on which variables are under examination, ICTs have been used to describe both sides of this discussion.

These more versatile information and communication technologies offer the potential to facilitate communication and interactions otherwise subject to the limitations of distance and physical accessibility in a way that goes beyond the long-used bidirectional telephone and broadcast technologies (Cairncross 1997; Helland, 2000). This is particularly true of groups with interests that are specialized, rare, or potentially perceived as less than socially acceptable, for which the virtual world offers a place to congregate in a way that would be impractical, risky, or inconvenient, in the physical world.

Some spiritual groups can be said to fall into at least one of these categories. Specific examples might include religious cults, obscure or New Age religions, or religion/belief structures with a foreign, exotic, or alien image—Buddhists, Islam, B'hais, and Hindus in the latter case—when viewed through the cultural lenses of western observers, especially from an American viewpoint.

The widespread adoption of ICTs and the subsequent emergence of first online personas or identities and then online communities, suggest that a re-conceptualization of the definition of community is necessary, one that takes into account a sense of connection beyond the immediate proximate context into a virtual space defined by the flow of data and communication of ideas, extending the traditional understanding of community linked to a sense of place (Castells, 1996). The emerging field of Internet research has led to the development of a variety of techniques to observe and interpret activities in virtual space in general and more recently to the study of online religion (Cowan & Hadden, 2000). This is reflected in the development of highly active professional groups such as the Association of Internet Researchers (AoIR) and the Association for Computing Machinery Special Interest Group on Computer Human Interaction (SigCHI). This chapter includes a theoretical/conceptual overview for mapping the activities of belief-based communities in virtual space, drawing on religious, communication, and hermeneutically based approaches, as well as on the insights arising from geographic approaches to online virtual spaces (Dodge & Kitchin, 2001). Virtual spiritual communities represent a rich and relatively understudied area of research, and the operation of communities with non-proximate cores presents an intriguing area of inquiry, both in terms of the sociology of group interactions as well as those of substantive, theological interest.

Communities, Context, and Virtuality

What, then, constitutes the substance of an online or spiritual community; what is the "virtual reality" of such a community? The expression virtual community, as used in discussions of the Internet and the related cyberspaces, generally refers to a construct generated by a non-geographic matrix represented by an electronic coordinate system used for routing communication protocols—the Internet, or more precisely, ICTs. Though retaining some elements of a spatial metaphor, virtual space is at least one step removed in abstractness from a physically characterized infrastructure. Thus, by stepping back from the physical characteristics of online/virtual spiritual communities and focusing on a functional characterization, we can reconceptualize the characteristics of a proximate community to capture the defining characteristic of a specifically online or virtual community.

While a variety of typological schemes have been constructed to describe online spiritual communities (see Bradley, 1997; Helland, 2000; Dawson, 2000), this paper classifies communities in terms of all the dynamic relations that constitute them. Accordingly, with a unit of analysis at the level of the individual, embedded in a variety of information, social, and neighborhood networks, linked by computer-mediated communication (CMC) and other ICT connections, "community" encompasses a variety of different types of relationships, depending on the context (Wellman & Gulia, 1997). All virtual communities, spiritual or otherwise, while operating in a nonproximate space, still must be physically realized (science fiction examples notwithstanding), that is, there is a real physical location occupied by computers, network, technologies, and support personnel. Accordingly, this notion of "virtual community" can be characterized as a collection of social interactions occurring online, in computer-mediated cyberspace, through repeated contact within a specified boundary or place (e.g., a listserv, chat room, or Web site-related discussion group) that is categorically delineated by topic of interest (Baker & Ward, 2000). For Buddhist groups it could be said that there is, by necessity, an attachment to the physical, even when engaged in nonattached virtual communication.

Community

The term community, quite common in usage and comforting in its familiarity, is in reality a complex concept frequently defined and understood by the context in which it occurs, either in terms of field of research (i.e., sociology, politics, religion) or locale (geographic, virtual). For any meaningful discourse to occur the observers (not to mention the participants) must negotiate a common understanding of the substance and nature of the specific aggregate entity (community) under examination.

While the literature on virtual communities has richly described the online communities that have emerged in the cyberspace realm (Rheingold, 1993, p. 5), in terms of proximate communities, what does community, in a sense of neighborhood, mean if cyberspace substitutes the flow of electrons for community churches, zendos, or ashrams? Is it possible to have a "here" when there is no "there"? If the geographic link is weakened, then what sort of connection exists among members of a community? Thus, if a community is defined by relationships or communication rather than place, then what is the nature of relationships? What linkages connect people in an analogous manner to proximate space or geographic place? Ward observed, "what had once been praxis, is now regarded as reality itself" (2001).

It is sometimes argued that virtual communities are "thin" communities, often communities of strangers with a single or narrow commonalty of interest, in contrast to physical communities based on strong, multidimensional linkages. This is in contrast to traditional "thick" or organic communities, grounded in common geography, history, and tradition, which offer constituents a "sense of community" through the allocation of roles and identities and the establishment of mutual trust

(McMillan & Chavis, 1986). Online spiritual communities, then, operating in a locale in the contemporary Internet, could be regarded as offering a global market of interests where strangers exchange information, engage in interpersonal transactions, and if a sufficient commonality and extended interaction develops, thus generates a "thin" community (Delanty, 2003).

Bender's (1982) definition of community described an involvement of a limited number of individuals in a somewhat restricted social space or network held together by shared understanding and a sense of obligation. Relationships are close, often intimate, and generally involve face-to-face interactions. Individuals are bound together by affective or emotional ties rather than by a perception of individual self-interest. There is a "we-ness" in a community; one is a member. Building on this, Galston (1999) suggested that at least four key structural components make up a virtual community:

- limited membership—a typical feature of online groups is weak control of admission and participation of members. Low barriers to entry, and little obligation to support or maintain the community potentially leads to rapid turnover and iteratively diluting the sense of intimacy and community from a point of stability.

- shared norms—virtual groups appear to develop protocols for behavior in response to three kinds of imperatives: promoting shared purposes, safeguarding the quality of group discussion, and managing scarce resources in the virtual commons.

- affective ties—as an explanatory aspect is complicated by debates among experts as to whether genuine community occurs or merely a type of "pseudocommunity." The intensity of "flaming" and the rather emotional language that can occur in online communications, however, might serve as an indicator that some type of emotional attachments are possible, even in non face-to-face settings. The aspect of what constitutes inappropriate communication is itself not always a given—many groups struggle with balancing a commitment to freedom of expression with a need to prevent decay of group civility, in an attempt to prevent a communication "tragedy of the commons."

- mutual obligation—while a sense of mutual obligation to the other members may or may not occur, ancillary face-to-face contact strengthens subsequent online interactions. Therefore, it might not be unreasonable to speculate that an online community with a geographic identity (and the possibility of further face-to-face re-enforcement) would be more likely to have a greater sense of mutual obligation develop.

Summarizing, an online community can be operationalized as a self-organizing, self-defining collection of individuals whose central principle is a shared interest, or set of interests. This definition draws conceptually, to some extent, from Howard Rheingold's 1993 definition of virtual communities as "social aggregations that emerge from the [Internet] when enough people carry on those public discussions long enough, with sufficient feeling, to form webs of personal relationships in cyberspace" (Dutton et al., 1999; Rheingold, 1993; Wellman, 1997).

Sometimes a community will self-organize because of minimal outside influences—for example, communities of scholars or organized soccer teams. In this case, the group is held together by a mutual attraction or commonality of interest. Conversely, they may self-organize in direct response to an outside influence, such as gay activists (or Evangelical Christians) mobilizing coalitions in response to social legislation, unions organizing against corporate interests, or in response to available resources such as a new stream of external funding. In these cases, the group is forming in response to or against an outside factor and held together by a common exterior influence or threat. Although some note is made of the factors that inhibit the formation of communities (McMillan & Chavis, 1986)—often lumped generically under issues of organization, this chapter focuses on factors influencing the successful formation of online (virtual) spiritual/religious communities oriented toward the contemplative, meditative, or mystic. Even though frequently used in a geographic sense, there is nothing that necessitates that the meaning of "community" be narrowly linked to a specific spatial location. For example, a metropolis is generally considered to be a large, sprawling urban center of culture and trade, or an incorporated municipality, whose boundaries may be legally precise and geographically vague in a cultural sense. Similarly, a religious community extends conceptually beyond the proximate and temporal into a conceptual realm encompassing soft communication and perceptual linkages. The notion of community, like many conceptual constructs, is undergoing cultural modifications in response to newly emergent forms. Ward (2001) comments that the reconceptualization of community blurs a variety of boundaries such as between real and virtual (communities of proximity and of interest), between human and machine, and type of activity. This transition makes the mapping and interpretation of communities more complex.

Proximity: Geographic and Corporeal

Because of the increasing sophistication of ICTs, individuals are no longer restricted to communication with people with whom they share primarily geographic locales. ICTs enable users to seek out people with whom they share a similar intensity of "concern" based on more general human interests, as well as concerns based on, and created by, widely disseminated information, such as television, radio, and "net" coverage. Concern about the ramifications of widespread use of these technologies as a substitution for in situ interactions has been expressed by Quentin Schultze (2001) who opined that overly focusing on the technology, and the wizard-like power that it conveys in terms of breadth and sheer amount of information available, will draw people away from spiritual contemplation, leading to superficial, shallow lives. This would seem to echo the traditional Buddhist admonition to beware of worldly attachments and even to be on guard against the seductive nature of the powers of advanced spiritual practice. Advanced communications technologies and computer-simulated environments enable one to completely bypass the effort required to achieve some characteristics of spiritual adepts without the practice that buffers against achievement (knowledge) without understanding of consequences (wisdom). The image that comes to mind would be the Karmic equivalent of Goethe's Sorcerer's Apprentice.

Beyond the geographic notion of proximity, there is also the physical, corporeal, component of spiritual communities. It would be expected that the import of body would have more or less of an impact depending on the nature of the group in question (Foltz, 2003). The nature of corporeality is particularly intriguing when parsed in the context of spiritual matters. Thus an online, virtual group focused on spirituality that is grounded in a physical reality presents some interesting contradictions. For instance, the question has been raised on more than a few occasions on how one sits in zazen online (perhaps unless one was an extraordinarily advanced practitioner), simply because the nature of the practice does not correlate well to an environment that is still primarily based on a flow of communication—in which logical word bits "paint" the space by flowing. The cessation of this, much like the ceasing of the painting of electrons on a television, results in the fading of the picture (and, by analogy, the group's existence) to nothingness.

Past as prologue (Bradley, 1997) offered an interesting take on the virtual spiritual communities, drawing from historical perspective to provide an alternative to techno-futurist speculation on net society. Bradley suggested that the Internet might be interpreted using a historical lens reflecting the role and activity of contemplative religious communities in the medieval period, aware of others and sharing in a common idea via letters and transmitted communications—the "virtuality" of its day. She reported that a common component of religious activity was those seeking community on the web—in this case an extension of extent communities—and documented the effort of many communities of the (proximate) religion rooted in the past. She observed that the character and flavor of many of the orders extend into cyberspace, their virtual presence mirroring their earthly practices. Here, she cited the visually complex Web sites of the Benedictines, the Dominicans' Web presence oriented toward ecumenical inter-religious dialogues, reflecting their teaching orientation, the inward-directed historical orientation reflecting their contemplative orientation, among others. She was surprised at the overwhelming presence of the religious orders that one would normally expect to disdain such worldly things. Rather, she found that there is in fact a connection with, and familiarity to, the "otherworldly"—thus the virtual world is a not-unfamiliar extension of their communities. Alternatively, one could say it is a way of engaging the world without being of the world.

Implementation/Practice

As noted above, virtual spiritual communities have a variety of conceptual limitations to the way they operate. The nature of the virtual (online) world is one that seems to manifest most frequently in the "library" or research function of a group—the transmittal of formalized, textual information, teaching, question and answer, and background information (Foltz & Foltz, 2003). If one envisions the operation of a spiritual group as providing the online analogue to bulletin boards, encyclopedias, or reference desks—the virtual "clubhouse wall," then this is a reasonable understanding. This manifested level of development, in essence "Web sites," does not require a high level of expertise to bring into being and is in fact not uncommon for a variety of religious groups (Hoover et al., 2004; Thumma, 2002b; 2002c). Surprisingly, some of the newer, more advanced ICT-based simulated environments such as Second Life, one of the many massively multiplayer (>15 million participants that might have 100,000 players at the same time) online simulations, would seem to be an ideal environment for virtual religious communities, yet very little activity of this nature has extensively materialized. As more and more educational and business collaborative activities begin to be built up online simulated environments such as Second Life—it is possible that religious groups will be more comfortable experimenting with this setting.

Much of the extent research on the function or presence of religion or spiritually focused groups, congregations, or institutions on the Internet is at the exploratory and descriptive level (e.g., Hoover et al., 2004; Thumma, 2002a; 2002b; 2002c; Larsen, 2000), and focuses primarily on the technology, and technological uses of the technology, rather than the actual sociology of the communities. Helland (2000) offered a heuristic device for differentiating the efforts of "online religion" (that which originates with formal institutions of religion) and "religion online" (the less institutionally supported expressions of faith and belief). Helland's analysis suggests that the Internet offers unprecedented opportunities for religious communities, although the Internet may not be as different from its precedents in other communication media as he would like to believe. Analysis of communications media has noted the way various media blur the boundaries of the public and private sphere, a characteristic not new to the Internet.

A 2004 empirical study (Hoover et al., 2004) provides some interesting insights into online religiously oriented behavior, and to some extent supports Helland's viewpoint (2000). According to this report, 64% of the online population—128 million Internet users (at that time) —have conducted online religiously related activity (Hoover et al., 2004, p. 4). This survey, conducted by the Pew Internet and American Life Project, found that contrary to previous theoretical speculation, online activity was less likely to consist of religious "seeking" among those outside of traditional religions and was used more by those already identified as religious to find out more about their own traditions (Hoover et al., 2004, p. 20). Online usage was more likely used to facilitate spiritual or religious interactions with others already engaged in traditional religious contexts and communities.

While the study was primarily conducted among those identifying as Christian (Protestants, Catholics, and Evangelicals) and Jewish, there was a category for those identifying as "Other," though they constituted a relatively small percentage of the participants. As noted above, it seems that a good deal of online activity falls more into the category of "expressing one's own spiritual beliefs" as evidenced by such reported activities as passing along religious or spiritual emails, prayer requests, or other communications (Hoover et al., 2004, p. 20). Finally those that identified as both spiritual and religious had the highest usage of the Internet, and, with Evangelical rural users, were the most ardent users.

Given the relatively small number of empirical studies, we can speculate additionally on how virtual communities of different philosophical bases might operate. Bradley (1997) noted that the proportion of Buddhist websites at the time was higher than the percentage of Buddhists in the U.S. populations. The recent Pew survey reported that the use of the Internet by categories of Protestants was relatively similar; Catholics were measurably less likely to use the Internet to explore aspects of their religion. A variety of reasons could be offered for this based on the demographic (income, age, education, cultural grouping) or the philosophical (the structural nature of Catholicism, which generally discourages non-doctrinal endeavors).

Virtual Habitus/Virtually Buddhist

As noted above, the fact that that numerous Web sites with a Buddhist orientation exist appears to be primarily an example of virtual community(ies) maintaining an identity culture, rather than attempting to engage in online practice—no zazen—an understandable limitation given the current state of online technology. In fact, very little "worship" activity, however one constructs it, seems to occur at present (Foltz & Foltz, 2003). Buddhists are not loath to use technology (Hershock, 1999; Hayes, 1999; Greider, 2000), however, the resource and physically intensive nature of the Internet might give some pause, and the seductive nature of immersion in the online flow of information and access to knowledge raises the possibly of unhealthy attachment to collection of information. Prebish (1999), in his early exploration of online Buddhist activities, observed:

> Perhaps the most consequential impact of the aggressive spread of Buddhism into cyberspace, along with the creation of a new kind of American Buddhist sangha never imagined by the Buddha, is the uniting of all the Buddhist communities or sanghas into one universal sangha that can communicate effectively in an attempt to eliminate the suffering of individuals throughout the world. (p. 232)

Hayes (1999, p. 177), another early observer, commented that much of the community (of the time) was generated by email and newsgroup traffic. The community focused a great deal on "westerners with misconceptions of the nature of Buddhism." Here, the focus of the communication seemed to be transmission of information and/or cultural aspects of Buddhism and was as much educational in nature as it was a conversation about the nature of community or the practice and maintenance of Buddhism in a non-proximate setting. To some extent, the shift that occurs in the intensity and nature of communication is a function of (a) the possibilities that advances in technology allow; (b) the rapid diffusion of technology so that participants are not only those with an interest in technology but also those for whom the technology is simply a tool rather than an interest, per se; and (c) the rapid decline in cost, and increased availability of broadband transmission of information, which in turn enables the use of more robust technologies of engagement.

Kim (2005) reported on the operation of a Buddhist community (Chollian Buddhist Community) that offers an interesting case. The online community of 300 sub-communities was formed in 1991 and operated using its own menu-driven system of communication for members until converting to a web-based one in 2001 (Kim, 2005, p. 143–145). Kim argued that in the case of this community, the development of an integrated system offered a robust system of information that provided interpretive and integrative functions as well as the more common interactive ones. The rather hierarchical system offered bifurcated options of "intimacy" (i.e., personal communications, open letters, "chat" opportunities) as well as "information" opportunities intended to increase the level and availability of religious information transmission and exchange.

The author concluded that the community (in this case it might be more appropriate to refer to it as an organization rather than a simple spiritual community), was especially effective in that it offered an opportunity to those who had a passing interest in Buddhism, especially urban dwellers, to explore without the commitment, demands, or inconvenience of offline (primarily) rural meetings (p.146). Here, the community (from 1996–97) performed the functions of (a) a belief community providing a system of beliefs and practices; (b) a relational community, satisfying a need for belonging; (c) an affective community, providing a group identity; and (d) a utilitarian community providing a means of resource mobilization. A more recent expression of the community (www.buddhasite.net) indicates that it is shifting from a structural/service model into more of an online community, offering a virtual "locale" oriented at more robust community interactions rather than more purely educational/informative ones.

As the Buddhist scholar Venerable Pannyavaro noted, "if the Buddha were alive today he would be using the Internet." Given the tradition of the transmission of knowledge and the way that Buddhism traveled, this seems likely. He raised, in balance, quite rightly, a concern about maintaining the authentic teaching of Buddhism but added that if one falls back on the validation of lineage, then this becomes less of a problem (2002).

Virtually (Essentially) Virtual

The example of individuals (gamers) engaged in participating in the complex simulated environment of Second Life represents an interesting alternative example of an online belief structure and was chosen more for the potential it represents rather than the actual practices yet occurring. At present, due to a combination of factors (e.g., a rapidly changing environment, a rapidly escalating—yet fluctuating—population, questions about data collection and validity) little actual data have been compiled on Second Life as a "place" (or space as it may be) beyond journalistic articles. It has begun to draw the attention of researchers from a variety of fields due to the tremendous possibilities it represents. Starting with the general, part of the power of the virtual world is that it frees individuals from some of the physical limitations (as well as advantages) of the body, especially in the case of people with disabilities (Forman et al., 2011; 2012), transforming the individual from a corporal presence, with the concurrent body habitus and practices, to a disembodied but emotionally connected avatar, a detached "toy" that focuses on communication rather than the complex connectivity of corporal presence. An obvious escapist attraction exists, not to mention the appeal of the ability to project virtually any physical, sexual, or other aspect of identity. In Second Life, you could be "a dog on the internet." The participants, as can be expected of a gaming environment, tended to be composed of libertarians, young males, and creative types, originally, but corporations, business people, and others are increasingly more common participants as the game becomes more mainstream.

While an extraordinary number of groups (or, in a liberal sense, "communities") exist in Second Life, a sampling of groups, conducted in March 2010, with identifiers using the keywords "religion, spirituality, Christian, Buddhist, Jewish or Islam" yields marginal results. Using the search terms listed above, some 456 groups were generated with total registered participants numbering 54,594. If compared to the total population of almost 19 million, this represents only 3% of the total metaverse. This represents the "joiners" and, given the ephemeral nature of relationships and contact in Second Life, can be expected to grossly underestimate individuals with an interest in religion.

A 2007 article on religion in Second Life noted that while much of the religious- (or more accurately, "spiritual-") identified activity involved alternative groups, "seekers" and architectural constructs of primarily visual appeal, it also involved an increasing amount of traditional, if virtual, spaces of prayer, study, support, and counseling (Grossman, 2007). For example, George Byrd, a real-estate broker from Columbus, Ohio, built the lavishly landscaped First Unitarian Universalist Church of Second Life, and organized weekly services that draw more than 60 people. He feels that virtual services in Second Life are as authentic as those in the physical-world church he attends in Columbus. "The spiritual connection is in your brain and in your soul. It's the same either way," Byrd says. Another member, who is disabled in real life, finds that attending services in Second Life affords her a community that she cannot easily access in the real world (Sutton, 2007). And another member, commenting on the nature of online interaction, noted:

> There's a real difference in goal and result....In real life . . . it's possible to come away with the glow of community, of whatever it is you've heard or absorbed, in music and reading and sermon. You can't come away with as much from a virtual service. It really has to rely on the sense of community more than anything that might reach you through music or even poetry or ambience. (Sutton, 2007)

Aside from the self-organizing groups created by community-oriented individuals seeking to utilize the virtual substrate, you are beginning to see the participation of the ecclesiastical equivalents of corporations. For instance, another 2007 article reported on the entrance of a large, technology-savvy church in "real life"—Lifechurch.TV (Biever, 2007). It viewed Second Life both as an experimental setting in another form of media (an extension of an existing community communication) and as a way to virtually replicate existing physical structures (a kind of attempt to recapture some of the characteristics of a proximate/geographic sense of community), and, of course, a huge pool of "unchurched." In this case the online community is not in place of geographic community but uses a variant of the televangelical church model—a broadcast type of relationship rather than a community- (interactive) focused one, per se. Another example of this type of activity is conducted by Larry Transue, pastor of the Second Life nondenominational Northbound Community Church, who sees Second Life as a mission field, is involved in evangelism and outreach at his real-world Northbound Church, and replicated it online to "practice what I preach no matter where I am" (Grossman, 2007).

Conclusions

While "place" and the impact of distance are significantly minimized as a function of use of ICTs, delineation of "place" in a virtual, or connected, context becomes increasingly a question of identity and choice rather than of geography and history. Frequently, virtual constructs are increasingly more robust analogues of the physical world, but it is questionable, as Ward (2001) noted, if they can be read as more than "toys." In physical, sometimes "unconnected" communities, relationships are impacted by distance so that a decay function occurs as one moves from the core to the periphery. In terms of virtual communities, we can posit that intensity of interest (or commitment), the habitus of the group, may be the analogue to distance in the "new spaces," so that increased intensity of interest places one closer to the conceptual center of a group. This becomes more important in thin communities such as virtual groups where, in the absence of other sorts of norms or context, the group practices are maintained by key actors, the community "elders." Could the concepts of "there" and "not there" among the connected be more concerned with how frequently a community member communicates, indicating a level of interest and hence how more or less "close" they are to the center of a virtual community?

Centralization vs. patchy-ness:

While the decentralizing spatial effect of ICTs has been noted, conversely an opposite effect is noted with respect to concentration of the "physical infrastructure"— i.e., the actual wires and servers, and access to bandwidth. ICTs enable a user to be anywhere, but the density of physical infrastructure underlying communication technologies enables a richer, denser flow (in this case, speed) of information. While a virtual community may spread over a large physical area, a fast and reliable connection to the Internet seems to provide a reason to re-centralize. Geography, while minimized, is still a factor even in virtual realms. Being virtually "connected," even metaphorically, still relies on "connectivity" technologically.

Maintenance of community:

Leadership of online spiritual communities becomes more complex than that of physical groups. Computer-mediated communication, while robust, is not as rich as the multi-channel communication that occurs in face-to-face physical interactions. Agreement upon and discussion of protocol require skill in written communication, which shifts leadership balance to those who are the most proficient in written communication, in distinction to the physical world where leadership may be a function of verbal skills and "presence." Without the contextual or proximate cues, subtlety and nuance can be lost as communication must be explicitly (textually) coded rather than inferred. How does a virtual community regulate the interactions of the members, and to what standard are they held? Further, given the "thin" or weak nature of online bonds, what factors enable sustainability of these online communities?

Norms of practice:

How do members of community "authenticate" the communication of participants' absent contextual clues? What protocol exists for the transmission of core community values and beliefs? In spiritual communities this poses a problem for validating transmissions of new teachings or interpretations. How do we know something is "true"? Where does Truth emanate from? How do we decide on what we agree on? Do different communities of faith operate differently in virtual communities?

The characterization of a community is more than a function of determining boundaries of place and space and is increasingly reliant upon the concept of community as based in identity. The growing deployment of advanced ICTs makes for alternative modes of online communication and information, enabling an entirely new array of relationships to emerge. Community can be expanded to include the loosely linked networks of interaction, with emphasis shifting from a locational requisite to one based in commonality of interest or purpose.

Cautious observers have warned that the use of ICTs will reduce social capital, diminish the nature of geographic community, and weaken (locale-based) community relationships. Others have championed ICTs as enabling a new wave of community participation due to the ease of network-based communication.

Empirical research to date has begun to suggest that contrary to early speculation, virtual communities do not eliminate or weaken the role of underlying geographic community, unless the community is weak in and of itself. Rather, online communities, spiritual or otherwise, are extensions of the experience, wants, and needs of the physical world. Online virtual communities can be thought of as extensions of the real world into a conceptual information overlay of the world. While creation of entirely new networks of connection (or community) is possible, it is more likely, as Calhoun (1998) speculated, that online communities reinforce existing interests or connections. Or, put another way, the "connected" and the "unconnected" can coexist.

If the current examples of spiritual communities presented in the literature are at all representative of the possibilities of the virtual world, then we may conclude that it is not the virtual world that is a competitive threat to belief structures or churches but a condition intrinsic to the existing physical communities. Virtual spiritual communities seem to act mainly as an augmented or richer form of community interaction rather than a replacement per se. Even as telephones and automobiles did not eliminate the need for "places," ICTs are unlikely to replace the need to meet face to face. We see that in those places where a geographic-related spiritual community exists, then ICTs can serve as intensifiers, or more efficient conduits for information flow.

On the other hand, the somewhat disappointing outcomes of some efforts to sustain virtual religious communities without an underlying recognized proximate connection seem to suggest that a core concept of community must exist, that the successful functional of a virtual community results from some extant interconnection and not the converse. Building a virtual spiritual community simply because it is possible will result in an empty space, unless there is reason to express communication and achieve "communion." If you build it they will come, but only if they have some other reason for going there.

Acknowledgments

I wish to acknowledge the assistance of my Georgia Tech research colleague, Ms. Jessica Pater, who assisted in data collection and provided editorial support.

References

Aarseth, E. (2001). Virtual worlds, real knowledge: Towards a hermeneutics of virtuality. *European Review, 9*(02), 227–232.

Abe, M. (1993). Buddhism. In A. Sharma (Ed.) *Our religions* (pp. 71–137). New York, NY: Harper Collins.

Baker, P., & Ward, A. (2000). Searching for "Civitas" in the digital city: Community formation and dynamics in the virtual metropolis. *National Civic Review, 89*(3), 203–216.

Baker, P. M., & Ward, A. C. (2002). Bridging temporal and spatial "Gaps": The role of information and communication technologies in defining communities. *Information, Communication & Society, 5*(2), 207–224.

Barrett, J. (2009, June). Religion in new places: Rhetoric of the holy in the online virtual environment of Second Life. Working Papers in Teacher Education presented at Changing Societies—Values, Religions, and Education Conference, Umea University, Sweden. Retrieved from umu.diva-portal.org/smash/get/diva2:357143/FULLTEXT01

Barzilai-Nahon, K., & Barzilai, G. (2005). Cultured technology: Internet and religious fundamentalism. *The Information Society, 22*(1), 25–40.

Bauwens, M., & Rossi, F. (1999). Dialogue on the cyber-sacred and the relationship between technological and spiritual development. *Cybersociology,* (7) Religion online/Techno-spiritualism. Sept. 1, 1999. Retrieved from http://www.cybersociology.com/files/7_bauwensrossi.html.

Bellinger, C. (n.d.). Wabash Guide to Internet Resources for Teaching and Learning in Theology and Religion: Buddhism. Wabash Center: Buddhism. Retrieved from http://www.wabashcenter.wabash.edu/resources/result-browse.aspx?topic=562&pid=361

Bender, T. (1982). *Community and social change in America.* New Brunswick, NJ: Rutgers University Press.

Biever, C. (2007). When pastors swap the pulpit for the webcam. *New Scientist, Vol. 193:* Issue 2591, p24

Bradley, R. (1997). Religion in cyberspace: Building on the past. Paper presented at Institute for the History of Religions, Abo Akademii University, Turku, Finland.

Brasher, B. E. (1996). Thoughts on the status of the cyborg: On technological socialization and its link to the religious function of popular culture *Journal of the American Academy of Religion, 64*(4), 809–830.

Brasher, B. (2001). The civic challenge of virtual eschatology: Heaven's Gate and Millennial fever in cyberspace. In P. D. Nesbitt (Ed.), *Religion and social policy* (pp. 196–209). Walnut Creek, CA: AltaMira Press

BuddhaNet-Worldwide Buddhist Information and Education Network. Retrieved from http://www.buddhanet.net/

Burnett, G. (2002). The scattered members of an invisible republic: Virtual communities and Paul Ricoeur's hermeneutics. *The Library Quarterly, 72*(2), 155–178.

Burnett, G., Dickey, M., Kazmer, M., & Chudoba, K. (2003). Inscription and interpretation of text: A cultural hermeneutic examination of virtual community. *Information Research, 9*(4), Retrieved from http://www.InformationR.net/ir/9-1/paper162.html

Cairncross, F. (1997). *The death of distance: How the communications revolution will change our lives.* Boston, MA: Harvard Business School Press.

Calhoun, C. (1986). Computer technology, large-scale social integration and the local community. *Urban Affairs Quarterly, 22*(2), 329–349.

Calhoun, C. (1991). Indirect relationships and imagined communities: Large-scale social integration and the transformation of everyday life. In P. Bourdieu & J. S. Coleman (Eds.), *Social theory for a changing society* (pp. 95–130). Boulder, CO: Westview Press.

Calhoun, C. (1992). The infrastructure of modernity: Indirect social relationships, information technology, and social integration. In H. Haferkamp & N. J. Smelser (Eds.), *Social change and modernity* (pp. 205–236). Berkeley, CA: University of California Press.

Calhoun, C. (1998). Community without propinquity revisited: Communications technology and the transformation of the urban public sphere. *Sociological Inquiry, 68*(3), 373–397.

Campbell, H. (2003). What is so "new" about new media? Considering how language and beliefs shape religious Internet usage. Paper presented at the 2003 AoIR Conference, Toronto, Canada.

Campbell, H., & Lovheim, M. (2011). Introduction: Rethinking the online-offline connection in the study of religion online. *Information, Communication & Society, 14*(8), 1083–1096.

Castells, M. (1996). *The information age: Economy, society and culture.* Oxford, England: Blackwell.

Cowan, D. E., & Hadden, J. K. (2000). (Eds.) *Religion on the Internet: Research prospects and promises.* New York, NY: JAI.

Dawson, L. L. (2000). Researching religion in cyberspace: Issues and strategies. In D. E. Cowan & J. K. Hadden (Eds.), *Religion on the Internet: Research prospects and promises.* New York, NY: JAI.

Dawson, L. L., & Cowan, D. E. (2004). *Religion online: Finding faith on the Internet.* New York, NY: Routledge.

Delanty, G. (2003). *Community.* New York, NY: Routledge.

Dodge, M., & Kitchin, R. (2001). *Mapping cyberspace.* London, England: Routledge.

Doheny-Farina, S. (1996). *The wired neighborhood.* New Haven, CT: Yale University Press.

Dutton, W. H., Peltu, M., & Bruce, M. (1999). *Society on the line: Information politics in the digital age.* Oxford, England: Oxford University Press.

Foltz, F. (2003). Religion on the Internet: Community and virtual existence. *Bulletin of Science, Technology & Society, 23*(4), 321–330.

Foreman, A., Baker, P., Pater, J., & Smith, K. (2011). Beautiful to me: Identity, disability, and gender in virtual environments. *International Journal of E-Politics, 2*(2), 1–17.

Foreman, A., Baker, P., Pater, J., & Smith, K. (2012). The not so level playing field: Disability, identity and gender representation in Second Life. In C. Romm-Livermore (Ed.), *Gender and social computing: Interactions, differences, and relationships* (pp. 144–161). Hershey, PA: Information Science Reference.

Galston, W. A. (1999). (How) does the Internet affect community? Some speculations in search of evidence. In E. C. Kamarck & J. S. Nye, Jr. (Eds.), *Democracy.com? Governance in a networked world* (pp. 45-62). Hollis, NH: Hollis Publishing.

Gethin, R. (1998). *The foundations of Buddhism.* Oxford, England: Oxford University Press.

Giddens, A. (1991). *Modernity and self-identity: Self and society in the late modern age.* Cambridge, England: Polity.

Greider, B. (2000, April). Academic Buddhology and the cyber-sangha: Researching and teaching Buddhism through multimedia Internet sources. Paper presented at American Academy of Religion Upper Midwest Regional Conference, St. Paul, Minnesota.

Gresham, J. (n.d.). A guide to religious studies—Resources on the Internet. Contents—John Gresham, J Retrieved from http://gresham.kenrickparish.com/contents.htm

Groothuis, D. (1999). *The soul in cyberspace.* Eugene, OR: Wipf and Stock.

Grossman, C. L. (2007, April). Faithful build a Second Life for religion online. Retrieved from http://www.usatoday.com/tech/gaming/2007-04-01-second-life-religion_N.htm

Gunderson, G. (1997). Spirituality, community, and technology: An interfaith health program goes online. *Generations, 21*(3), 42–45.

Hayes, R. (1999). The Internet as a window onto American Buddhism. In D. R. Williams & C. S. Queen (Eds.), *American Buddhism: Methods and findings in recent scholarship* (pp. 168–180). Surrey, England: Curzon.

Helland, C. (2000). Online-religion/Religion-online and virtual communities. In D. E. Cowan & J. K. Hadden (Eds.), *Religion on the Internet: Research prospects and promises.* New York, NY: JAI.

Hershock, P. D. (1999). *Reinventing the wheel: A Buddhist response to the information age.* Albany, NY: State University of New York Press.

Hoisgaard, M. (2005). Introduction: Waves of research. In M. Hoisgaard & M. Warburg (Eds.), *Religion and cyberspace* (pp. 1–11). New York, NY: Routledge.

Hoover, S. (2003). Religious seeking religious finding: The new age in the digital world. Paper presented at 2003 AoIR Conference, Toronto, Ontario.

Hoover, S., Clark, L., & Rainee, L. (2004). Faith online: Pew Internet & American Life Project. Retrieved from http://www.pewinternet. org/Reports/2004/Faith-Online.aspx

Jones, S. (1999). *Doing Internet research: Critical issues and methods for examining the Net.* Thousand Oaks, CA: Sage Publications.

Kim, M. (2005). Online Buddhist community: An alternative religious organization in the information age. In M. Hoisgaard & M. Warburg (Eds.), *Religion and cyberspace* (pp. 138–148). New York, NY: Routledge.

LaReau, R. (2001, October). Net gains: How the Internet is changing the church. *U.S.Catholic,* October, 2011. Retrieved from http://www. onlineministries.creighton.edu/CollaborativeMinistry/uscath-oct-01.html

Larsen, E. (2000). *Wired churches, wired temples: Taking congregations and missions into cyberspace.* Washington, DC: Pew Internet & American Life Project.

McMillan, D., & Chavis, D. (1986). Sense of community: A definition and theory. *Journal of Community Psychology, 12*(1), 6–23.

Nocera, J. A. (2002). Ethnography and hermeneutics in cybercultural research accessing IRC virtual communities. *Journal of Computer-Mediated Communication, 7*(2).

Pannyavaro, V. (2002). E-learning Buddhism on the Internet. Retrieved from http://www.buddhanet.net/gds-speech.htm

Phra, T. (1995). *Buddhadhamma: Natural laws and values for life* (G. A. Olson, Trans.). Albany, NY: State University of New York Press.

Poplin, D. E. (1972). *Communities: A survey of theories and methods of research.* New York, NY: Macmillan.

Prebish, C. S. (1999). *Luminous passage: The practice and study of Buddhism in America.* Berkeley, CA: University of California Press.

Preece, J., & Maloney-Krichmar, D. (2003). Online communities. In J. Jacko & A. Sears (Eds.), *Handbook of human-computer interaction* (pp. 596–620). Mahwah, NJ: Lawrence Erlbaum.

Rasmussen, T. (2000). *Social theory and communication technology.* Aldershot, England: Ashgate.

Religion and the Internet. (2002). Retrieved from http://web.mit.edu/comm-forum/forums/religion.html

Rheingold, H. (1993). *The virtual community: Homesteading on the electronic frontier.* Reading, MA: Addison-Wesley.

Rodin, S., Brauch, M., Brown-Woodard, M., Hailson, D., Sider, R., & Ellmore, P. (2001). A theology of technology: Raising the theological questions,Eastern Baptist Theological Seminar. Retrieved from anthonyfoster.com/charter/af/Theology_techno.doc

Sample, T. (1998). *The spectacle of worship in a wired world: Electronic culture and the gathered people of God.* Nashville, TN: Abingdon Press.

Schultze, Q. (2000, February 16). Lost in the digital cosmos. *The Christian Century,* 178–183.

Schultze, Q. (2001, January 31). Going digital. *The Christian Century,* 178–183.

Sutton, K. (2007, February 19). Going to church in Second Life. Retrieved from http://www.uuworld.org/life/articles/16206.shtml

Thumma, S. (2002a). Of mice and members: Using the Web to research religious phenomena. Paper presented at Annual Meeting of the Society for the Scientific Study of Religion in Salt Lake City, Utah.

Thumma, S. (2002b). A Sunday drive on the information superhighway: The use of Web-based research by religious groups. Paper presented at Annual Meeting of the Society for the Scientific Study of Religion, Salt Lake City, Utah.

Thumma, S. (2002c, April 18). Religion and the Internet. Paper presented at Communications Forum Lecture in Massachusetts Institute of Technology, Cambridge, Massachusetts.

Ward, G. (2001). *Cities of God.* London, England: Routledge.

Wellman, B. (1997). An electronic group is virtually a social network. In S. Kiesler (Ed.), *Culture of the Internet.* Mahwah, NJ: Lawrence Erlbaum.

Wellman, B., & Gulia, M. (1999). Virtual communities as communities: Net surfers don't ride alone. In M. A. Smith & P. Kollock (Eds.), *Communities in cyberspace* (pp. 167–194). London, England: Routledge.

Wellman, B., & Haythornthwaite, C. A. (2002). *The Internet in everyday life*. Malden, MA: Blackwell.

Wertheim, M. (1999, September). Is cyberspace a spiritual space? *Cybersociology*, 7. Retrieved from http://www.cybersociology.com/files/7_wertheim.html

Zaleski, J. P. (1997). *The soul of cyberspace: How new technology is changing our spiritual lives*. San Francisco, CA: HarperEdge.

Section 4

Communication

Chapter 10:
Democracy to Technocracy: Tyranny of the Majority in the Information Age

Andrew C. Ward

Introduction

A common claim about the public use of information communication technologies is that they act as both a safeguard to democracy in societies in which they already exist and as principal tools to introduce public use into societies that are not democratic. However, information technologies, like so many other kinds of technology, are not without their dangers. One danger is that dependence for political participation on these technologies may lead to under-representation for those people who are unconnected from the network created by the technologies. In such cases, the "connected majority" (who may be a minority in the society as a whole) may impose its will on both the connected and unconnected minorities. A second kind of danger is that the connectedness of one or more organizations may give them an unfair advantage relative to the message they seek to deliver. This chapter explores some of these concerns about the possible slide from a democracy into a technocracy in which the interests of the "connected majority" limit the freedoms of others in the society.

Background

The development and diffusion of inexpensive, reliable, and easy-to-use public Internet access in the closing years of the twentieth century provided connectivity to large portions of the U.S. and the world. For example, according to the United Nations' International Telecommunication Union (2011), 62.5% of U.S. households in 2008 had Internet access. The Pew Research Center reported that 54% of adults used the Internet to "get news or information about the 2010 midterm [U.S.]

elections, or to get involved in the campaign in one way or another" (Smith, 2010). Globally, the Internet World Stats Website (http://www.internetworldstats.com/stats.htm) reported that, as of March 31 2011, over 30% of the world's population use the Internet, representing a 480% growth from 2000. Moreover, by "2010, developing world Internet users accounted for 58% of the global total, with 1.2 billion in the developing world, compared to 900 million in the developed world" (International Telecommunications Union, 2011).

A distinguishing characteristic of the history of the Internet's creation and development is the transition from the use of computer-medicated communication (CMC) by a relatively small number of people and organizations for specialized purposes to its use by many stakeholders for a multitude of purposes (Kwak, Zinkhan, Pan, & Andras, 2008). With the advent of "Web 2.0" technologies (e.g., social networks, blogs), the communication focus has moved from interconnecting documents and Web pages to "linking up people, organizations and concepts" (Maciel, Roque, & Garcia, 2010). This movement is likely to gain further momentum as people continue to transition from traditional personal computers (PCs), to mobile computing technologies (Kleinrock, 2008). Some people, using the language of Alvin Toffler, refer to this further shift from information dissemination to the creation of a virtual public domain/public sphere as the "fourth wave" (Jalali & Mahmoodi, 2009).

This expansion of the Internet has led to what Daniel Burton (1997) called "The Brave New Wired World." Some speculation is general and provocative, focusing on the nature of the cyberspaces (Strate, 1999) created by networks of interconnected computers (Yen, 2002). For example, in his 1993 book, *The Metaphysics of Virtual Reality*, Michael Heim wrote that cyberspace is:

> The juncture of digital information and human perception, the "matrix" of civilization where banks exchange money (credit) and information seekers navigate layers of data stored and represented in virtual space. Buildings in cyberspace may have more dimensions than physical buildings do, and cyberspace may reflect different laws of existence. It has been said that cyberspace is...where electronic mail travels, and it resembles the Toontown in the movie *Roger Rabbit*.

In contrast, Rain Ottis and Peeter Lorents (2010) wrote that cyberspace "is a time-dependent set of interconnected information systems and the human users that interact with these systems," while in Wikipedia (http://en.wikipedia.org/wiki/Cyberspace), a classic example of Web 1.0, "cyberspace" is defined as "the global network of interdependent information technology infrastructures, telecommunications networks and computer processing systems." Although Heim's (1993) characterization focused on the absence of traditional borders in the "spaces" created by Internet use, it shares an acknowledgment that use of the Internet permits the creation and sharing of information of various types. In 1987, Mitchell Moss wrote that "[M]any observers believe that new information systems will ultimately lead to the demise of cities by allowing electronic means of communication to substitute for face-to-face exchanges."

In the past five years we have been witness to the analogue of this predicted demise of cities in the failures of newspapers lacking electronic presence and the shift from brick-and-mortar bookstores to online book retailers. It remains an open question whether virtual communities linked by information technologies will "de-place" traditional cities, or to what degree the transformations of newspapers and book retailers will spread to other businesses. Contrary to some of the earlier speculation, we have not reached the point where online realities, activities, and interactions entirely supersede their physical counterparts.

What is perhaps more important at this point in time is not worries about the imminent dissolution of geographically defined and bounded communities (such as cities) and businesses but instead that use of the Internet often "supplants physical space" (Heim, 1993), permitting people to do what would otherwise be difficult or impossible. When our communications with one another are mediated electronically through technologies such as the Internet, "where we are physically" need not determine "where and who we are socially" (Meyrowitz, 1985). In the same vein, communities "often sundered in the real world by traffic, the threat of violence or the self-sufficiency encouraged by modern domestic appliances" are, as Stallabrass (1995) remarked, being reborn "in the ether, as people with the same interests but who are perhaps geographically distant, virtually meet." The Internet changes

social relationships as well as communities with a geographic orientation.

Mills (2002) observed that the "ways we experience reality, encounter ourselves and others, participate in daily activities, and, of course,
act politically, are in the process of being dramatically redefined and
remade." Given that a "decade after the first graphics-based web browser became widely available, the Internet has become a mainstream
avenue for political participation in the United States" (Best & Krueger,
2005), a challenging socio-political question arises: "Will the increasing
penetration of the Internet into the social and political lives of people
facilitate adoption and maintenance of democracy within the public
domain/public sphere?" Many people believe that the answer to this
question is "yes," and further, there are claims that use of the Internet is
one of the principal tools to introduce democratic characteristics into
societies that would otherwise be ambivalent or hostile to democracy.
Beverly Pappas (2011) observed the use of social media technologies
such as Twitter and Facebook by people living in "oppressive, authoritarian societies" to challenge governmental authority, exchange information with one another, and broadcast information to the "outside"
world.

While some writers focus their attention on citizens' use of the
Internet to facilitate and encourage democratization of politics and
social relations, other writers suggest that governments' increasing
utilization of the Internet will have a democratizing effect. In this
connection, Michael Dertouzos, in his 1997 book, *What Will Be: How
the New World of Information Will Change Our Lives*, claimed that use of
the Internet will promote what he calls "computer-aided peace." "Once
governments really begin using the Information Marketplace to alter
their internal practices," wrote Dertouzos, "they will be a short step
away from improving intergovernmental activity." If correct, then, it
seems reasonable to take seriously the claim of Mitch Kapor (1993) that,
at its best, life in a world interconnected by the Internet would be
"more egalitarian than elitist, and more decentered than hierarchical."

While a more peaceful, just, and equitable world is surely something we would all welcome, even a perfunctory examination of the
history of the introductions of new information technologies reveals

how common such optimistic claims about the positive transformative power of the technologies are. For instance, in 1898, in his book *Submarine Telegraphs*, the British electrician and telegraph expert Charles Bright wrote:

> An entirely new and much-improved method of conducting diplomatic relations between one country and another has come into use with the telegraph wire and cable. The facility and rapidity with which one government is now enabled to know the "mind"—or, at any rate, the professed mind—of another, has often been the means of averting diplomatic ruptures and consequent wars during the last decade. (Standage, 1999)

Given that introduction and use of the telegraph and other "modern" information technologies such as the telephone have not created idyllic, just, and equitable communities, it seems reasonable to be chary of claims that, by itself, the availability of communications through the agency of the Internet will create new, more equitable, and just social and political relationships (Weare, 2002).

The very characteristics of Internet use that are conducive to, and facilitate adoption of, democratic principles of association are also characteristics that, left unchecked, can create conditions leading to what Alexis de Tocqueville (2000) called "tyranny of the majority." Dependence of political participation on information technologies may lead to under-representation for those people who are unconnected from these networks, where the "connected majority" (who may be a minority in the society as a whole) may tyrannically impose its will on the connected minority as well as on the unconnected. On the other hand, the connectedness of one or more actors may give them an unfair advantage relative to the message they seek to deliver to members of the communities in which they exist. In both cases, increasing reliance on the Internet as a principal tool of communication and creative interaction within the public domain/public sphere may result in a slide from a democracy into a technocracy in which the interests of the "connected majority" limit the freedoms of others. The conclusion is that to better understand the promises and challenges of the future it is important to reflect critically on how the use of the Internet has transformed the character of the public domain/public sphere (Crang, 2010) and the deliberations about governance that occur within that domain/sphere.

Communities and Public Domains/Public Spheres

According to Margaret Somers (1993), the concept of "public domain/public sphere" refers to "a contested participatory site in which actors with overlapping identities as legal subjects, citizens, economic actors, and family members form a public body and engage in negotiations and contestations over political and social life." Thus, the relevant worries relate to how use of the Internet may alter the "negotiations and contestations" that occur within the public domain/public sphere, and so affect governance of the "public body." Expressed in language drawn from Jürgen Habermas (1991), the worry is that widespread, easy use of the Internet permits self-interested stakeholders to shape the communicative interactions of people in ways that do not represent the interests of private people (private stakeholders) as the public.

In this context, the appropriate unit of analysis is the community; the grouping of people both necessary and sufficient for the creation and maintenance of a public domain/public sphere (Dewey, 1954). Jan Fernback (2007) observed that, "[S]ince the late 19th century, sociologists, anthropologists, political scientists and cultural prophets have kept the social quest for community in the limelight of popular discourse." As multiple stakeholders have used the word "community" to meet their own needs, its meaning can be consequentially vague (Bellini & Vargas, 2003). D. J. Walmsley (2000) wrote that the,

> notion of community has been of interest to human geographers for many years. However, as in much of the rest of social science, the concept has been interpreted loosely, with a result that the term has a high level of use, but a low level of meaning. (p. 5)

Although some writers believe that these vagaries associated with the use of community justify avoiding the term altogether (Etzioni, 2000), addressing the issues involved with the meaning of community and thus providing a clear starting point for understanding how use of the Internet may affect governance of people within communities. Consider the *Oxford English Dictionary's* (OED's) definition of community as a "body of people who live in the same place, usually sharing a common cultural or ethnic identity" (Simpson & Weiner, 1989). Although this is only one of over 10 different definitions of community found in the

OED (in his classic "Definitions of Community: Areas of Agreement," George Hillery, 1955, identified 94 different definitions of community), it captures many of the elements found in the other definitions and provides a starting point for operationalizing the concept of community. The first thing to note is that a collection of people living in the same place is not a sufficient condition for existence of a community. The members of a single family may all live in the same place (e.g., a household) but, generally, are not a community (or at least, in the Aristotelian sense, do not constitute a political community). A step up from this, several families may live in close proximity to one another and so live "in the same place" but have no interaction and so do not constitute a community (Hoffer, 1931). What is missing, in the words of John Dewey (1954), is a shared set of meanings that serve as an "integrated principle" transforming the conjoint desires and activities of individuals "into a community of interest and endeavor." Although the spatial proximity of people to one another may increase the likelihood of community formation, proximity does not guarantee the existence or formation of a community.

Information technologies such as the Internet (and earlier, technologies such as the telegraph and telephone) have demonstrated that a collection of people living in the same place is not a necessary condition for existence of a community qua civitas (Mitchell, 2000; Wellman & Gulia, 1999). As remarked by Robert Chaskin (1997), the "networks of connection that bind individuals of a given group to one another as a community may or may not be rooted in place." Consider the case of the social-media tool Facebook. Started in February 2004, Facebook (2011) reported having over 500 million active users who spend over 700 billion minutes per month using the social media (http://www.facebook.com/press/info.php?statistics). With over 900 million objects (e.g., pages, groups, events, community pages) that people access and use, Facebook provides an electronic network (synchronous and asynchronous) in which members with shared desires and interests can communicate with one another using Internet connections.

One of the most active applications for exchanging real-time information and communicating current events is Twitter. According to Steven Johnson (2009), "[A]s a social network, Twitter revolves around the principle of followers. When you choose to follow another Twitter user that user's tweets appear in reverse chronological order on your main Twitter page." Although Twitter was formed only five years ago in 2006, Website-monitoring.com (2010) reported that there are currently more than 106 million accounts on Twitter and that approximately 40 percent of Twitter users generally follow at least 10 user accounts simultaneously (http://www.website-monitoring.com/blog/2010/05/04/twitter-facts-and-figures-history-statistics/). Organizations as diverse as Phi Kappa Phi (Schubert, Riechert, &Wicksall, 2011) and the American Red Cross (Briones, Kuch, Liu, & Jin, 2011) use Twitter (as well as Facebook) to create, expand, and maintain their "communities of interest." Even U.S. President Barack Obama has used Twitter; on July 6, 2011, he used Twitter to hold a "town hall-"style meeting to answer questions and advocate his economic agenda (Mason & Holland, 2011). The upshot is that while it is common to restrict the connotation of community to a bounded geographic area, the use and capabilities of social media technologies such as Facebook and Twitter demonstrate that nothing demands that we accept this restricted connotation of community.

Traditionally, people living in the same geographically bounded place were subject to two consequences: First, living in the same place, the people were more likely to share common interests and so have overlapping conceptions of "the good." Second, people increased the likelihood that they would have robust communications and interactions with one another relevant to satisfying their common interests and realizing their shared vision of the common good (Aristotle, 1998). Together, these consequences manifested themselves in a "heritage narrative;" "selective [shared] representations of the past that feed into, and are partially driven by the demands, sentiments, and interest of those in the present," thus functioning to create the synchronic and diachronic unity constituting the community (Bridger, 1996). However, with the advent of information technologies such as the Internet, it is possible for these constitutive heritage narratives to emerge from communicative activities that take place through use of the electronic information exchange technologies.

Joseph Gusfield (1975) wrote that we should distinguish between a territorial, geographic conception of a community and a relational conception of community that is concerned with the "quality of human relationship, without reference to location." Acknowledging and building on Gusfield's distinction, David McMillan and David Chavis (Galston, 2004) identified criteria whose satisfaction they believe is sufficient for an association of people being a community in either the territorial or the relational sense. The criteria are:

a) the "feeling of belonging or of sharing a sense of personal related-ness" (Membership);

b) a "sense of mattering, of making a difference to a group and of the group mattering to its members" (Influence);

c) the "feeling that members' needs will be met by the resources re-ceived through their membership in the group" (Integration); and

d) the "commitment and belief that members have shared and will share history...and similar experiences" (Shared Emotional Connec-tion). (McMillan & Chavis, 1986)

What is important in these closely related characterizations of community is not the spatial, geographic propinquity of the members to one another, but the relationships, manifested in the constitutive heritage narratives, existing between the members of the community (Baker & Ward, 2002; Bellini & Vargas, 2003; Bridger, 1996; Chaskin, 1997; Parrish, 2002). Thus, it is possible to understand why both a small town with clearly delimited geographic boundaries and a profes-sional group (e.g., the American Medical Association) "without physical locus" and "whose founding fathers are linked only rarely by blood with the present generation" (Goode, 1957), are both communities.

There are ongoing and vibrant debates about the adequacy of the characterizations of community presented above. What makes geo-graphically based groupings of people, as well as the social networks created by the use of social media tools such as Facebook and Twitter, communities, is a constitutive heritage narrative having four principal elements (elements based on the criteria identified above):

1. It is a narrative representing and expressing shared interests.

2. It is based in the perceived need of cooperation to satisfy those interests.

3. A sense of membership matters.

4. As a shared, constitutive narrative, it provides a set of guidelines for what counts as permissible or impermissible, as well as appropriate or inappropriate interactions.

Communities range from what Gerald Suttles (1972) called "communities of limited liability," created when people form voluntary associations that focus on limited and often specialized issues, to more long-lasting associations based on broader, more important and sustained interests, to associations whose principal function is to provide "emotional and peer group support" (Wellman & Gulia, 1999). A voluntary association of people who come together, either virtually or physically, in a "shared space" (Driskell & Lyon, 2002) to play "fantasy football" is an example of a community of limited liability. What Jaren Fisher, Kenton Unruh and Joan Durrance (2003) called "information communities" are examples of more long-lasting associations based on broader, sustained interests. An information community is "a partnership of institutions and individuals forming and cultivating a community of interest around the provision and exchange of information, aimed at increasing access to that information or increasing communication, and thereby increasing that knowledge-base." Finally, peer group support for "recovering alcohol and drug addicts" and "SeniorNet," which provides "access to grief counselors who would otherwise be unavailable," are examples of Internet-based associations providing emotional and peer support (Wellman & Gulia, 1999). A key point here is that the conception of community broad enough to cover neighborhoods, professional groups, and online networks (associations) of people is not a purely functional conception. The people who belong to the community, the community citizens, bring their own characteristics to the community (Parrish, 2002).

The conception of community as constituted by heritage narratives is not a conception that starts with individuals as "social atoms" and then defines communities as those complex concatenations of individuals created by properties entirely endogenous to the individuals. The heritage narrative conception of communities is a view that sees people as both constituting and constitutive of heritage narratives (Tilly, 1995). Communities, as the basic units of social analysis, emerge because of the "relational processes of interaction between and among" individuals whose own identity is, at least in part, itself a product of the constitutive narrative activity (Somers, 1998; Lyotard, 1991).

How does this help us understand what it means to predicate "virtual" to community and to the public domain/public sphere of the community? The term virtual generally implies that the focus of attention is on communication (narrative processes) flowing through a non-geographic matrix represented by an electronic coordinate system used for routing communication protocols. This use of virtual fits rather neatly into a Clifford Geertz-like (1973) characterization of communities as "webs of significance," and what we can say is that appropriately bounded human-made webs of information exchange (narrative associations) and the protocols (regulative norms of narrative, communicative action) that govern those exchanges are the heritage narratives that constitute communities. When essential and significant portions of these heritage narratives emerge because of computer-mediated communications, the communities are, in at least partial but important ways, virtual communities (Castells, 1996; Rheingold, 1994). Just as urban geographers often abstract from the physical characteristics of metropolitan areas and focus on the interrelations of services and various governance structures, so we too can more generally conceptualize communities in terms of their narrative (information) flows and relationships (Baker & Ward, 2002).

This conceptualization permits us to capture the defining characteristic, the appropriate bounds, of specifically "virtual communities" without denying that, in some important and critical sense, it is necessary to base a virtual community on physical reality (Strate, 1999). Those who use the Internet and, by that use, create virtual (computer-mediated) heritage narratives, are people whose identities and characteristics are formed, at least in part, separately from their computer-mediated communicative activities. This conceptualization uncouples the concept of community from a traditionally physical, geographic characterization and, in its place, offers a "higher-level" characterization of communities in terms of the norm-governed narrative roles the members play relative to one. Here the "flow of information" (Castells, 1996) is less constrained by the physical boundaries of distance than by the boundaries of information density, the ability to manipulate and coordinate information, and the limitations of interest and desire. Geography may, and traditionally often did, play an important role in creating the conditions conducive for the emergence of these "flows of information" (narratives), but the technologically mediated public domain/public sphere created by use of the Internet "is a non-localized space in that it is not bounded by a particular spatial-temporal locale" (Slevin, 2000).

Those connected with one another by computer-mediated communications use ontological narratives—heritage narratives—to define who they are in the context of their information-sharing connections and to make sense of and regulate their interconnections with other people (Somers, 1994). In defining themselves and their relationships to one another, these people create a new narrative and so too a new community and public domain/public sphere; a domain/sphere that incorporates governance rules for the community and permits opportunities for discourse leading to decisions regarding community governance.

Democracy and the Internet's Transformation of Public Domains/Public Spheres

As reported in the Pew Internet and American Life Project's report on the Internet's role in the 2008 U.S. political campaigns, three-quarters "of internet users went online during the 2008 election to take part in, or get news about the 2008 campaign," a number that "represents 55% of the entire adult population" (Smith, 2010). This raises the question as to whether democracy is facilitated or inhibited in those communities where electronic information exchanges (electronically mediated heritage narratives) play a significant role in constituting their public domain/public sphere. This question merits some discussion of what counts as democracy. "Democracy" is a word used widely in political and socio-political discussions and means, generally, "rule of the people" (Shepard, 1935; Wollheim, 1958); offering a more precise definition is neither trivial nor easy. For example, in his 1999 book on political ideologies, Leon Baradat (2000) wrote that "[T]here are almost

220 national constitutions in the world today, and almost all of them claim to be democratic." Similarly, Robert Dahl (2006), in his *A Preface to Democratic Theory*, wrote that "there is no democratic theory—there are only democratic theories." The Wikipedia article on democracy includes discussions of other forms of democracy, including socialist, anarchist and cosmopolitan democracy, (http://en.wikipedia.org/wiki/Democracy), while Austin Ranney and Willmoore Kendall (1951) noted that for some writers, democracy is not simply a form of government but, as in the case of Dewey, a "way of life." The problem, then, is that democracy has become, as Carl Becker (1941) wrote, "a kind of conceptual Gladstone bag which, with a little manipulation, can be made to accommodate almost any collection of social facts we may wish to carry about in it."

Even though there are multiple senses of democracy, three elements common to most connotations of democracy are important in the present context. The first element is the assumption that democracies, as instances of "rule by the people," assume that "there is more enlightenment and wisdom in many men united than in one alone" (Tocqueville, 2000). The second element is that, ideally, democracies require a "public space" in which it is possible to discuss and debate issues of importance to the community (that is, important to communities characterized as democratic) in an open and free manner. The third element is that, again ideally, the discussions (although not necessarily the final governance decisions vis-à-vis rules, regulations and laws governing behaviors in the community) must be open to participation by all members of the community. The idea then, resting in the idea of the community as constituted by heritage narrative practices, is that the characterization of a community as democratic is a characterization referring to the nature of the narrative practices within, and constituting, the community. A necessary, though not sufficient, condition for a community to be properly characterized as democratic is that the resources for free and open constitutive narratives by everyone in the community are present, used, and institutionalized in the regulations, rules, and laws that govern the behaviors of the community and its citizens.

Widespread and nearly universal access to and use of the Internet may provide the conditions for, and encourage the creation and maintenance of, free and open narratives (Dahlberg, 2001). To the extent that access to and use of the Internet has this effect, it is reasonable to believe that it is a force for democracy. On the other hand, to the extent that use of the Internet distorts the public domain/public space of the community by inhibiting free and open narrative, or by restricting the information needed for thoughtful, rational discussions about the issues the community believes important, the Internet is an antidemocratic force. Since it is only through a cognizance of the potential antidemocratic consequences of Internet use that its potential for facilitating democracy can be realized, the balance of this section focuses on the antidemocratic potentials.

A common element in different forms of democracy is the belief that there is "more enlightenment and wisdom" in the many members of the community than in one member or a small "elite" class. This does not mean that democratic governance excludes regulations, rules, and laws created by some subset of the entire community, since in at least some forms of representative democracy (e.g., Madisonian Republics), elected delegates are responsible for the creation of the appropriate modes of governance. However, what it does mean is that in all genuine democracies, the public domain/public sphere must be genuinely public; it must be free and open to participation by all community members. In the case of the availability and use of the Internet, we can refer, following Tocqueville (2000), to the possibilities of tyranny as the possibilities of the tyranny of the majority.

In this sense of the tyranny of the majority, the threat is that the choices by the majority stop any further discussion of the issues about which the majority has decided, and in so doing, close the public domain/public sphere to further free and open discussion. Matters of majority opinion become settled "matters of fact" rather than provisional points of agreement about which further thoughtful, rational discussion is always permitted (and encouraged). The question is, how might the Internet actually facilitate rather than inhibit this antidemocratic possibility?

Three characteristics of the Internet are salient to the claim that its use may lay the groundwork for tyranny of the majority and inhibit democracy. The first is the presence of a "digital divide." Although there is general agreement that there is a digital divide within and between societies/communities (Dobransky & Hargittai, 2006), its "complex, dynamic, multifaceted" (Bruno, Esposito, Genovese, & Gwebu, 2010) character leads to various definitions.

Whether participation in the public domain/public sphere created by, or accessed by, the Internet and associated information technologies is due to lack of access or lack of skills (Belanger, 2009), the existence of the digital divide means that there will be differential participation in the formation and maintenance of the heritage narratives that constitute the community. This, in turn, means that the deliberative narratives that constitute the public domain/public sphere may not reflect the interests and perspectives of the people who fall on the "have not" side of the digital divide.

To the extent that people in the community cannot participate in the deliberative narratives or cannot participate in the informed selection of delegates to represent their interests and perspectives, the result is an antidemocratic distortion of the public domain/public sphere. Thus, to the extent that the narratives of the public domain/public sphere take place through the mediation of the Internet and associated information technologies, and to the extent that groups of people are, because of this, excluded from the deliberative narrations of the public domain/public sphere, the community is antidemocratic. Even "if status inequalities concerning technical equipment and digital experience were to decline, status-based differences in Internet usage would likely persist" (Zillien & Hargittai, 2009).

Many people feel uncomfortable with, or are unwilling to use, the social media tools of Web 2.0. For these people, most political communication takes place in a one-way environment, and "the model of subjectivity that is being reinforced is that of a passive agent" (Koch, 2005). In this usage, the Internet, as noted by Andrew Koch, "takes on the character of a sophisticated billboard for advertising purposes" and, rather than supporting reasoned, deliberative narrative, "provides the perfect public relations tool for the government." Without satisfaction of the requisite material and social conditions, or assurance that the members of the community share in minimal technical skills, there is reason to be skeptical of claims that use of the Internet and associated information technologies will facilitate democracy within the community. The existence of digital divides provides the opportunity for the majority of "haves" to structure and control the deliberative narratives of the public domain/public sphere and so create one form of the "tyranny of the majority."

The second characteristic of the Internet salient to the claim that its use may lay the groundwork for tyranny of the majority and inhibit democracy is the presence of "cloaked websites" (Daniels, 2009). According to Daniels, a cloaked Web site is one "published by individuals or groups that conceal authorship or feign legitimacy in order to deliberately disguise a hidden political agenda." For example, following Hurricane Katrina, a number of Web sites such as www.katrinafamilies. com appeared with digital photos of distressed people. These Web sites redirected people to Internet Donations.org where people could make donations. What was not at all evident was that the "domain name was registered to Frank Weltner, a St. Louis, MO-based white supremacist" (Daniels, 2009). Thus, donations were supporting, if only indirectly, a white supremacist group, even though there was nothing on the Web site to indicate this connection. Rather than being a problem of "too much information," an issue to which some critics of the Internet's ability to foster democracy refer (see Noveck, 2000), the problem posed by the existence of such Web sites is that they compromise the "open" character of the deliberative narrative of the public domain/public sphere.

The compromise takes two general forms: First, groups may gain material resources and thus, additional abilities to influence the narratives of the public domain/public sphere. When people unknowingly support organizations whose political ideologies are different from their own, the result is that private interests supersede genuinely public interests. Second, because of the "information" promulgated by the Web sites, people may have false beliefs and advocate biased or distorted positions based on those beliefs. In such cases, the narrative deliberations may reflect, in one sense, the majority view of the community, but in another sense may reflect a view shaped by the special interests of groups or organizations within the community. Thus, "cloaked websites" create a possibility of tyranny of the majority, wherein the views of the majority reflect the private and partial special interests of organizations (or people) within the community, and disagreement with the so-called majority views is stifled by control of access to the deliberative narratives or to the "facts" against which competing deliberative claims are judged. Quite generally, this is an "epistemic challenge" to democracy, posed by the use of the Internet and associated information technologies. Although the challenge is not unique to the Internet, the sophisticated nature of the technology and the inability of most people to differentiate "cloaked" from non-cloaked Web sites exacerbates the problem.

The third characteristic of the Internet salient to the claim that its use may lay the groundwork for tyranny of the majority and inhibit democracy relates to the perceived credibility of Web-based information. Empirical work by Andrew Flanagin and Miriam Metzger (2007) shows that credibility assessments of Web-based information "appear to be primarily due to website attributes (e.g., design features, depth of content, site complexity) rather than to familiarity with Web site sponsors." Flanagin and Metzger found that "fictitious sites were able to achieve credibility ratings that were largely equal to those of major organizations, presumably based on their sophisticated site attributes, including design and content." Since political information "is a central aspect of democracy" (Gronlund, 2007), to the extent that people form opinions based on information from Web sites they use because of design features, their deliberations within the public domain/public sphere will reflect the creators of those Web sites. In such cases, there is no guarantee that the deliberations, and decisions based on those deliberations, will reflect the public view as opposed to the private views of the creators of those Web sites.

Dissenting perspectives and opinions can either be "drowned out" by people using information from Web sites whose design features are more appealing, or, even worse, criticized and invalidated by those Web sites. In either case, the majority view is really a view created by private interests and, once again, the problem posed by the use of the Internet and associated information technologies for the public domain/public sphere is a variant of "tyranny of the majority." While the moral that writers such as Beth Noveck (2000) draw from this is that "[D]eliberate, participatory democracy requires careful editors [of information] and good filters [of information] to engage a mediated, educated debate," this seems to be decidedly antidemocratic in its reliance on "experts" and "gatekeepers" of information.

These three characteristics of the Internet demonstrate that, as is often the case, technology creates new dynamics and new possibilities and requires that we carefully rethink the social boundaries and definitions of communities and the individuals who constitute and interact with the community. The users of the electronic information technologies such as the Internet not only adapt the technologies to meet their needs and desires, the technologies in turn transform the users. The narrative practices made possible by use of the Internet and associated information technologies provide, in part, the temporally constructed backdrop against which, in the words of Mustapha Emirbayer and Anne Mische (1998), the interplay of "habit, imagination, and judgment, both reproduces and transforms those structures in interactive response to the problems posed by changing historical situations."

There is, consequently, no compelling reason to believe that widespread use of the Internet, by itself, supports one political organizational principle better than any other political organizational principle. A free and open public domain/public sphere, which many see as the future offered by the widespread dissemination and use of the Internet and associated information technologies, is not guaranteed. As Barry Wellman (2004) wrote, "technology [by itself] does not determine anything"; instead, it is how people use technology, for good or bad, that matters.

Conclusion

In his 1927 book, *The Public and Its Problems*, Dewey made the following remark on the connection between technologies that connect people together and democracy:

> Carlyle was no admirer of democracy, but in a lucid moment he said: "Invent the printing press and democracy is inevitable." Add to this: Invent the railway, the telegraph, mass manufacture and concentration of population in urban centers, and some form of democratic government is, humanly speaking, inevitable. (Dewey, 1954)

The current view that widespread, ready use of the communication capabilities provided by the Internet and associated information technologies will facilitate and support democratization is a natural extension of Dewey's observation. The Internet, according to this line of reasoning, facilitates the possibility for the creation of a public domain/public sphere in which an open "network of pragmatic considerations, compromises, and discourses of self-understanding and of justice" occur, and these discursive deliberations constitute "the central element of the democratic process" (Habermas, 1998).

The increasing use of the Internet as a means for public discourse about governance presents new possibilities for interactions by community members, whether geographic, virtual, or a hybrid combination in nature. As the intensity and volume of public discussion shift from face-to-face, printed (e.g., newspaper), and one-way telecommunication interactions (e.g., television) to dynamic social media forums made possible by technologies such as Web 2.0, administrators, elected officials, and other interested stakeholders must proactively attempt to understand the possibilities occasioned by the virtual realm. Without this understanding, they risk marginalization by those stakeholders who may well be more adept at accessing and using extant and emerging electronic information technologies. Thus, stakeholders with the greatest facility in accessing the Internet and making use of communicative possibilities of the Internet could frame and control the critical discussion occurring in the public domain/public sphere regarding governance. When this happens, "public opinion," which, as public, is, in the words of Bernard Bosanquet (1899) "sound and true, and contains the ethical spirit of the State," becomes the expression of "individuals in their particular judgments, on which they plume themselves," and is "full of falsehood and vanity."

Without careful, thoughtful examination of the possibilities and perils of increasing use of the Internet, we may find ourselves more shaped by technological forces we do not fully comprehend than active, engaged participants in the opportunities afforded by the Internet and associated information technologies. We need to avoid slipping from the promises of a "Brave New Wired World" to the technocracy of a "Brave New World," where the persuasive force of "public opinion" shaped by the electronic medium of the Internet takes the place of reasoned, thoughtful discussion. Private, partial interests hold sway in the public domain/public sphere (Habermas, 1991), and the moral validation of the public domain/public sphere becomes lost. Fortunately, for all its perils, the Internet also offers the promise of improving "the methods and conditions of [public] debate discussion and persuasion" (Dewey, 1954) and, as Dewey remarked, how to make these improvements "is the problem of the public."

References

Aristotle. (1998). *Politics*. Indianapolis, IN: Hackett.

Baker, P. M. A., & Ward, A. C. (2002). Bridging temporal and spatial "gaps": The role of information and communication technologies in defining communities. *Information, Communication & Society, 5*(2), 207–224.

Baradat, L. P. (2000). *Political ideologies: Their origins and impact* (7th ed.). Upper Saddle River, NJ: Prentice Hall.

Becker, C. (1941). *Modern democracy*. New Haven, CT: Yale University Press.

Belanger, F. (2009). The impact of the digital divide on e-government use. *Communications of the ACM, 52*(4), 132–135.

Bellini, C. G. P., & Vargas, L. M. (2003). Rationale for Internet-mediated communities. *CyberPsychology & Behavior, 6*(1), 3–14.

Best, S. J., & Krueger, B. S. (2005). Analyzing the representativeness of Internet political participation. *Political Behavior, 27*(2), 183–216.

Bosanquet, B. (1899). *The philosophical theory of the state*. London, England: Macmillan.

Bridger, J. C. (1996). Community imagery and the built environment. *The Sociological Quarterly, 37*(3), 353–374.

Briones, R. L., Kuch, B., Liu, B. F., & Jin, Y. (2011). Keeping up with the digital age: How the American Red Cross uses social media to build relationships. *Public Relations Review, 37*, 37–43. doi:10.1016/j.pubrev.2010.12.006

Bruno, G., Esposito, E., Genovese, A., & Gwebu, K. L. (2010). A critical analysis of current indexes for digital divide measurement. *The Information Society, 27*(1), 16–28. doi:10.1080/01972243.2010.534364

Burton, D. F. (1997). The brave new wired world. *Foreign Policy, 106*, 22–37.

Castells, M. (1996). *The rise of the network society*. Cambridge, MA: Blackwell.

Chaskin, R. J. (1997). Perspectives on neighborhood and community: A review of the literature. *The Social Service Review, 71*(4), 521–547.

Crang, M. (2010). Cyberspace as the new public domain. In C. W. Kihato, M. Massoumi, B. A. Ruble, & A. M. Garland (Eds.), *Urban diversity: Space, culture, and inclusive pluralism in cities worldwide* (pp. 99–122). Baltimore, MD: Johns Hopkins University Press.

Dahl, R. A. (2006). *A preface to democratic theory (expanded edition)*. Chicago, IL: University of Chicago Press.

Dahlberg, L. (2001). The Internet and democratic discourse: Exploring the prospects of online deliberative forums extending the public sphere. *Information, Communication & Society, 4*(4), 615-633. doi:10.1080/13691180110 097030

Daniels, J. (2009). Cloaked websites: Propaganda, cyber-racism and epistemology in the digital age. *New Media and Society, 11*(5), 659-683. doi:10.1177/ 1461444809105345

Dertouzos, M. (1997). *What will be: How the new world of information will change our lives*. San Francisco, CA: HarperEdge.

Dewey, J. (1954). *The public and its problems*. Athens, OH: Swallow Press/Ohio University Press.

Dobransky, K., & Hargittai, E. (2006). The disability divide in Internet access and use. *Information, Communication & Society, 9*(3), 313-334. doi:10.1080/ 13691180600751298

Driskell, R. B., & Lyon, L. (2002). Are virtual communities true communities? Examining the environments and elements of community. *City & Community, 1*(4), 373-390.

Emirbayer, M., & Mische, A. (1998). What is agency? *American Journal of Sociology, 103*(4), 962-1023.

Etzioni, A. (2000). Creating good communities and good societies. *Contemporary Sociology, 29*(1), 188-195.

Fernback, J. (2007). Beyond the diluted community concept: A symbolic interactionist perspective on online social relations. *New Media Society, 9*(1), 49-69. doi:10.1177/1461444807072417

Fisher, J. E., Unruh, K. T., & Durrance, J. C. (2003). Information communities: Characteristics gleaned from studies of three online networks. *Proceedings of the ASIST Annual Meeting, 40*, 298-305.

Flanagin, A. J., & Metzger, M. J. (2007). The role of site features, user attributes, and information verification behaviors on the perceived credibility of Web-based information. *New Media & Society, 9*(2), 319-342. doi:10.1177/ 1461444807075015

Galston, W. A. (2004). The impact of the Internet on civic life: An early assessment. In V. A. Gehring (Ed.), *The Internet in public life* (pp. 59-77). Lanham, MD: Rowman and Littlefield.

Geertz, C. (1973). Thick description: Toward an interpretative theory of culture. In C. Geertz (Ed.), *The interpretation of cultures* (pp. 3–30). New York, NY: Basic Books.

Gergen, K. J. (2005). Narrative, moral identity and historical consciousness: A social constructionist account. In J. Straub (Ed.), *Narration, identity and historical consciousness* (pp. 99–119). New York, NY: Berghahn Books.

Goode, W. J. (1957). Community within a community: The professions. *American Sociological Review, 22*(2), 194–200.

Gronlund, K. (2007). Knowing and not knowing: The Internet and political information. *Scandinavian Political Studies, 30*(3), 397–418. doi:10.1111/j.1467-9477.2007.00186.x

Gusfield, J. R. (1975). *Community: A critical response.* New York, NY: Harper Colophon Books.

Habermas, J. (1991). *The structural transformation of the public sphere: An inquiry into a category of bourgeois society.* Cambridge, MA: MIT Press.

Habermas, J. (1998). *Between facts and norms: Contributions to a discourse theory of law and democracy.* Cambridge, MA: MIT Press.

Heim, M. (1993). *The metaphysics of virtual reality.* New York, NY: Oxford University Press.

Hillery, G. A. (1955). Definitions of community: Areas of agreement. *Rural Sociology, 20*(2), 111–123.

Hoffer, C. R. (1931). Understanding the community. *American Journal of Sociology, 36*(4), 616–624.

International Telecommunications Union. (2010). Measuring the Information Society: 2010. Geneva: International Telecommunications Union.

International Telecommunications Union. (2011, April). From billions to trillions: Ubiquitous ICTs? Retrieved from http://www.itu.int/net/pressoffice/stats/2011/02/index.aspx

Jalali, A. A., & Mahmoodi, H. (2009). Virtual age: Next wave of change in society. Paper presented at the 2009 Joint Conferences on e-CASE and e-Technology, Singapore. Retrieved from http://userwww.sfsu.edu/~mahmoodi/papers/paper_C50.pdf

Johnson, S. (2009, June 5). How Twitter will change the way we live. Retrieved from http://www.time.com/time/business/article/0,8599,1902604,00.html

Kapor, M. (1993, August). Where is the digital highway really headed? *Wired,* 53–59, 94.

Kedzie, C. (1997). *Communication and democracy: Coincident revolutions and the emergent dictators.* Retrieved from http://www.rand.org/pubs/rgs_dissertations/RGSD127.html#toc

Kleinrock, L. (2008). History of the Internet and its flexible future. *IEEE Wireless Communications*, 8–18.

Koch, A. (2005). Cyber citizen or cyborg citizen: Baudrillard, political agency, and the commons in virtual politics. *Journal of Mass Media Ethics*, 20(2/3), 159–175. doi:10.1207/s15327728jmme2002&3_5

Kwak, H., Zinkhan, G. M., Pan, Y., & Andras, T. L. (2008). Consumer communications, media use, and purchases via the Internet: A comparative, exploratory study. *Journal of International Consumer Marketing*, 20(3–4), 55–68. doi:10.1080/08961530802129243

Lyotard, J.-F. (1991). The postmodern condition: A report on knowledge. *Theory and History of Literature* (10). Minneapolis, MN: University of Minnesota Press.

Maciel, C., Roque, L., & Garcia, A. C. B. (2010). Interaction and communication resources in collaborative e-democratic environments: The democratic citizenship community. *Information Polity*, 15(1–2), 73–88.

Mason, J., & Holland, S. (2011, July 6). Obama tweets for the first time, tweaks Republicans. Retrieved from http://www.reuters.com/article/2011/07/06/us-obama-twitter-idUSTRE7652VO20110706?feedType=RSS&feedName=topNews&rpc=71

McMillan, D. W., & Chavis, D. M. (1986). Sense of community: A definition and theory. *Journal of Community Psychology*, 14, 6–23.

Meyrowitz, J. (1985). *No sense of place: The impact of electronic media on social behavior*. New York, NY: Oxford University Press.

Mills, K. (2002). Cybernations: Identity, self-determination, democracy and the "Internet effect" in the emerging information order. *Global Society*, 16(1), 69–87.

Mitchell, W. J. (2000). *City of bits: Space, place, and the Infobahn*. Cambridge, MA: MIT Press.

Moss, M. L. (1987). Telecommunications, world cities, and urban policy. *Urban Studies*, 24, 534–546.

Noveck, B. S. (2000). Paradoxical partners: Electronic communication and electronic democracy. *Democratization*, 7(1), 18–35. doi:10.1080/13510340008403643

Ottis, R., & Lorents, P. (2010). Cyberspace: Definition and implications. *Proceedings of the 5th International Conference on Information, Warfare and Security*, Dayton, OH, 267–270.

Pappas, B. (2011). Click here for democracy: Analysis of social media in Egypt and Iran as a process towards democratization. *Arete*, 20, 1–8.

Parrish, R. (2002). The changing nature of community. *Strategies, 15*(2), 259–284.

Ranney, A., & Kendall, W. (1951). Democracy: Confusion and agreement. *The Western Political Quarterly, 4*(3), 430–439.

Rheingold, H. (1994). *The virtual community: Homesteading on the electronic frontier.* New York, NY: HarperPerennial.

Schubert, D. C., Riechert, B. P., & Wicksall, S. G. (2011). Society online networks reach 15,000 members. *Phi Kappa Phi Forum, 91*(1), 30.

Shepard, W. J. (1935). Democracy. *Annals of the American Academy of Political and Social Science, 180*, 94–101.

Simpson, J., & Weiner, E. (1989). *Oxford English dictionary (2).* New ed. York, NY: Oxford University Press.

Slevin, J. (2000). *The Internet and society.* Cambridge, England: Polity Press.

Smith, A. (2010). *The Internet and campaign 2010.* Washington, DC: Pew Internet and American Life Project. Retrieved from http://www.pewinternet.org/~/media//Files/Reports/2011/Internet%20and%20Campaign%202010.pdf

Somers, M. R. (1993). Citizenship and the place of the public sphere: Law, community, and political culture in the transition to democracy. *American Sociological Review, 58*(5), 587–620.

Somers, M. R. (1994). The narrative constitution of identity: A relational and network approach. *Theory & Society, 23*(5), 605–649.

Somers, M. R. (1998). "We're no angels": Realism, rational choice, and relativity in social science. *American Journal of Sociology, 104*(3), 722–784.

Stallabrass, J. (1995). Empowering technology: The exploration of cyberspace. *New Left Review, 78*, 3–32.

Standage, T. (1999). *The Victorian Internet.* New York, NY: Berkeley Books.

Strate, L. (1999). The varieties of cyberspace: Problems in definition and delimitation. *Western Journal of Communication, 63*(3), 382–412.

Suttles, G. D. (1972). *The social construction of communities.* Chicago, IL: University of Chicago Press.

Tilly, C. (1995). To explain political processes. *American Journal of Sociology, 100*(6), 1594–1610.

Tocqueville, A. de. (2000). *Democracy in America.* (H. C. Mansfield & D. Winthrop, Eds. &Trans.). Chicago, IL: University of Chicago Press.

Walmsley, D. J. (2000). Community, place and cyberspace. *Australian Geographer, 31*(1), 5–19.

Weare, C. (2002). The Internet and democracy: The causal links between technology and politics. *International Journal of Public Administration, 25*(5), 659–691.

Wellman, B. (2004). Internet and community. *Ideas, 1*(1), 26–29.

Wellman, B., & Gulia, M. (1999). Virtual communities as communities. In M. A. Smith & P. Kollock (Eds.), *Communities in cyberspace.* (pp. 167–194). London, England: Routledge.

Wollheim, R. (1958). Democracy. *Journal of the History of Ideas, 19*(2), 225–242.

Yen, A. C. (2002). Western frontier or feudal society? Metaphors and perceptions of cyberspace. *Berkeley Technology Law Journal, 17*(4), 1207–1263.

Zillien, N., & Hargittai, E. (2009). Digital distinction: Status-specific types of Internet usage. *Social Science Quarterly, 90*(2), 274–291. doi:10.1111/j.1540-6237.2009.00617.x

Jarice Hanson

Introduction

Many images of the "information society" suggest a fast-paced society where (hypothetically) "everyone" can be instantly connected to (hypothetically) "anything" in milliseconds. The image of technology looming above the collectivity of individuals, benevolently facilitating and mediating their needs, suggests a utopian vision that projects an image of technology in the service of humanity. The popular notion of cloud computing suggests a comfortable blanket over the populace, quietly and unobtrusively connecting people to all of their desired information. These comforting thoughts are often juxtaposed against a different image that is far more brutal. A more dystopian vision of technology may appear to be similar to Orwell's "Big Brother," with technology monitoring people and their behaviors from every elevator, lamp-post, and wireless connector, limiting personal freedom and free will. There is no doubt that both of these competing visions exist in popular culture, but in the world of policy studies, practical applications of technology often view socially responsible policies as the bridge that leads from the dystopian sense of inequality and lack of personal expression toward the more utopian ideas of social justice.

For those who like to believe in the inevitability and the sanctity of the information society, a term such as "the digital divide" suggests a chasm that has finally been crossed. Information technology in the industrialized world is no longer new, and the deployment of broadband technology, as well as the proliferation of smart phones, has bridged a gap that once was thought to have been "uncrossable" in industrialized, as well as developing, nations.

This chapter focuses on the assumptions that undergird urban living in the early part of the twenty-first century and discusses some examples of typical, middle-class urban residents who have willfully chosen not to use the digital technologies that many assume permeate contemporary urban life. The study focuses on adults who have chosen to opt out of the information society for a number of personal, political, and economic reasons. These *willfully unconnected* individuals know that their choices have consequences, and yet they choose not to use some technologies—particularly digital technologies that would give them Internet access or cell phone access, and therefore, they have made conscious decisions to marginalize themselves in some ways from the information society. I call them the *new minority*. They remind us that sometimes using technology is a choice and not a requirement for living in contemporary society.

As major urban areas become even more populated, the new minority is likely to grow, but with what consequences? This chapter addresses the choices of the new minority (the willfully unconnected) and compares their values to the assumed challenge of creating public policies that are responsive to the perceived needs of the polis to be "connected."

The New Minority

In-depth interviews were conducted with 26 individuals who are self-professed "non-digital" users. These individuals are not Luddites, nor do they exhibit any desire to be self-sufficient or anti-social. They use "old" technologies, such as televisions, wired phones, radios, and, occasionally, desk-top computers, but they have chosen not to own or regularly use cell phones, laptops, tablets, electronic readers, or other more recent digital technologies that most of us see people using in public every day. Many of them consider portable digital technologies as unnecessary communications and information devices, though almost every one of them considered themselves well informed on topical issues within their localities and nations and in terms of global events. Many of them share similar characteristics, and all of them are educated members of the middle class, and gainfully employed. But in examining their communication preferences, we are reminded that not everyone feels inclined to be "connected" in the information age—at least not everywhere, all of the time. Their resistance to popular values that seemingly assume that anyone who can afford portable devices must have them has implications for some public policy matters, such as the ubiquity of municipal Wi-Fi, pricing of communications systems, emergency notification procedures, and delivery of services that favor the continuously connected.

This study did not start as an in-depth inquiry into the biases of urban dwellers but rather, with a simple conversation. "Arthur" (all interviewees will be described by pseudonyms) runs a news-stand in downtown Philadelphia. While purchasing a newspaper from him during a short stay, we began to talk about the customers who came to buy newspapers, magazines, candy, and soft drinks. As we conversed, we talked about what types of people still buy print media, what they talk about, and the way they think of time and the act of reading. "Arthur" had wonderful observations from his perch within the news-stand, and in subsequent conversations with him, he raised my consciousness about contemporary urban behavior and increased social pressures to conform to using small digital technologies that, in his words, "create more anxiety than I want."

Arthur's comments and situation led me to ask other people about their use of digital technologies in public, and I was surprised to find how easy it was to locate middle-class adults who have made strategic decisions to give up, or never buy, cell phones, laptops, electronic readers, or other portable communications technologies. At the same time, I was investigating social policies to increase municipal wireless systems, ways of funding a wireless infrastructure, and policies intended to include people who could not afford their own technologies.

Ironically, while I was thinking of the potential for developing a study on people who chose to be unconnected, I was teaching an online course for my university. Of the 30 registered students, seven did not own their own computers or have easy access to the Internet. They assumed that it would be easy enough to find public communication systems and took it for granted that all systems used in the course delivery would be transparent. While I scratched my head and wondered why they would spend so much money to take an online course when they didn't have the basic technology to take the course, I thought about how the Internet playing field favored those who had their own computers and broadband access, while some of the students relied on using technology at work. I did not see these students' perspectives as a variation on the traditional digital divide but rather as an assumption that technology could be accessed and that a little initiative on their part would enable them to do the work when they wanted to and when they could. Some of the students were dependent upon the public library, which limited their access to one hour at a time and filtered information so the students could not take online exams without special permission. The experiences of the willfully unconnected and those students who scrambled to find alternative ways to use computers and the Internet made me re-think some of the policies that have been written for purposes of inclusion and wonder what had become of early definitions of the digital divide and whether new definitions and concepts might pose more important questions for today's consumers and policy-makers. These questions will be addressed later in this chapter.

From Being Connected to Becoming Willfully Unconnected

The 26 individuals interviewed for this study had some remarkable similarities:

- Almost all of the participants (24) had a cell phone at one time, but gave it up;

- Most (19) are self-employed;

- None of them currently had children living at home;

- Most (21) considered the use of digital technology in public to be annoying or invasive;

- Most of the 26 (22) said they liked to work in solitude;

- A majority of the 26 were single and lived alone (18);

- Several (14) cited close relationships to people in religious organizations or social organizations;

- Only 1 person did not have access in the home to a wired phone though he did have access to a wired phone at work;

- Only 3 did not have a traditional television set in the home;

- A majority (23) had a traditional radio in the home, but only 18 claimed to listen regularly;

- Many (12) of the participants claimed that they attended free cultural events "often";

- All of the 26 considered their interpersonal relationships to be "fulfilling";

- All of the 26 enjoyed participating in cultural activities with other people in live settings.

While the experiences of the 26 interviewees will not be discussed in depth in this chapter, the Participant Table (Table 1) provides the interviewee's pseudonym, occupation, and reason for not using portable digital technology in public. Though a brief summary of the new minority's reasons for opting out of using some specific technologies is warranted, the experiences of these adults will be contrasted with the growing urban movement of social life today, and the consequences for being willfully unconnected in an environment that creates policies for inclusion. Therefore, the experiences of the new minority will provide a different perspective on urbanization and socially relevant public policies that favor "connectivity."

Table 11.1: *Participants*

Pseudonym	Location	Occupation	Reason for Being Unconnected
Arthur	Philadelphia	News dealer	Too expensive; unnecessary
Betty	Boston	Writer	Don't need it
Carol	Philadelphia	Designer	Other people handle this for me
Daryl	Trenton, NJ	Mechanic	I talk to people at work

Evelyn	Boston	Yoga instructor	Prefer peace and quiet
Fred	NYC	Train conductor	I like to read; I like it quiet
Gary	NYC	Political aide	I use equipment at work
Herman	Philadelphia	Store owner	I would probably lose a cell phone
Irene	Boston	Teacher	I like to listen to music at home
James	Philadelphia	Waiter	I don't need it; keep costs down
Kevin	Philadelphia	Law student	I don't need it; too expensive
Lucy	NYC	Shoe store clerk	Don't need it
Marie	Trenton	Activist	Kept losing it; didn't need it
Nancy	NYC	Printing Business	I don't need it
Otis	Philadelphia	Book Store Clerk	Too expensive; don't need it
Perry	NYC	Musician	I have a wired phone
Quint	Boston	Librarian	No need
Robin	New York City	Photographer	Prefers solitude
Sally	Stamford, Ct.	Editor	Old stuff works fine
Tom	Boston	Professor	Don't need it; I like quiet
Una	Amherst, MA	Health Club Owner	I don't need it
Valerie	Westport, CT.	Radio DJ	Too expensive
Walter	Amherst, MA	Television Director	Don't need it
Xena	Amherst, MA	Dancer	I'd probably lose it
Yves	NYC	Owns book store	Those technologies are annoying
Zef	NYC	Bookstore clerk	Who need them? I don't

Several of the interviewees commented that at some point in their lives (if there were children at home, elderly parents who might need immediate help, a change of job), they might purchase a cell phone or laptop in the future, but almost all of the interviewees said they saw no reason for tablets, electronic readers, or portable audio devices. Instead, the interviewees overwhelmingly claimed they enjoyed listening to a natural soundscape or thought that these portable technologies were anxiety-producing or would upset the balance in their lives.

For now, however, the majority of the 26 members of the new minority claimed that society puts too much pressure on people to spend money on items they don't need and disdained the pressure of "constant communication" when they did have portable devices. For many, the stress induced by constant interruptions or the tendency to continually check messages ultimately resulted in a feeling of loss of control over their lives (Hanson, 2007a, pp. 49-63). Their comments indicated that they were aware that personal control is largely an illusion when using portable technologies, and the majority of the new minority preferred to exhibit a clear distinction between public and private life.

The Willfully Unconnected and
Adult Technology Consumption

While once it may have seemed that portable, digital technologies were more likely to be owned and used by younger adults and teens, the Pew Internet and American Life Trend data provide a more inclusive picture of the technologies Americans own.

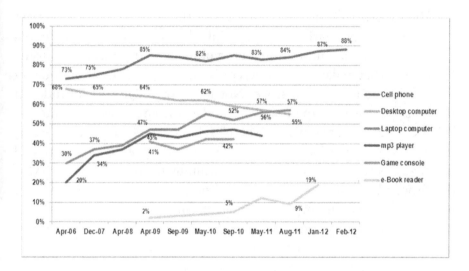

Figure 11.2: Pew Internet and American Life Project. http://pewinternet.org/Trend-Data-(Adults)/Device-Ownership.aspx

According to Pew, 87% of American adults have a cell phone; more than half (57%) have a laptop, and more than half go online wirelessly with one of those devices. When it comes to some of the newer technologies, fewer own an e-book reader (19%), and the same number have a tablet computer (19%) (http://pewinternet.org/Static-Pages/Trend-Data/~/media/Infographics/Trend Data/August 2011/Adult gadget ownership over time 2006-2012.jpg?w=530&h=428&as=1). In comparing "old" technologies to the Pew Study, the new minority still chose to engage in fewer technologies, though the biggest gaps in their technology usage undoubtedly reflected portable technologies that we often say "extend someone's communication ability" beyond the household.

These figures indicate that in general, the adult use of portable technologies reported in the Pew study is not lagging significantly;

therefore, those members of the willfully unconnected new minority are bucking the trend. Their personal reasons for not wanting portable technologies that they can afford attest to choice, not necessity, and indicate a willingness to share different values that reflect their own, personal, social realities.

Does Being Unconnected Matter?

The experiences of the 26 subjects in the original study may seem anomalous, or even frivolous; after all, they do maintain traditional technologies of communication, entertainment, and information in the home, but what makes them different is that they have clear boundaries between home and public space. Not many years ago, the attitudes of these individuals were the norm; but today, the emphasis has shifted to being connected "anytime/anywhere" (Hanson, 2007a, p. 1). So, why are the values and attitudes of these people worthy of investigation, and how likely is the new minority of the willfully unconnected to grow? If the group does indeed grow, what would be the consequences for public policy, communication, and information infrastructures, and assumptions about digital connectivity? As Ward has written (in the previous chapter), there is a social cost to being "unconnected."

In the interviews, it was also possible to see that the 26 individuals who preferred to be willfully unconnected were very aware of the stress of the cities in which they worked. Many referred to their own homes as "refuge" and said that they felt enough sensory stimulation in the day that they sought "solitude" and "peace and quiet." Philosophically, there is a long history of understanding the stress caused by, and through, urbanization, and the need for individuals to seek control over their lives. Anderson's *Imagined Communities* (1983) forewarned of the stresses of nationalism; Postman (1992) wrote that "A new technology does not add or subtract something. It changes everything" (p. 18). Postman also wrote about the power of *illusion* and how we choose to see things in certain ways that influence the way we make sense and narrate the story of our existence vis-à-vis a technologically constructed infrastructure that re-orders our relationships to the things that surround us (2000, p. 99–115). In many ways, what the new minority are reacting to is the nature of (a) change to their levels of comfort with other people and with technology; and (b) resistance to external pressures from advertisers, other individuals, and the accelerating pace of life brought about by portable technologies that raise anxiety and ask us to enter the proverbial "network" or the "hive mind" (Kelly, 1995, p. 8) of contemporary urbanity.

In part, the reason the new minority is worthy of watching is the rate of change in our urban landscape. Gregg Easterbrook likened the speed of change to a *Sonic Boom* (2009) that changes entire geographic regions and nations by the necessity for reacting to global change. The anxiety created by this change hovers above all things that seem to be in flux, whether good or bad. In projecting from a position of what created the economic downturn in 2008 toward the future, he wrote:

> Here's the catch: just as favorable economic and social trends are likely to resume, many problems that have characterized recent decades are likely to get worse, too. Job instability, economic insecurity, a sense of turmoil, the unfocused fear that even when things seem good a hammer is about to fall—these also are a part of the larger trend, and no rising tide will wash them away. (p. xii)

Similarly, the growth of cities around the world is resulting in rapid urbanization that puts tremendous strain on the urban character. Citing the 2002 United Nations Department of Economic and Social Affairs, Population Division, Mike Davis (2006) wrote in *Planet of Slums*:

> The earth has urbanized even faster than originally predicted by the Club of Rome in its notoriously Malthusian 1972 report *Limits of Growth*. In 1950 there were 86 cities in the world with a population of more than one million; today there are 400, and by 2015 there will be at least 550 (p. 1).....New megacities with populations in excess of 8 million, [will be created] and hypercities with more than 20 million. (p. 5)

Davis wrote that one of the most disturbing aspects of rapid urbanization is the emergence of slums, where the influx of immigrants from surrounding rural areas puts a particular stress on the traditional middleclass, and the distribution of rich, middle class, and poor throughout urban areas becomes the focus of public policy. Davis cited UN-Habitat, which tells us that the world's highest percentage of slum-dwellers are currently in Ethiopia (99.4% of the urban population) (p. 28), but at the same time, shifts in urban distribution within the United States have created populations in urban areas that cause extreme social stress on traditional communities.

In Thomas L. Friedman's best selling *The World Is Flat: A Brief History of the Twenty-first Century*, he developed the thesis that because the world is becoming "flat" through globalization, we humans have to "run faster in order to stay in place" (Friedman, 2005, p. 341). The result is that ultimately, individuals, communities, companies, countries, and governments must adapt to the rapidly changing forces within their confines. These three authors all agree that the stress and anxiety caused by rapid changes to our social structures—especially within urban settings—have raised the level of social anxiety and the need for some, like the new minority, to draw proverbial lines in the sand to demarcate their environments. These ideas portraying the social stress of urban life may well be one of the trade-offs of living in an increasingly technologized world, where it becomes harder to find the "naturalness" provided by nature or more stress-free environments.

The Social Cost of Being Willingly Unconnected

There is a social cost to being *willingly unconnected*, even when the forces of advertising, government, media, friends, and family raise expectations about how "everyone" may be instantly accessible, and that the imperative for constant communicative ability is part of living in an industrial society. Therefore, the willfully unconnected may well pay a social price. They may be thought of as Luddites or as anti-social but in each case of the 26 subjects in this study, these labels don't matter. Personal control over their environments is far superior to the need to be socially perceived as "reachable" at any hour. In fact, the willfully connected elevate the value of privacy above that of the necessity of connectivity.

For each of these individuals, people matter far more than institutions, the pressures of society, or the social need to be like others. In fact, *there is perhaps a strong correlation between the choice of these individuals to be self-employed, or in control of their careers*, and less subject to the whims or pressures of corporate life or group activity. The new minority's iconoclastic attitude is the result of an understanding of what urban life exacts from them; they exercise their choice to be with people when they want to be and value solitude and solitary pursuits—such as reading. It is also perhaps not surprising that so many of the 26 subjects are deeply involved with print media by choice, as both a career and as a solitary pursuit.

Policies and Prospects for Inclusion

The social costs are exacerbated by the economic costs to the surrounding urban areas as well. Nathan Newman's 2002 book, *Net Loss*, examined how "state and local government finances are becoming road kill on the information highway" (p. 254). Newman's attention to the Internet-driven economy and the way public finances are shifted in the wake of efforts to meet public needs for a communication and information infrastructure to support the growing need for trade and work using wired and wireless Internet connections is a frightening prelude to considering how public policies may change. He warns of traditional regional subsidies that could significantly impact the way poor and working families have traditionally received some aid (or at least public access) to communication technologies, and he warns that the most hard-hit areas will start with communities at the local level and then spread to broader constituencies. The new economies that result are likely to levy "new standards" that he identifies as "intangible assets" for economies (p. 158).

If individuals withdraw from the network that constitutes the human/technological matrix of relationships, those intangible assets could well be lost. By marginalizing (or rejecting) technology, an entire group of individuals can undermine the policies designed for the benefit of the maintenance of society.

For example, Manuel Castells, the great interpreter of the social effects of the millennial period, has written that "informational black holes" will undoubtedly contribute to instability and a rift between social action and public policy (1998). Castells developed his ideas on informational "black holes" in his book *The Informational City* (1992), in which he identified a number of problems for the social structure of the future urbanized city. In particular, he warned that a good number of people in the increasingly multicultural city may flee to gated communities in search of finding solace with people like themselves. The city, he predicted, is one with both face-to- face communication but also an equally vibrant virtual community for those who seek ubiquitous communication. But, for those people like the willfully unconnected, both social connections as well as marginalization may occur.

In an edition of *Wired* magazine, Jay Ogilvy interviewed Castells and asked specifically about his interpretation of the idea of "black holes":

> By "black holes" I mean areas of social exclusion that can be marginalized and the system doesn't suffer at all. They're not valuable as producers, consumers—in fact, if they would disappear, the logic of the overall system would improve. If you are outside the network, in other words, you don't even exist (pp. 1–2).

> An increasing number of people not only are being disconnected, but are reacting to their disconnection. We have the global criminal economy swallowing up entire states: Mexico, for example; Russia is in a similar process. Markets are a fundamental element to ensure the dynamism of an economy, but society needs institutions, society needs values, society needs rules that can interact with the markets productively. In the short term, I fear a nationalist, populist reaction in Russia. This is a script for a nightmare (p. 2).

Whether marginalization is caused by "black holes" or inadequate infrastructural policies to make technology more user-friendly, and generally more affordable for all, several of the interviewees were adamant that they "don't need" more technology than they already have and that our current economy makes them think long and hard about the cost of buying technologies they may not need as well as supporting public works that they don't use.

Efforts of many communities to introduce municipal Wi-Fi systems provide one such example. While different models of providing wireless service to communities may involve any combination of privately funded projects, publically funded projects, or a mix of private and public infrastructure selection and deployment, ultimately the cost of distribution of the wireless signal falls to taxpayers, at least to a certain extent (Hanson, 2007b).

In each of the cities where the interviewees lived, large-scale municipal Wi-Fi systems had been planned, and in most cases they existed, though not in their original form. Each of the interviewees knew of the availability of the systems in their areas, but some stated that even though the cities had spent a lot of money on developing the infrastructures, they knew of dead zones and of architectural barriers that mitigated against some peoples' use of the municipal wireless systems. Two participants in particular, Robin and Otis, were outspoken about the amount of money taxpayers had been asked to contribute to their respective local municipal wireless systems, which each thought were entirely unnecessary and a reflection of poor decision-making on the part of their legislators.

Surveillance and Loss of Privacy as the Great Reality of the Twenty-First Century

While none of the participants shared great concerns about their own personal privacy and portable technologies, several indicated that they realized surveillance could be a major issue for people who use portable devices in public. Several of the interviewees thought that other peoples' conversations in public places were out of line and often embarrassing, if not to the person on the phone, then to those who were within earshot.

Almost on cue, after having a personal conversation with "Fred," a train conductor, I was travelling on a train from New York to Philadelphia. Seated on the other side of the aisle, about two seats ahead of me, a man was watching a pornographic video on his laptop computer. The sound from the video echoed through the train car, and several people, walking from the club car or restroom, made a sound when they passed him and saw what was on the screen in a public train. Very shortly afterwards, a conductor was dispatched to ask the man to turn down the sound and to reposition his computer so passers-by wouldn't be offended, but the relationship of personal technology use in public places hit home.

For many of the interviewees, episodes such as this one contributed to their antipathy toward portable devices, and while many said they could easily ignore unwanted conversations or noise from other peoples' devices, it became clear that the noise pollution was viewed as inappropriate and breached personal ethics and general etiquette.

In his fascinating prediction of the use of the Internet in *The Future of the Internet and How to Stop It*, Jonathan Zittrain (2008) forewarned of the dilemma of the loss of privacy due to the Internet and the undermining of traditional values and legal interpretations of policy decisions. He warned, "the Net enables individuals in many cases to compromise privacy more thoroughly than the government and commercial institutions traditionally targeted for scrutiny and regulation" (p. 200). While Zittrain posed his questions through the lens of the law, the willfully unconnected do so through resistance to succumbing to situations that challenge their comfort levels. Since portable digital technologies primarily distribute messages that are distributed on the Internet, the new minority may well have the clue to avoiding uncomfortable breaches of their own privacy by resisting temptation.

Revisiting the Digital Divide

As mentioned in the introduction to this chapter, traditional notions of the digital divide were predicated on access to technology. As we lived with the concepts of this inequity, with the desire to create more equitable surroundings, we learned that other aspects of the digital divide could be considered. Hargittai, for example, referred to the "secondary digital divide," which relies on the ability of the individual to develop skill in using technology (2003). Other authors in this edition have described the inequities among able-bodied and disabled individuals as a "disability divide" (Baker, Hanson, & Myhill, 2009).

More recently, Hampton has written about another aspect of the digital divide, calling attention to the contexts in which "social and civic inequalities are reproduced" (2010, p. 1111). His study investigated how digital inequities are perpetuated within social contexts, such as cities. In this vein, we see the dilemma of the willfully unconnected in major urban areas, such as the 26 individuals who provided background for this essay, along with the large-scale global phenomena that address the ties that bind within the globe's regions. Are the new minority the newly divided, when it comes to digital technology? The question raises several threads related to the present and future of those who choose to withdraw, resist, or reject public policies and social practices.

On the international scene, as more urbanization occurs, the new digital divide could have an effect on modes of production within regions. In an interview with Manuel Castells, Olgivy (1998) quoted Castells as saying:

> Many, many segments of societies, countries, and regions are being excluded. Africa lives in a technological apartheid. Yes, maybe it could leapfrog, but for the moment you don't have the minimum technological and educational infrastructure. Instead of

pulling at least southern Africa out of this black hole, the new democratic South Africa is increasing its economic development by using the other countries as markets, annihilating potential industries there.

Hampton (2010) cited the growing problem between the haves and have nots within changing regions as reflecting the Matthew Effect—in which the rich get richer, and the poor get poorer, but in his thoughtful analysis he identified how the rich get access to more technology, while the poor are increasingly marginalized (p. 1128).

The evidence of the interviewees and their commentaries on personal values in changing public places took on the tenor of having to survive in hostile territory. For those who were willfully unconnected, many causes related to the increasing urbanity of social life in the areas in which they lived demonstrated an attitude of knowing that their personal choices may not be popular, but that it was perfectly fine to step outside of mainstream behaviors and choices.

There is no doubt that the economy has a significant impact on how people make choices, but at the same time, it seems as though the choices of policy makers are guided by notions of crossing the digital divide, while the new minority think of the digital divide as a "moat" that protects them from unwanted social stress. These ideas were examined well in a 2010 issue of *The Nation*, in which several prominent authors reflected on "Inequality in America, and What to Do About It." As Robert Reich wrote:

> If nothing more is done, America's three-decade-long lurch toward widening inequality is an open invitation to a future demagogue who misconnects the dots, blaming immigrants, the poor, government, foreign nations, "socialists" or "intellectual elites" for the growing frustrations of the middle class. The major fault line in American politics will no longer be between Democrats and Republicans, liberals and conservatives. It will be between the "establishment" and an increasingly mad-as-hell populace determined to "take back America" from them. (p. 15)

The new minority then, becomes one of the most powerful agents in predicting more urbanization and social action within the community and country.

Globalization and Urbanization: The Built Environment

To round-out the discourse on issues of access and responsible public policy within a context of ever-changing relationships, we might wonder whether planned cities would fare differently than those twentieth-century cities attempting to grapple with twenty-first century technologies and social practices.

By returning to the snapshots of a growing urban area we can see just how the juxtaposition of old values and new values collide. Easterbrook (2009) profiled the city of Shenzhen, China, the fourth-largest port city in the world, which did not exist 30 years ago but now has "nearly 9 million residents, about the same population as the five boroughs of New York" (p. 3). The city was planned to handle incoming and outgoing goods to other countries as China began to trade on the global level, but the city has also become the focus of emerging labor practices in the growing urban areas with the controversy over Apple products manufactured in the city and reports of sub-standard working conditions for laborers:

> Nothing like Shenzhen has ever happened before: there has never been a great city built so fast, nor a productive economy established from so little, nor a society transformed in such a short time from isolationist and repressed to outward-focused and eager to be free. (p. 5)

And yet, Shenzhen is not immune from social and economic stress. Most of the residents came from poor, rural communities. Some have been bussed to the city from rural areas with the promise of jobs, dormitories for living space, and the guarantee of clean work.

And yet, Shenzhen, and the Foxconn corporation that manufactures a good deal of the world's electronic components, seems like a throw-back to slave labor and hazardous conditions. If Shenzhen is a bellwether for the new urban megacity, we may expect to see a proliferation of policies and practices that continue to marginalize human beings while reifying the presumed need for more portable, electronic gadgets, no matter what the human cost.

Conclusions

As the new minority demonstrate within the confines of the changing urban metropolis, growing inequality can contribute to the shaping of social values. In the case of our interviewees—the willfully unconnected—we see how the vicissitudes of urban life and the availability of portable, digital technology have exceeded the needs of some, and how they have contributed to behaviors and values that reject increasing technologizing.

The anxiety and stress that come with one finding one's place in the urban environment may contribute to a choice of marginalization for personal reasons, but those personal reasons can create class struggle within specific urban environments. A new digital divide may actually be the result of more digital technology availability, and the divide will be re-evaluated as a choice of separation rather than an accident of birth or economic circumstance.

When we think about the extreme shifts from poverty to the working conditions in one of the new global cities, such as Shenzhen, we may well question the ability of the working class to negotiate the built environment. Will they accept, or reject, a blurring between private and public activity, and will they have a choice at all? Are the problems of urbanization that we understand, avoidable?

As history has shown, minorities often ultimately become majorities. If this is the case in the increasingly urbanized global society, we may well see, despite greater access to technology, a newly created digital divide, with individual human choice as the context for examining the relationship of the networked society.

References

Anderson, B. (1983). *Imagined communities: Reflections on the origins and spread of nationalism*. NY: Verso.

Baker, P. M. A., Hanson, J., & Myhill, W. N. (2009). The promise of municipal WiFi and failed policies of inclusion: The disability divide. *Information Polity, 14*(1,2), 47–59.

Castells, M. (1992). *The informational city*. Oxford, England: Blackwell.

Castells, M. (1998). *End of millennium*, Vol III. Oxford, England: Blackwell.

Davis, M. (2006). *Planet of slums*. London, England, New York, NY: Verso.

Easterbrook, G. (2009). *Sonic boom: Globalization at mach speed.* New York, NY: Random House.

Friedman, T. L. (2005). *The world is flat: A brief history of the twenty-first century.* New York, NY: Farrar, Straus, and Giroux.

Hampton, K. N. (2010). Internet use and the concentration of disadvantage: Glocalization and the urban underclass. *American Behavioral Scientist, 53*(8), 1111–1132. Retrieved from http://abs.sagepub.com/content/53/8/1111

Hanson, J. (2007a). *24/7: How cell phones change the way we live, work, and play.* Westport, CT: Praeger.

Hanson, J. (2007b). Is this the global village?: VoIP and wire/wireless convergence. In S. Park (Ed.), *Strategies and policies in digital convergence* (pp. 14–25). Hershey, PA: Idea Group.

Hargittai, E. (2003). The digital divide and what to do about it. In D. C. Jones (Ed.), *New economy handbook.* San Diego, CA: Academic Press.

Kelly, K. (1995). *Out of control: The new biology of machines, social systems and the economic world.* New York, NY: Basic Books.

Newman, N. (2002). *Net loss: Internet prophets, private profits, and the costs to community.* University Park, PA: The Pennsylvania State University Press.

Ogilvy, J. (1998). Dark side of the boom. Retrieved from http://www.wired.com/wired/archive/6.11/castells_pr.html

Pew Internet and American Life Project. Retrieved from http://www.pewinternet.org/Trend-Data-(Adults)/Device-Ownership.aspx

Postman, N. (1992). *Technopoly: The surrender of culture to technology.* New York, NY: Alfred A. Knopf.

Postman, N. (2000). *Building a bridge to the 18th century.* New York, NY: Vintage Books.

Reich, R. (2010, July19/26). Inequality in America and what to do about it. *The Nation, 291*(3,4), 13–23.

Shapiro, R. J. (2008). *Futurecast: How superpowers, populations, and globalization will change the way you live and work.* New York, NY: St. Martin's Press.

Zittrain, J., (2008). *The future of the Internet and how to stop it.* New Haven, CT, London, England: Yale University Press.

Martha Fuentes-Bautista

Introduction

This chapter explores the potential of community media projects to foster social inclusion in the U.S. While the European Community, Canada, Australia, and other OECD countries have in recent years promoted community-based or "third sector" media projects as a means to support community cohesion, pluralism, and digital inclusion in their societies (CRTC, 2002; European Parliament, 2008), community media remain an unrecognized and under-valued component of U.S. media ecology and public policy. Through the case study of chan- nelAustin, one of the oldest and most active public access communities in the country, this research explores the contributions of digital community broadcasting to bridge social divides in the city of Austin, Texas. Austin has gained a reputation as one of the top technologoy- based creative economies in the U.S. However, the city also exhibits poverty and residential segregation indicators above national averages (Flores & Wilson, 2009; Straubhaar et al., 2012). What is the role of community media institutions in this environment?

Since the early days of the Internet, public policy to promote the adoption and use of information and communication technologies (ICT) in the United States has privileged a diffusionist approach to technological innovation that assumes the progressive and natural spread of technology and its benefits through market forces. A vibrant, competitive market of IT products is the primary social space where diffusion networks operate, and early and late majorities of adopters are able to observe, try, and experiment with, Internet-based innovations (Rogers, 2003).

From this standpoint, shared Internet access and use at public and community institutions and spaces such as libraries, schools, and community centers are considered transient solutions and a substitute for individual home access, and only "third" in importance after access at work. These "third places" are mostly thought of as demonstration sites where late and non-adopters can get online and learn about common uses and desired applications of the technology for job training and access to government information. This diffusionist interpretation of community-based Internet access is limited, and instead I propose a communication-commons approach to evaluate the social function of these projects and their potential contribution to inclusion and social change. This approach emphasizes open access, participation of diverse local publics, and social collaboration to increase the communicative capacities of a community and its members.

Scholars from different disciplines have theorized public and community media as forms of communication and information commons. They highlight the role of third-sector media as a non-market (Aufderheide, 2002; Flew 2006), open, and participatory public forum (van Vuuren, 2006; Rennie, 2006) that serves diverse publics (Steemers, 2004) and builds sustainability through collaborative practices that support innovation and social change (Rennie, 2007; Tacchi & Grubb, 2007). This chapter evaluates the impact of these practices on social inclusion and the general well-being of participants in a digital community media project.

Refocusing attention on questions of equity and justice in ICT diffusion is an urgent matter. Today's unprecedented boom in digital production of information and culture is taking place in a world of exacerbated inequalities (Tilly, 2004; Castells, 2010). A social stratification perspective informs this assessment (DiMaggio, Hargittai, Celeste, & Shafer, 2004; van Dijk, 2005) that tries to identify how institutional dynamics and media practices reproduce disparities, or on the contrary, how they help participants in community media production to avoid exclusion. Narrow understanding on these issues stems from limited conceptualizations of technological gaps as a "digital divide" associated with different group characteristics and individual endowments (i.e., income, education, age, and ethnicity) and consumer preferences.

This chapter advances the discussion by focusing on the experience of users of services provided by Austin's Public Access Center between 2007 and 2009, as channelAustin was transitioning to full digital operations. Specifically, I ask: (a) What are the patterns of public participation in training programs, production, and distribution of content at channelAustin? (b) Why do citizens use community access services in an increasingly available new media environment? (c) How does this experience relate to their livelihoods and sense of well-being?

Inequalities and the Wealth of Networks

ICT are complex goods, and their value stems from the combined effect of powerful information processing and networking capacities. These capacities, and their ability to expand the productivity of other resources, such as labor, capital and land, have transformed ICT into key "value-producing resources" in our times (Tilly, 2004, 2007). The wealth of digital networks is derived from powerful externalities unleashed by social networking capacities, but their benefits are not always equally distributed. Furthermore, negative externalities mostly threaten the disconnected and those with marginal participation in different forms of network power, restricting their ability to create ties, direct flows, produce content, frame meaning, and program the logics of digital networks (Castells, 2009).

In a historical overview of the literature, sociologist of inequalities Charles Tilly (2004) concluded that in today's world, social inequalities are increasingly the result of unequal control over ICT, the media, and scientific-technical knowledge. Two macro-level processes, characteristics of ICT and media development, have amplified such effects. First, in a global system of exchanges that increasingly relies on informational capitalism, more sources of productivity depend on the accumulation and control over technologies of knowledge generation, information processing, and symbolic communication (Castells, 2006). Second, public reasoning, the representation of social problems, and social assessments about what is equitable and just in one's society have grown more dependent on social mediation processes facilitated by media institutions and electronic communications (Sen, 2010). In the network society, privileged social groups and actors seeking to retain and increase their advantage engage in a number of inequality-generating mechanisms of accumulation, scarcity, polarization, and differentiation of information and communication resources. Accumulation and scarcities are typically generated through market capitalism and property regulation that affect the cost of access and consumption of information services and products (i.e., copyrights, patents, licensing, subscription fees, etc.), and appropriate creative labor and knowledge in the hands of the few (Tilly, 2004). Mechanisms of differentiation rely to a great extent on cultural distinction and social norms that underline class divides and the cultural domination of privileged groups based on accumulation of prestige and recognition or symbolic capital (Bourdieu, 1984). Through formal and informal processes of social inculcation, such norms also result in distinct dispositions and practices (habitus), and differential accumulation of social and cultural capitals that further reinforce social gaps (Bourdieu & Wacquant, 1992). These dynamics come together in the naturalization of social disparities and norms that legitimatize them. The result is the reduction in the autonomy of some social groups to access, use, produce, exchange, and share information and knowledge that circulates through high-performance technologies, with negative consequences for their livelihood. The relationship between technological development and the acute stratification and polarization of wealth in today's world is best illustrated by the paradox of "creative cities" or "technopoles" in the U.S., such as Austin, that in the last decades have achieved economic growth and low rates of unemployment through technological development but still cope with historical inequalities crystallized in high poverty rates, income polarization, and residential segregation.

Austin, TX, and the Technopolis Paradox

The knowledge-based economy is the primary arena for the interaction of citizens, organizations, and local powers in Austin, framing the social recognition they enjoy within the Austin community and serving as the main path for the accumulation of economic, social, and cultural capital. Modeled on Silicon Valley's development plan, Austin's technopolis strategy of the 1980s also included creating science parks, investing in university research and training programs, providing capital assistance, creating business incubators, and building advanced infrastructure. What has made the Austin model unique is its emphasis on "institutional networking arrangements" and "affordable quality of life" as catalytic forces of economic growth (Smilor, Kozmetsky, & Gibson, 1988). First designed as a cluster economy of semiconductors and semiconductor manufacturing equipment, Austin has also become the home of computer manufacturers such as Dell, software development firms, game developers, and most recently, of networking and wireless industries.

The technopolis model follows a post-industrial logic about the relationship between technology, labor, and social mobility. The assumption was that as more people engage in technology and creative work, their work will be better rewarded, and overall social conditions will tend to improve. The creation of the modern technology city-state builds on public-private partnerships where each actor is assigned a role. Private companies are the leading forces in economic and job creation initiatives. Meanwhile, the local government serves as a promoter and convener of private initiatives, fostering affordable living and supporting training and education, all necessary conditions to attract firms in search of affordable, highly skilled workers. Educational institutions provide the know-how and educated workforce needed for these ventures. Finally, non-profits and citizens groups are expected to share and leverage resources for the promotion and strengthening of technology corporations established in Austin (Smilor et al., 1988).

Despite positive employment indicators and the widespread quality of life rhetoric, in the last decade the poverty ratio in Austin has consistently been above the national average (Table 12.1). The rapid growth of the technology industry has also fostered high real-estate prices and growing income gaps and added to existing issues of land use, residential segregation, and the concentration of communities of color at the east side of the city (Flores & Wilson, 2009).

Table 12.1: Poverty indicators – City of Austin

Poverty	2000 Austin (%)	2000 U.S. (%)	2005 Austin (%)	2005 U.S. (%)	2010 Austin (%)	2010 U.S. (%)
Families below poverty level	9.1	9.2	13.8	10.2	11.9	11.8
Individuals below poverty level	14.4	12.4	18.1	13.3	20.8	15.1

Source: U.S. Census Bureau (2010), American Community Survey

Problems of uneven growth in Austin predate the technopolis experiment. As aptly described by Orum (1987), since the days of the city's infamous 1928 Master Plan that moved African American and Latino communities from all over the city to the east of downtown—transforming the Texas capital into an institutionally segregated city for almost 40 years—the social history of Austin has been characterized by the continuing, episodic struggle between two competing visions: one led by great wealth, industrial development, and private property; and another inspired by social struggles to make the benefits of growth available to ever-larger numbers of people. Anchored in the first tradition, planners of the technopolis assumed that technological growth would finally bridge the city's historical class and race divides (Straubhaar et al., 2012).

Instead, since the mid-1980s the city has experienced increasing wage inequality and the income polarization characteristics of other creative epicenters of the U.S. economy. Proponents of the creative economy model such as Richard Florida (2002) usually normalize this phenomenon, explaining that creative workers earn more than "people who do low-end service work or rote manufacturing" since they "contribute more" to local economies "by adding creative value" (p. xv). In reality, two main restructuring processes have led to growing disparities. First, the model has grown through stratification of the technology labor market creating low-skill, low-paid assembly jobs for technology and service industries (Tufekci, 2012). Second, the lack of integration between creative activities and other business activities in the city creates residual economies for populations who live at the margins and who are increasingly seen as "techno-cultural laggards" (Straubhaar et al., 2012). As a result, new technology infrastructure and services such as wireless hotspots that provide public Internet access for many Austinites tend to flourish in commercial and more affluent areas of Austin while bypassing areas on the east side of the city (Fuentes-Bautista & Inagaki, 2012).

Exploring why families in disadvantaged communities in Austin do not have, do not use, or do not seek access to ICT, Rojas, Straubhaar, Roychowdhury, & Okur (2003) found that everyday life practices of working-class families reinforce a demotivating class habitus that acts as a barrier to the development of proactive techno-dispositions among members of these families. Some of the parents perceived the technology to be for the "rich and educated," while their children (many of them avid users of videogames and computers), do not identify technology with careers or job opportunities "made for them." The question still is, how can the cycle of reproduction of inequalities be broken in the American technopolis?

Information Commons and Social Justice

In the last decade scholars in diverse fields have persuasively argued that the time is ripe to seize the generative power of digital networks and reconfigure current dynamics of uneven distribution through new systems of intellectual property, knowledge, and cultural production that operate in the public domain and generate a new "information commons" (Boyle, 2003; Benkler, 2006; Krikorian & Kapczynski, 2010). Information or communication commons are decentralized, open, collaborative, non-proprietary forms to generate information and knowledge through social production. Open-source software projects, creative commons licensing, open publishing journals, Wikipedia, community wireless initiatives, and community-based media are organizational projects where loosely connected individuals cooperate and share resources, seeking to enhance their communicative power in networked environments. The commons, Yochai Benkler (2006) argued, is potentially an autonomy-enhancing form of social organization, and is thus able to support more democratic ways of production, exchange, and use of information and culture.

The promise of the information commons is based on conditions of openness, collaborative practices, enhanced information processing capacities, and flexible forms of organization that enable social production (Benkler, 2006). Openness, the cornerstone principle of the information commons, crystallizes into "access to opportunities for one's own action, and access to the outputs and inputs of the information economy" (p. 302).

The influence of these ideas on media policy has been articulated by scholars and public interest advocates who oppose media concentration and the enclosure practices of corporations that could lead to anti-competitive behavior, could threaten open access for newcomers and consumers, and could stifle innovation (Aufderheide, 2002; Garcelon, 2009; Melody, 2010). In reality, proponents of open-access policies can be found across the political spectrum, offering diverse interpretations of what "openness" means. From a liberal, market-oriented perspective, openness is thought of as an anti-discriminatory mechanism that reduces the cost of entry of competitors to information and communication markets. Information commons are not seen in complete opposition to markets but rather as coexisting and supporting them through information sharing, innovation, and creativity. From a social democratic perspective, openness and sharing practices are interpreted as acts of resistance to capitalism and market dynamics of accumulation, and preconditions for the articulation of new, non-proprietary relations of social production. Participatory democratic articulation of the commons approach for the public interest would stress direct participation of diverse publics in governance and different functions of media institutions as an open-access practice aimed at the expansion of collaborative relations and information and communication capacities of less-privileged groups. Benkler (2010) stressed this capacity-building approach to information commons in his most recent writings about the Access to Knowledge (A2K) movement and its implications for social justice. He wrote that:

> access to the information commons in the abstract is insufficient...freedom, justice, and innovation all require effective agency, not merely formal permission to act. An effective agency in the domains of information and knowledge production requires access to material means, as well as, to a knowledge commons—not the same access as

was required in the industrial age, but access to a minimal set of material capabilities and educational faculties nonetheless. (p. 233)

These ideas are inspired by the work of Nobel Prize winning economist Amartya Sen, (1999) who proposed to understand poverty as "capability deprivation" and a form of unfreedom. In Sen's view, overcoming poverty and achieving inclusion in one's society demands a minimum "set of capabilities" to be functional or able to participate in it (i.e., being literate, well-nourished, in good health etc.). Refocusing attention on the development of human capacities for action in the information commons leads us to interrogate the social and cultural conditions that enable participation in social production. Participation is a multidimensional and complex concept inherently linked to the process of reproduction of social power structures within media organizations and fields (Carpentier, 2011).

In order to consider how effective agency or engagement is materialized, I borrow ideas from critical communication scholars who have examined the implications of Sen's work for issues of cultural citizenship, welfare, and communication policy (Couldry, 2009; Garnham, 1999; Mansell, 2002). These authors stress that any effort to define the set of communicative resources needed to participate in today's society impinges on discussions about people's communication rights, and how they support different modes of democratic governance. From a participatory democratic perspective, Couldry (2009) powerfully argued that in these discussions we should consider both material and symbolic conditions that facilitate dialogue and interactions based on mutual recognition and respect that allow citizens to participate creatively and effectively in their national culture. In terms of creating conditions for effective agency to emerge in the commons, beyond access to information and to the means of communication, one might also need educational opportunities to develop skills (i.e., literacy and the ability for expression across media platforms), the ability to access and engage particular publics (i.e., those with certain cultural and social capital), and to be able to be heard by them (i.e., enjoying their respect and recognition). In this context, developing a "voice" within a community carries more than self-expression; it denotes the ability to articulate issues, enter dialogue, and negotiate and articulate solutions by being part of the community or group.

Authors such as Garnham (1999) and Mossberger, Tolbert, and McNeal (2008) claimed that the critical question is how communicative resources are used to enable a wider range of functions in economic, political, social, and cultural life. In other words, how individuals use the communicative resources at their disposal to find a job, have access to education, make informed political decisions, vote and use their political rights, be healthy, and enhance their general well-being. In the same way, social production projects would be capability enhancing and contribute to equity when they share and produce resources needed for social and economic justice programs, civic life, education, and healthcare, directing their benefit to less privileged social groups. There is the case, for instance, of the many groups around the world that organize through Free and Open Source Software (FOSS) and use their technical expertise to support the work of environmental causes, disaster relief efforts, preservation of indigenous knowledge systems and cultures, coalitions of groups seeking affordable treatments for people with AIDS, and direct access of farmers to markets, articulating global agendas with local needs and concerns.

To summarize, overcoming issues of unequal control over information-based resources demands more than the creation of market opportunities to access and use ICT. The commons-based approach offers new possibilities to rethink information and communication policy in terms of equity and development. Avoiding exclusion and promoting social inclusion call for the expansion of conditions and competencies that foster autonomy to determine one's communicative environment. They include open access and the expansion of digital skills and collaborative capacities at the local level; respect and recognition, in particular among underprivileged groups; and the development of "voice," or capacities for public reasoning and action. However, this has not necessarily been the focus of policies that in the last 15 years have attempted to tackle the problem of technological gaps in the U.S.

From Digital Divide to Capable Use

Even some proponents of the commons sometimes consider technolog-ical gaps as a "transient problem" that mostly affects people in develop-ing nations and that has been mostly overcome in the developed world (Benkler, 2006, p. 337). This view conflates availability of ICT with their effective adoption and use, equating technological access to social access. The concept of social access was introduced by Kling (1999), who referred to knowledge-based and institutional resources that shape effective use of ICT in organizational and social contexts. The miscon-ception of Internet access exclusively as a problem of technical access took root in the policy debates of the Clinton administration that in mid-1990s traced the diffusion of technology, drawing a binary distinc-tion between people with or without computer and home Internet connectivity and suggesting that this "digital divide" was the main factor preventing disconnected populations from enjoying the wealth of the emerging digital economy (NTIA, 1995). Under a diffusionist approach, government reports typically highlighted how younger, non-Hispanic, white males—those with higher income, more education, and who resided in urbanized areas—tended to be better "connected" than their counterparts. Public policy to ameliorate the divide identified "tradi-tional providers of information access for the general public" such as public schools, libraries, and community access centers as "safety nets" that "at least during an interim period" would provide a means for electronic access to all those who might not otherwise have such access" (p. 10).

The analytical and policy inadequacies of the digital divide meta-phor became apparent between 2002 and 2003 as more than half of Americans went online. Government reports offered celebratory accounts of increasing numbers of Internet users, the variety of uses supported by the market, and the advances in the adoption of high-speed services (NTIA, 2002), and while this rhetoric suggested that Internet use was almost universal and evenly spread, increasing stratifi-cation of use persisted. However, based on such assessments, policy concerns about the digital divide faded away, and government and private support for public and community-based Internet access initia-tives was cut or considerably reduced during Bush's administration.

Analyses based on binary divides later proved insufficient in explaining increasing disparities in ICT uses and their implications. Even today, when 79% of Americans have gone online, only a third of adult Internet users have ever employed social media applications (Lenhart, 2008).

Applying insights of the social stratification literature and critical cultural sociology, social researchers now reject the view of Internet use as a one-dimensional category, concluding that a more nuanced view of digital inequalities is needed (DiMaggio et al., 2004; Mossberger et al., 2008; van Dijk, 2005; Warschauer, 2003). They argue that it is important to consider factors such as cost and ability to choose among different types of connectivity and equipment; frequency, proficiency, and autonomy of use; ability to complete life-enhancing tasks online (e.g., apply for a job, look for health care information, find relevant political information); and capacity to produce and share different types of online content, and to participate and find support in social networking spaces (Hargittai, 2008, 2010; Kvasny, 2006; Dailey, Byrne, Powell, Karaganis, & Chung, 2010; Hargittai & Hsieh, 2010; Mossberger et al., 2008; Rojas et al., 2003; van Dijk, 2005).

Methodology

This study emerged as collaborative project with channelAustin to develop a framework for evaluating its operations and services and responded to the station's concerns regarding the restructuring of its operations in order to adapt to the technological and regulatory changes of the networking media environment (Fuentes-Bautista, 2009). The project employed empowerment evaluation techniques (Fetterman, 2000), involving stakeholders (channelAustin management, staff, producers, and other users of access resources) in defining the goals of the study, data collection efforts, and self-reflection on their practice.

The study followed a case study design to generate data (Yin, 2002). First, the external conditions that influenced channelAustin's operations were analyzed, including the regulatory environment, and stakeholders' understanding of the mission of community access. Second, framework was developed to assess public participation in four media functions of digital community projects: (a) public participation in training programs; (b) public use of production and creative resources;

(c) public input in the programming mix and distribution of citizen content; and (d) station outreach and engagement with local publics.

Data for the analysis were collected from channelAustin's operation database and focus group discussions with 49 people, including: 20 new producers (recently certified producers with less than three years at the station, who volunteer on others' productions while learning the production process); 17 established producers (producers of series or several one-time productions, with more than three years at the station); and 12 channelAustin staff members. Focus groups with users explored motivation for involvement in access productions and their experience with, and attitudes toward, emerging technology. The station's archival data included producers' registration records, listings of more than 4,000 hours of programming, and records of equipment and facilities use and reservations. These records were examined through exploratory geographic and statistical analyses, matching Zip Code socio-demographic data to users' Zip Codes. Additionally, 12 semi-structured interviews with established producers and representatives of non-profit organizations examined factors encouraging their continued participation at the station and the benefits they derived from this experience.

The Digital Transition of channelAustin

Austin epitomizes the experience of a thriving public-access community in the U.S. One of its three public-access channels, Channel 10, is the longest continually running access channel in the country, and every year Austinites produce more than 4,000 hours of local programming at the DeWitty access center, which is located in the African American and Latino district of East Austin. After 37 years of strong municipal sponsorship, PEG access resources have grown to seven channels, with clear administrative divisions among them: two educational channels, run by the Austin Independent School District and Austin Community College, respectively; two government channels, one dedicated to City of Austin programming and one for Travis County programs; and three public access channels (10, 11, and 16) managed by channelAustin, a local non-profit organization. In 1994, the City of Austin also funded the Austin Music Network (AMN), but this channel was finally privatized in 2005. Since the privatization of the music network, the channels managed by channelAustin (10, 11, and 16) remain the city's only local television outlets for citizen-produced content.

Under the auspices of the City, since 2005 a new administration has sought to transform the old public access community television station (PACT) into a digital community media center that "provides the means for community dialogue through media technology." According to the management, fulfilling this mission would require more technology education and digital media literacy classes, as well as equipment and Web streaming and digital cable distribution capacity, to promote various digital forms of citizen productions through television, film, and music.

Under local policies that promote arts and culture as part of the creative economy, "economic development" emerged as a new and important rationale for justifying local investment in channelAustin (Fuentes-Bautista, 2009). In 2008, the station changed its historic name—ACTV—to become channelAustin, a one-stop community solution for digital media access. Although the station's plans seemed in sync with those of the municipal government, the digital transition confronted Austin's access community's many challenges. Municipal support was limited to funding to equipment and infrastructure and simply ignored increasing organizational and operational demands generated by the transition. Through partnerships with local, regional, and national organizations, channelAustin was attempting to build sustainability for its operations and programs, but their financial viability was not assured.

Findings

Geographic and statistical analyses of the center's membership data reveal that in 2008, the majority (52.2%) of its 1,204 active users were residents of economically challenged and ethnically diverse Zip Codes of Austin. As illustrated in Figure 12.1, the public access studios serve residents in almost all Austin zip codes. These maps represent the density of users of access resources among Austin residents in relation to the geographical distribution of the median household income and the non-Hispanic white population across the city's Zip Code areas.

Geographic and statistical analysis revealed two important features; first, there is a great distribution of access producers across the city. This speaks to one level of connection between the community access center and Austin communities: its ties to diverse neighborhoods and populations of the city.

Figure 12.1: Users of access resources in Austin (N/10,000 by Zip Code)

Second, the majority of producers, crew, and other users of access services come from economically challenged areas of the city. More than half (52.2%) of Austin's producer population live in Zip Codes with an annual median household income of $40,000 or less (Figure 12.2). Statistical analysis indicates a significant relationship between a higher density of access users and lower median household income of Zip Codes. Third, producers also tended to be residents of ethnically diverse areas of the city. A similar statistically significant relationship was found in the case of a high number of producers living in Zip Codes with a lower percentage of non-Hispanic, white population.

Although the results do not indicate diversity of the access community per se, they underscore the center's ability to serve residents of all areas in a city with a long history of ethnic and economic divides, overcoming one of the greatest paradoxes of the technopolis: residential segregation. ChannelAustin is located in the DeWitty Center in the heart of Austin's Eastside, historically home to the majority of its African American and Hispanic residents and home to a vibrant artistic community that identifies with, and gives character to, the city. The location of the station's facilities enables access for residents of this area and neighboring Zip Codes.

Views expressed by participants of our focus groups also echoed the socioeconomic diversity of the center, characterizing it as an open space where citizens can freely mingle and interact. A recently certified white female producer described how the center's social diversity invites participation, enriches users' experience, and helps to build community:

> Here I saw a Baptist Pastor invited to an Atheist variety show. And these things happen because this is a very open place. Here you have every race, people from every socioeconomic level, from people who are well off to people who don't have two nickels to rub together. You have every age group, from grannies down to kids. Access is a place where all these people come together, not like in a forced way....We're all here together and help each other. We meet each other here where we wouldn't be doing it otherwise in our daily lives....And it's real; it's a wonderful place to build good relationships in the community....that's one of the great things about how [access] helps the community. It's hard to have an attitude towards a group of people when you're actually running into them, and they're helping you with the soundboard and the cameras or whatever. This experience completely changes your attitudes, I think. And that's different from commercial media in that we can come here

and do it....With my [college] degree I've even tried to get an internship at a commercial radio station and it's not like this. (March 21, 2008)

This statement and other testimonies of focus-group participants are consistent with the findings of studies of community broadcasting stations from around the world (Meadows, Forde, Ewart & Foxwell, 2007; Rennie, 2006; Tacchi et al. 2009) that have established the contributions of these projects to social inclusion, social cohesion, and community based on community media's ability to engage diverse social groups and publics in the process of training, participatory content production, distribution, and discussion of local media content.

Enhancing Social Access

Focus groups described patterns of public engagement in channelAustin; participants identified four main factors that keep users involved in public access (Figure 12.2). Access users highly value the availability of both affordable video training and the high-end digital equipment used in their productions, pointing out that there is no other place in Austin that offers better rates for these services. In fact, digitization of the station's equipment and operations seems to stimulate public demand for field equipment and post-production services. Producers talked about the advantages of the new Apple computers with Final Cut Pro software, as well as the convenience of working with digital files instead of videotape.

Table 12.2: What keeps you coming back to access?

Reason	Frequency	Percent
Affordable access to training & equipment	13	35.1
Connecting with local publics	10	27.0
Free expression and creativity	9	24.3
Friendships and community at the station	5	13.5
Total	37	100.0

Technical access is not the main reason attracting users to the center. Participants identified a number of factors associated with the center's capacity to enhance their social access to ICT (Kling, 1999), including skills and training programs, and the ability to reach local publics, create networks of collaboration and support at the station, and develop a voice and find ways for self-expression. Media literacy and training programs are important stepping-stones to the empowerment of audiences through community media. Historically, part of the core mission of access centers nationwide is to transform their audiences from passive spectators into individuals who can critically analyze, understand, and create content.

Austin's access center also enjoys a positive symbolic capital among individuals interested in filmmaking, performance, and visual arts careers in the city. They are attracted by the center's reputation as an open space for Austin's "creatives," and by stories of former access users who went on to develop successful careers as filmmakers. Richard Linklater, for instance, checked out equipment from the Austin Access Center to film part of *Slacker* (1991), the mythically low-budget ($23,000) film about Austin's counter-culture that became a reference point for the U.S. independent film movement of the 1990s. In his book *Rebel Without a Crew: Or How a 23-Year-Old Filmmaker with $7,000 Became a Hollywood Player*, screenwriter and director Robert Rodriguez talks about how he used Austin's access services in the post-production of El Mariachi. Focus group participants referred to the stories of these prominent access users and explained how their own volunteer work in access productions related to artistic pursuits and filmmaking career aspirations:

> I've done theater and some courses on film production...but I keep coming back be-cause I'm utilizing the services and equipment here to learn more about it. So I'm helping out with a couple shows that are generally shorthanded and kind of pick up some slack and learn at the same time. (March 20, 2008)

Access users articulated the advantages of training and production services in terms of affordability, flexible learning formats, and oppor-tunities to experiment with the different production process phases in a collaborative and welcoming environment. A young female producer said she values all these aspects of her experience at channelAustin.

> I made a movie using the commonly available technology at home for my father-in-law who had a stroke. He loved that so much he was just so tickled by it that I decided I was going to try to learn how to actually make a production—because I was very ama-teurish—I found out about PACT just sort of by Googling it after getting extremely

frustrated with the university and community college systems where classes are more theoretical and very expensive. And I came over here and I was so impressed with how well run this place is, how clean it is, and how professional it is. (March 29, 2008)

Participatory content creation denotes the ability of individuals to creatively engage with ICT and advance their communicative capacities (Tacchi et al. 2009). This "capable use" is most essentially autonomous use that enhances previous abilities and allows individuals to achieve career, political or personal interests.

Connecting Local Publics

Connecting local producers and publics is another important function of digital community media in Austin. Most focus group participants see community television as a unique vehicle to gain exposure to local audiences without censorship. Users consider the station as a content-neutral, open platform to address the issues that matter to the local community. This characteristic of channelAustin is regarded as a very valuable one that distinguishes it not only from commercial media but also from other alternative media outlets that serve the city:

> [I keep coming back because] I actually want to document what's going on here, that event is....How many people can I reach on my access TV channel? Well, you're not always trying to reach everybody; you're trying to reach that demographic that you're interacting with out there in the community....

> There's also a sense of access and uncensored television...You don't have somebody over your shoulder telling you what to say or do. Even though there are [community] radio stations or even the Music Network, they all have their own focus and make a lot of decisions about what gets on the air. The only rules that we have here are pretty much FCC rules. If you produce your own content, it gets on the air and you're responsible for it. That's it. (March 21, 2008)

Non-profit informants consulted by this study highlighted that their participation in access productions is "unfiltered," and they appreciate the opportunity to explain their issues in "their own terms." This freedom is highly valued by community organizers and social service providers who want to communicate with local audiences. Although some commercial TV and radio stations do offer free community service announcements in local news and talk shows, these are typically very short. Informants value their experience with access television because they have more exposure and media time to convey their message. For instance, non-profit representatives who have participated in channelAustin's *Austin Commons* show think that community access television is an effective and affordable way to reach local audiences. They report increased awareness of their programs, particularly among lower-income households.

The online presence of Austin's community content producers is organic and has developed as a result of the interactions among producers, the station, and audiences. Many producers currently use Web-based distribution services such as YouTube, Google Video, and MySpace pages to promote their productions and reach online audiences for their shows. The geographic dimension of community media means that members of these communities have the unique opportunity to share and participate in making media messages in both real and virtual spaces. Access productions in particular rely on the work of volunteers who sometimes come from their audience and/or local community groups. With the introduction of Web-based distribution systems such as Google Video or YouTube, this process has not changed, as illustrated by the account of a producer who participated in one of our focus groups.

> I watched the show [*The Atheist Experience*] on Google Videos. You'll probably laugh about this but I haven't watched TV in about five years! I stopped watching TV a long time ago. I found out that the show was on Google Videos through a friend and kept watching it on the Web. One day, talking to my friend about it, he said we should help out with the show. So that's what happened and we came down here and joined. (May 29, 2008)

Online audience members participate in access productions in different ways. MySpace fans have also been invited to, and interviewed on, access shows such as *Sacrebleu TV!* (http://www.youtube.com/SacrebleuLive). Other shows use e-mail and social networking sites to stay in touch with fans, inviting them to volunteer in access productions. The Web also facilitates cooperative work and exchanges between audience members and producers. Shows such as *The Perry Logan Show* developed a Web presence (http://perrylogan.org/) thanks to the volunteer work of fans who helped design the site. Through all these different interactions, the Web enables higher producer/audience cooperation, thus encouraging audience participation in access productions. However, this also underscores that the articulation of online networks and community resources needs to be supported by an outlet in the real space.

These participatory experiences also illustrate how the use of Web tools and access resources can foster more public involvement and community dialogue. These occurred in an unplanned and informal manner in the Access Center. The station lacked detailed information about who was actually online, which digital skills producers have, and how producers use the Web to distribute content. In the last years, station management has tried to harness some in-house expertise and initiative by promoting the online networking of the station's Web sites to producers' social networking sites. But producers also spoke about the disadvantages of using commercial video distribution systems such as YouTube. Some of the challenges posed by the new environment to local producers include:

- exposure to an audience that is fragmented and non-local. This aspect was seen as a significant disadvantage by producers whose programs are directed to local audiences, as they speak to particular realities of the Austin community;

- limited space to store large quantities of quality video;

- the inability to reach local audiences who do not use computers and lack Internet access; and

- a very important point for producers: the inability to manage and administer copyrights of content distributed over commercial video sharing Web sites.

Finally, in order to harness the potential of networking technologies to connect local publics, producers suggested that the station develop an "umbrella" site with archival capabilities that preserves producers' rights over their content and enables them to link to the commercial social networking spaces they currently use. Likewise, they asserted, such a site would increase the visibility of the wealth of Web content produced by the Austin access community. All these factors indicate that channelAustin needed to devote more attention to archiving and curation activities necessary to consolidate a networked local public sphere with the ability to serve as an interface between online and offline publics.

Supporting Local Creative Cultures

Young, college-educated individuals who want to pursue careers in filmmaking are not the only beneficiaries of resources available at channelAustin. For years, Austin's Access Center has been the cradle where many popular and community artists are born. Robert Rodriguez, a veteran access producer who was born in Mexico and raised in Texas, offers an account that illustrates the particular appeal of available access resources to community members. His pioneering show promoting Tejano music, *Estamos en Tejas*, has received recognition from the City of Austin and the Mexican American communities throughout Texas:

> In 1985 I was a carpenter and sometimes played in bands. I played in a Country-Western band, and with a banda tropical, but there was not much for Tejanoconjuntos and musicians in those days. One day, flipping through the [cable] channels, I saw some kind of information about [access TV], like "come and make your own TV." So I thought, why not? I came here, liked it, and started to take classes in my spare time in the evenings, and made my first show of Tejano music. And then you have to continue taking new classes because the equipment and things change....It sounds easy and fun but it's a lot of work. But this work is really rewarding because after you see what you have created, and that really has an impact on the community, you just want to keep doing it. (Interview with Robert Rodriguez translated from Spanish, March 19, 2008)

The skills learned and developed in community-video production easily transfer to other media production and career opportunities. Producers' testimonies indicate that participants employ skills acquired at the center in a wide range of professional and personal activities, including video game and Web design, event preparation and planning, promotion and community outreach, film, theater, music, and radio production, performance, and public relations. Focus-group participants were very vocal about how their experiences at channelAustin have impacted their careers. An African American male producer with five years at the station explained how his community television experience had a vocational function and helped him to change careers.

> After being laid off I was kind of seeking a new career path and after I attempted various things, I came here and this was the only thing that stuck with me...I finished school in November in the CSB [Connecticut School of Broadcasting] here in Austin, and now I'm the chief editor for a cooking show. We were on PBS but now we're going to network television in September... Access television gives you a chance to be very creative. I'm still producing my church's television shows and working on a couple other Christian events around here. We produce a show called *Sweet Aroma*, which is a conglomerate of various Christian artists, from gospel music and Holy Hip Hop to Praise Dance and Christian poetry. We have an event at The Victory Grill every three or four months, and we're looking to make that an actual television show once we get enough people to get into it to make a regular production....I feel public access is a very important key in our community to get a lot of things out to people who don't see them on a regular basis that you don't see in the mainstream broadcasts. (May 28, 2008)

Focus group discussions also revealed that users of access resources produce more than "TV programs." They see cable channels as one of the outlets they commonly employ in the distribution of their productions. Other commonly used venues include festivals and community radio programs, local non-profit organizations, circles of local artists (musicians, other video producers), religious communities and churches, and producers' Web sites and popular video-sharing sites.

The Atheist Experience, a program of the Atheist Community of Austin, illustrates this trend. The Atheist Community is a non-profit educational corporation that promotes secular viewpoints and encourages positive community dialogue on these issues. For many years, its show has been cablecast, but its Web presence enabled new forms of distributing content and reaching new audiences. The show started Web-streaming in 2008 through UStream and kept an archive of more than 200 90-minute shows that is available on Google Video. The group also maintains a blog and a Wiki, used for keeping up with daily news and discussions of various topics raised in the program. More recently, the group's Web site started featuring *Non Prophets Radio*, an Internet audio show that offers live and podcast transmissions. Since the inception of Web-streaming transmissions, the show has attracted the attention of viewers around the country and the world who remix their programs and distribute them on YouTube and call in to the live show cablecast every week from the studios of channelAustin. But who would have the opportunity to participate and be heard in this local-global dialogue enabled by digital networks?

It was difficult to answer this question at the time this study was completed. The station was in the process of building its online "channel" and archive; secondly, producers virally distributed their digital content in many ways. Locally produced programs accounted for 90% of the total hours of programming (N = 4,443) distributed by Austin's three public-access channels from January to November 2008. The percentage was equally high in the case of first-run or premiere programming. The geo-statistical analysis of these records (Figure 12.2) revealed that residents of almost all areas of the city contributed to the programming mix of the stations, but the density of programs produced was only significantly correlated to levels of education (r41) = 0.396, p =009).

The dissemination of local news services and public affairs programming is generally deemed to be the most important function of local broadcasting. However, in community media productions, local entertainment, cultural events, and activities typically make up the greatest portion of content. Community-driven programming is seen as an expression of people's motivation and ability to produce. In the case of Austin (Table 12.3), religious or spiritual programming dominates the content offering of public access (41.5%), followed by public affairs (37.1%) and entertainment programs (21.2%).

According to participants in the study, churches commonly underwrite the cost of producers' training, access to equipment, and materials needed for religious productions, providing an incentive to produce spiritual programming. Some churches have their own production and editing equipment, so channelAustin's content-neutral policies facilitate the distribution of their programs. Churches and religious individuals see community productions as a natural extension of their mission and community outreach efforts. Finally, religious communities also offer ready-made audiences for these programs, and religious producers in our focus groups talked proudly about their popularity among members of these local communities.

Table 12.3: *Programming Mix (Number of Hrs by Category, Jan.–Nov. 2008)*

Categories	Hrs	Percent
Spiritual & Religious	1467.4	41.5
Public Affairs & Education	1311.7	37.1
Public Affairs	519.9	14.7
Community Service	155.2	4.4
International	165.1	4.7
Politics	130.6	3.7
Minority Issue	162.1	4.6
Education	121.9	3.4
Government	37.3	1.1
Health	19.6	0.6
Entertainment & Culture	750.9	21.2
Music	370.3	10.5
Arts/Culture	211.2	6.0
Comedy	115.9	3.3
Experimental & Hobby	15.4	0.4
Christmas & Halloween	25.9	0.7
Sports	12.3	0.3
Other	7.0	0.2
Total	3537.0	100.0

Institutional capacities can bolster the ability of some community groups to dominate the local public sphere. The open-access approach demands a capacity-enhancing mechanism to give representation to more voices within a larger community. In order to support other forms of programming and public affairs in particular, in 2007 channelAustin launched an outreach program, *Austin Commons*, offering technical assistance to non-profits and groups who do not have the economic and organizational resources to actively engage in media productions. Interestingly, statistical analysis of the density of programming categories reveals that residents of ethnically diverse areas of the city tend to be the main contributors to public affairs programming (r (37) = .377, p= .03).

Conclusions

Building on a communication-commons approach to media policy and practice, this chapter has attempted to provide a broader framework to evaluate the contributions of digital community media projects to social inclusion and community building. First, continuing its historical function, the Austin Digital Community Center functions as a communication-commons infrastructure that provides open and affordable access not only to equipment but also to training and various online and offline distribution platforms. What is remarkable about the Austin Digital Community Center is its ability to engage diverse publics functioning as a mechanism for the redistribution of "the wealth of networks" in a Technopolis characterized by its uneven economic growth. Scholars have argued that community-based media best fit the dynamics of the networking media environments engaging citizens in participatory content production (Rennie, 2006; Tacchi et al., 2009). I found that "innovation" in these environments is manifested through empowered participation of citizens who become autonomous users of communicative resources that they employ to pursue well-being in different spheres of their lives, from community engagement and self-expression, to education, vocational, and career development.

Digital community access also supports local creative cultures by proving a welcoming environment where different individuals and social groups find affordable equipment, flexible learning formats, and opportunities for expression. Through their cooperative work, these local creative cultures produce hyperlocal content and more important-ly, develop a voice and recognition in the Austin community. As nicely illustrated by the stories of the two Robert Rodriguezes (the filmmaker and the Tejano musician), local creative cultures can potentially follow fairly different trajectories but highly beneficial outcomes for partici-pants. Robert Rodriguez "the filmmaker," who arrived in Austin as a young Chicano student from South Texas two decades ago, has devel-oped a professional career with national and international reputation and has gone on to open his production company, Troublemaker Studio, in Austin. Robert Rodriguez "the musician," a former carpen-ter, and an immigrant from Mexico, who uses his access television show to promote emergent local talent and Tejanoconjuntos not typically featured in commercial media has won municipal and state awards for the show's contributions to Latino and Chicano cultural heritage. These stories stand out essentially as examples of inclusion in a city with a long history of racial discrimination and social differentiation. They also illustrate the potential of community-access resources to act as what Fraser (2002) called "transformative remedies for injustice," that is, redistribution mechanisms that help citizens to avoid economic margin-alization, and redress "underlying cultural-valuation structures of disrespect" and "stigmatization," substituting them with structures of cultural respect and recognition (p. 24). This is perhaps the main contribution of community broadcasting to harness the power and wealth of networks.

References

Aufderheide, P. (2002). Competition and commons: the public interest in and after the AOL-Time Warner merger. *Journal of Broadcasting & Electronic Media, 46*(4), 515–531.

Benkler, Y. (2006). *The wealth of networks: How social production transforms markets and freedom.* New Haven, CT: Yale University Press.

Bourdieu, P. (1984). *Distinction: A social critique of the judgment of taste.* Cambridge, MA: Harvard University Press.

Bourdieu, P. & Wacquant, L. (1992). *An invitation to reflexive sociology.* Chicago, IL: University of Chicago Press.

Boyle, (2003). The second enclosure movement and the construction of the public domain. *Law & Contemporary Problems, 66,*(1–2), 33–34.

Carpentier, N. (2011). *Media and participation: A site of ideological-democratic struggle.* Bristol, UK: Intellect.

CRTC (2002). Broadcasting Public Notice CRTC 2002-61. Retrieved from http://www.crtc.gc.ca/eng/archive/2002/pb2002-61.htm

Castells, M. (2010). *The rise of the network society (2nd ed.).* Oxford, England: Blackwell.

Castells, M. (2009). *Communication power.* Oxford, England: Blackwell.

Couldry, N. (2009). Communicative entitlements and democracy: The future of the digital divide debate. In R. Mansell, C. Avgerou, D. Quah, & R. Silverstone (Eds.), *The Oxford handbook of information technologies* (pp. 383–403). Oxford, England: Oxford University Press.

Dailey, D., Bryne, A., Powell, A., Karaganis, J., & Chung, J. (2010, March). Broadband adoption in low-income communities. A Social Science Research Council Report.

DiMaggio, P., Hargittai, E., Celeste, C., & Shafer, S. (2004). Digital inequality: From unequal access to differentiated use. In K. M. Neckerman (Ed.), *Social inequality* (pp. 355–400). New York, NY: Russell Sage Foundation.

European Parliament (2008). Community media in Europe. European Resolution 2008/2011(INI), A6-0263/2008.

Fetterman, D.M. (2000) *Foundations of empowerment evaluation*. Thousand Oaks, CA: Sage

Flew, T. (2006). The social contract and beyond in broadcast media policy. *Television & New Media, 7*(3), 282–305.

Flores, C., & Wilson, R. H. (2009). Changing patterns of residential segregation in Austin. In B.R. Roberts & R. H. Wilson (Eds.), Urban segregation and governance in the Americas (pp. 187–204). New York, NY: Palgrave Macmillan.

Florida, R. (2002). *The rise of the creative class*. New York, NY: Basic Books.

Fraser, N. (2002). From redistribution to recognition? In N. Fraser (Ed.), *Justice interruptus: Critical reflections on the postcolonialism condition*. New York, NY: Routledge.

Fuentes-Bautista, M. (June 2009). Beyond television: The digital transition of public access. A Social Science Research Council Report.

Fuentes-Bautista, M. & Inagaki, N. (2012) Bridging the broadband gap or recreating digital inequalities? The social shaping of public Wi-Fi in Austin, TX. In Joseph Straubhaar, Jeremiah Spence, Zeynep Tufekci and Roberta Lentz (Eds) *Race, class and the digital divide in Austin: The persistence of inequity in the technopolis*. Austin, TX: University of Texas Press.

Garcelon, M. (2009). An information commons? Creative commons and public access to cultural creations. *New Media & Society, 11*(8), 1307–1326.

Garnham, N. (1999). Amartya Sen's "capabilities" approach to the evaluation of welfare: Its application to communication. In A. Calabrese & J.-C. Burgelman (Eds.), *Communication, citizenship, and social policy: Rethinking the limits of the Welfare State* (pp. 113–124). Lanham, MD: Rowman & Littlefield.

Hargittai, E. (2008). The digital reproduction of inequality. In D. Grusky (Ed.), *Social stratification: Class, race and gender in sociological perspective* (pp. 861–892). New York, NY: Russell Sage Foundation.

Hargittai, E. & Hsieh, Y. P. (2010). Predictors and consequences of differentiated practices on social network sites. *Information, Communication & Society, 13*(4), 515–536.

Hargittai, E. & Walejko, G. (2008). The participation divide: Content creation and sharing in the digital age. *Information, Communication & Society, 11*(2), 239–256.

Kidd, D. (2002). Indymedia.org: The development of the communications commons. *Democratic Communiqué, 18*, 65–86.

Kling, R. (1999). Can the "next generation Internet" effectively support ordinary citizens? *The Information Society, 15*(1), 57–63.

Krikorian, G. & Kapczynski, A. (2010). *Access to knowledge in the age of intellectual property*. Cambridge, MA: MIT Press.

Kvasny, L. (2006). Cultural (Re)production of digital inequality in a US community technology initiative. *Information, Communication & Society, 9*(2), 160–181.

Lenhart, A. (2008). Adults and social network Website. Report for the Pew Internet and American Life Project. Retrieved from http://www.pewinternet.org/PPF/r/272/report_display.asp

Mansell, R. (2002). From digital divides to digital entitlements in knowledge societies. *Current Sociology, 50*(3), 407–426.

Meadows, M., Forde, S., Ewart, J., and Foxwell, K. (2007). *Community media matters: An audience study of the Australian community broadcasting sector*. Melbourn, Australia.

Melody, W.H. (2010). Openness: The central issue in telecom policy reform and ICT development. *Information Technologies & International Development 6 (Special Ed.)*, 89–91.

Mossberger, K., Tolbert, C., & McNeal, R. (2008). *Digital citizenship*. Cambridge, MA: MIT Press.

Orum, A. (1987). *Power, money and the people: The making of modern Austin*. Austin, TX: Texas Monthly Press.

Rennie, E. (2007). Community media in the prosumer era. *Journal of Community, Citizen's and Third Sector Media and Communication, 3*, 24–32.

Rennie, E. (2006). *Community media: A global introduction*. Lanham, MD: Rowman & Littlefield.

Rogers, E. (2003) *Diffusion of innovation theory*. New York: Free Press.

Rojas, V., Straubhaar, J., Roychowdhury, D., & Okur, O. (2003). Communities, cultural capital and the digital divide. In E. P. Bucy & J. E. Newhagen (Eds.), *Media access: Social and psychological dimensions of new technology use* (pp. 107–130). Mahwah, NJ: Lawrence Erlbaum.

Sen, A. (2010). *The idea of justice*. Cambridge, MA: Harvard University Press.

Sen, A. (1999). *Development as freedom*. Oxford, UK: Oxford University Press

Smilor, R., Kozmetsky, G., & Gibson, D. (1988). *Creating the technopolis: Linking technology commercialization and economic development*. Cambridge, MA: Ballinger.

Steemers, J. (2004). Building a digital cultural commons: The example of the BBC. *Convergence: The Journal of Research into New Media Technologies, 10*(3), 102–107.

Straubhaar, J., Spence, J., Tufekci, Z., & Lentz, R. (2012). *The persistence of inequity in the technopolis: Austin, Texas.* Austin, TX: University of Texas Press.

Tacchi, J. (2005). Supporting the democratic voice through community media centres in South Asia. *3C Media Journal of Community, Citizens' and Third Sector Media and Communication,* 1(1), 25–36.

Tacchi, J. (2004). Researching creative applications of new information and communication technologies. *International Journal of Cultural Studies,* 7(1), 91–103.

Tacchi, J., & Grubb, B. (2007). The case of the E-Tuktuk. *Media International Australia Incorporating Culture & Policy,* 71–82.

Tacchi, J., Watkins, J., & Keerthirathne, K. (2009). Participatory content creation: Voice, communication and development. *Development in Practice,* 19(4–5), 573–584.

Tilly, C. (2007). Unequal access to scientific knowledge. *Journal of Human Development* 8,(2), 245–258.

Tilly, C. (2004). Historical perspectives on inequality. M. Romero & E. Margolis (Eds.), *The Blackwell companion to social inequalities* (pp. 15–30). Malden, MA: Blackwell.

Tufekci, Z. (2012). Past and future divides: Social mobility, inequality and the digital divide in Austin during the tech-boom. In J. Straubhaar, J. Spence, Z. Tufekci, & R. Lentz (Eds), *The persistence of inequity in the technopolis.* Austin, TX: University of Texas Press.

van Dijk, Jan (2005). *The deepening divide: Inequality in the information society.* Thousand Oaks, London, New Delhi: Sage.

van Vuuren, K. (2006). Community broadcasting and the enclosure of the public sphere. *Media, Culture & Society,* 28(3), 379–392.

Yin, R.K. (2002) *Case study research: Design and methods.* Newbury Park, CA: Sage.

Chapter 13:

Black Holes in the Electronic Galaxies:
Metaphor for Resistance
in the Information Society?

Barry Vacker and Agreen Wang

Introduction: "GOING DARK"

In September 2010, United States law enforcement officials announced their intent to seek new regulations that will provide the legal and technological powers to "wiretap" the Internet. The first two paragraphs in *The New York Times'* story perfectly summarized the issues:

> Federal law enforcement and national security officials are preparing to seek sweeping new regulations for the Internet, arguing that their ability to wiretap criminal and terrorism suspects is "going dark" as people increasingly communicate online instead of by telephone.

> Essentially, officials want Congress to require all services that enable communications—including encrypted e-mail transmitters like BlackBerry, social networking Web sites like Facebook and software that allows direct "peer to peer" messaging like Skype—to be technically capable of complying if served with a wiretap order. (Savage, 2010)

Of course, these requests should not be surprising, given the evisceration of the Bill of Rights by the 2001 USA PATRIOT Act, the 1994 CALEA legislation that mandated that phone companies empower government eavesdropping in their digital phone systems, and the fact that the National Security Agency (NSA) has built massive eavesdropping systems within the United States since 2001. Among the many expanded programs and powers sought by the U.S. government, perhaps the most philosophically provocative is the "Going Dark Program," which is operated by the Federal Bureau of Investigation (FBI) and includes a $9-million budget dedicated to enhancing its electronic surveillance capabilities. Apparently, "Going Dark" began in 2009 with a budget of $234 million to fund "the research and development of new tools, technical support and training initiatives" (Zetter, 2009). For the purposes of this chapter, the budgets and technologies of this program are much less important than the symbolism in the name of the program, "Going Dark."

With the name, Going Dark, the government has tapped into powerful symbolic imagery that may anticipate a *strange* future of technological resistance within a culture of total surveillance–a future of "black holes in the electronic galaxies." In pointing toward such resistance and what it might look like, metaphorically and technologically, this chapter charts several broad cultural patterns that juxtapose "light" with "dark" across the seemingly disparate realms of: (a) philosophy, (b) cosmology, (c) film, (d) media theory, and (e) media technologies. These patterns are outlined in Table 13.1. The pattern can be summarized as follows: The information society exists within a network of electronic galaxies in an expanding media universe, aglow with light, seemingly destined for total surveillance and total representation. Total light is generating conditions such that the trajectory of the enlightenment project has begun a strange reversal, where representation is resisted through disconnection and disappearance, in a self-chosen unconnection.

This may seem utterly strange or ridiculous to the empiricist scholar or pragmatic policy expert. Yet, these patterns are very real, and to deny their existence and potential symbolic powers would be to overlook the complex cultural relations between art, science, technology, and interdisciplinary theory. Drawing from Plato, Marshall McLuhan, Guy Debord, Jean Baudrillard, and a host of scientists, filmmakers, and media theorists, this chapter connects the cultural dots to reveal a powerful pattern, however strange, for further exploration.

Table 13.1: The Evolution of a Metaphor For a New Resistance

1. THE EVOLUTION OF "LIGHT"	2. BLACK HOLES IN COSMOLOGY	3. EXITS FROM "LIGHT" IN FILM	4. "BLACK HOLES" IN MEDIA THEORY	5. "BLACK HOLES" IN MEDIA TECHNOLOGIES
360 BC: Plato, *The Republic* • The Cave: exit shadows into light. 1626: Francis Bacon, *New Atlantis* • "Multiplications of light" are source of knowledge. 1944: *No Exit*, Jean-Paul Sartre • No exit from total electric light. 1948: *Nineteen Eight-Four*, George Orwell • Winston imprisoned in room of light. 1964: *Understanding Media*, Marshall McLuhan • Electric light is pure information. 1967: *The Society of the Spectacle*, Guy Debord • Society and "reality" are dominated by all encompassing techno-media spectacle.	1915: Albert Einstein, *General Theory of Relativity* • Space-time warped by gravity. 1939: Robert Oppenheimer • Massive stars collapse to a single point. 1967: John Wheeler • Coined term: "black hole."	1963: *X: The Man with X-ray Eyes*, Roger Corman • Exit total transparency; total vision, total light; eyes gouged out. 1965: *Alphaville*, Jean-Luc Godard • Exit light, total surveillance.		

Table 13.1: The Evolution of a Metaphor For a New Resistance (continued)

1. THE EVOLUTION OF "LIGHT"	2. BLACK HOLES IN COSMOLOGY	3. EXITS FROM "LIGHT" IN FILM	4. "BLACK HOLES" IN MEDIA THEORY	5. "BLACK HOLES" IN MEDIA TECHNOLOGIES
	1970s-2010: Steven Hawking • Pioneering work on black holes. • Hawking radiation: black holes not 100% black. • Black hole: "cosmic censorship."	1968: *2001: A Space Odyssey*, Stanley Kubrick • Exit light, total gaze of HAL, to enter darkness of deep space. 1970: *Colossus: The Forbin Project*, Joseph Sargent • No exit from total surveillance. 1971: *THX 1138*, George Lucas • Exit from illuminated futurist city. 1973: *Westworld*, Michael Crichton • No exit from light in theme park. 1976: *Logan's Run*, Michael Anderson • Exit futurist city of surveillance. 1982: *Tron*, Steven Lisberger • Exit from electronic light.		

Table 13.1: The Evolution of a Metaphor For a New Resistance (continued)

1. THE EVOLUTION OF "LIGHT"	2. BLACK HOLES IN COSMOLOGY	3. EXITS FROM "LIGHT" IN FILM	4. "BLACK HOLES" IN MEDIA THEORY	5. "BLACK HOLES" IN MEDIA TECHNOLOGIES
1984: *Neuromancer*, William Gibson • Coined term: "cyberspace" • Envisions cyberspace as electronic universe, with galaxies of information. • Data in cyberspace protected by "Black ICE" (Intrusion Countermeasures Electronics). 2000: *The Internet Galaxy*, Manuel Castells • The internet galaxy is the message for the globally networked society.		1997: *The Truman Show*, Peter Weir • Exit from light, total media universe. 1997: *Cube*, Vincent Natali • Exit glowing cubes (silicon chips?) into darkness, beyond which is light. 1998: *Enemy of the State*, Tony Scott • Exit from U.S. surveillance system. 1999: *The Matrix*, Wachowski Brothers • Exit from light, onslaught of information, media universe.	1983: *In the Shadow of the Silent Majorities*, Jean Baudrillard • The masses, messages, and meaning have imploded in a mediated black hole. 1995: *Burning All Illusions*, David Edwards • Politically "unsuitable" truths disappear into media black holes. 1998: *End of the Millennium*, Manuel Castells • Black holes of social exclusion effected by informational capitalism.	

Table 13.1: The Evolution of a Metaphor For a New Resistance (continued)

1. THE EVOLUTION OF "LIGHT"	2. BLACK HOLES IN COSMOLOGY	3. EXITS FROM "LIGHT" IN FILM	4. "BLACK HOLES" IN MEDIA THEORY	5. "BLACK HOLES" IN MEDIA TECHNOLOGIES
2009: *Total Recall*, Gordon Bell and Jim Gemmell • Everyone's entire lives to recorded and stored in electronic memories.	2008: Leonard Susskind • Information not lost in black holes. • Black holes are holographic.	2002: *Minority Report*, Steven Spielberg • Exit from light, total surveillance. • Eyes are replaced, echoing *X: The Man with X-ray Eyes.* 2003: *The Matrix Reloaded,* Wachowski Brothers • Create black hole to hack the system. 2008: *Wall•E*, Andrew Stanton • Humans exit electronic spectacle of a consumer spacecraft floating in deep space, in a return to nature on Earth. 2010: *TRON: Legacy*, Joseph Kosinski • Flynn lives "off the grid" in secluded, hidden realm of light surrounded by darkness.	2013: "Black Holes in Electronic Galaxies," Vacker & Wang • Black holes as metaphor for disappearance as resistance.	2007: Hubble Project, U. of Washington • System finds black holes in the internet. 2008: Fiber-optical black hole, Ulf Leonhardt, Friedrich Königa • Artificial event-horizon via intense light pulses. 2008: Micro black holes, Brian Greene • LHC might create micro black holes to study. 2009: Desktop mini black hole, Cui & Cheng • Circuit boards absorb electro-magnetic radiation. 2009: Blackest material ever, Mizuno, et al. • Layers of nanotubes absorb 99% of all light. 2010: Slow light, U. of California-Santa Cruz • Speed of light slowed down using "quantum interference" on photons in a silicon chip. 2010: Black Hole 1.0 • Delete information from Mac with single click.

The Evolution of Light

Since at least the time of Plato, philosophers have associated "dark" with falsehood and ignorance, while "light" has been associated with the pursuit of truth and enlightenment (Table 13.1, Column 1). This is illustrated by phrases and eras such as:

- "being in the dark"—having a lack of knowledge.

- "seeing the light of truth"—discovering or acquiring knowledge.

- "the Dark Ages"—the era often characterized as being dominated by ignorance and lack of knowledge of the empirical world.

- "the Enlightenment"—the era characterized by the growth of science and increasing knowledge of the empirical world, along with recognition of human rights.

A key origin of "light" as "truth" is likely to be Plato's famed allegory of "the Cave" (1974, pp. 167–170). The allegory tells the story of several prisoners in a cave, chained to the ground in the darkness and facing a wall opposite the entry to the cave. The prisoners can only view shadows on the cave wall, shadows caused by people passing between the prisoners and the light outside the cave. One prisoner manages to break free and escape the cave to the light outside, which hurts his eyes at first but remains the new and ultimate source of "truth." When the prisoner returns to the cave to alert the other prisoners to the world of light outside, they are skeptical and choose to remain chained in the darkness, gazing at the shadows, the only "reality" they have known. Echoing across the millennia, Plato's tale of shadows in the cave and the "light" outside has served as a metaphor for the discovery of truth and human enlightenment.

For Francis Bacon, "light" was a condition for the birth of the modern utopia. In the famed 1626 essay, "New Atlantis," Bacon envisioned an island-based utopia of science with the power to acquire knowledge from around the world. New Atlantis possessed "inter-knowledge" of world affairs and Houses of Light, in which light was multiplied to carry information around the world via reflections, refractions, and multiplications, of visual beams of objects (pp. 133-134).

It is no coincidence that Bacon was writing during the emergence of the Enlightenment. Preceding Marshall McLuhan (1964) by three centuries, Bacon seems to have anticipated the alteration of space-time to be effected by the electronic media and the spectacle of electric light. He also anticipated the conditions of surveillance, the power of seeing from afar through the magnification and amplification of light.

For McLuhan (1964), electric light was "pure information," a medium that is "totally radical, pervasive, and decentralized" (pp. 23-25). McLuhan remarked that light was the only "medium without a message," but it is not clear that claim holds up today. The global surveillance system relies on this existential and technological condition, using many of the different types of light waves. The typical surveillance camera relies on the band of light visible to the human eye, seen in the spectrum of colors (violet, blue, green, yellow, orange, and red). Deployed in airports and in many public or urban spaces, x-ray machines use light that travels in wavelengths less than the distance between atoms, much shorter than the spectrum visible to the human eye. If there is a message for this medium, then it might be total surveillance and total representation.

Perhaps such pervasive light is, in existential terms, less about spectral truth than total spectacle. Guy Debord (1994) theorized the spectacle as the outcome and goal of the dominant mode of production, with the spectacle reigning supreme over the structures of society. The spectacle is more than the technological proliferation of images and commodities, for the spectacle is "a weltanschauung that has been actualized, translated into the material realm, a worldview transformed into an objective force" (pp. 12-13). For Debord, the worldview of the spectacle is the logical progression of Western philosophy, which privileges sight in seeking to represent and understand social and natural phenomena. The effects of the spectacle are both subtle and profound, for the spectacle is not merely realizing philosophy, but rather the spectacle "philosophizes reality, and turns the material life of everyone into a universe of speculation" (p. 17). Light has become less the path to enlightenment, than to entertainment, distraction, and simulation. Today we see this phenomenon happening on a global scale, from simulated conquests in sports spectacles on TV, flat-screen universes of Times Square, simulated cities in Las Vegas, and simulated friends, micro-celebrities, and self-surveillance in Facebook. What else are the Super Bowl, Times Square, and Las Vegas other than microcosms of our 24/7 media environment's culture, sites for spectacle and simulation in movie-set galaxies of blazing lights?

In response to the events of September 11, the U.S. and the Pentagon have made their ultimate goals very clear: "Total Information Awareness." Within the Pentagon's Defense Advanced Research Projects Agency (DARPA), the Information Awareness Office (IAO) was created to oversee the Total Information Awareness surveillance system, to be effected in a massive computer and electronic network functioning on a global scale. This ambition was clearly illustrated in 2002 with the controversial logo for the Information Awareness Office.

Under public criticism, the name was changed to "Terrorist Information Awareness" and the program was then apparently defunded by Congress. Others question if the program died or was merely relocated to other classified programs (Williams, 2006). Given the ambition to wiretap the Internet, can we seriously doubt the U.S. government's desire for total global surveillance? Such goals and trajectories were made clear in the logo for the IAO. Gazing down at Earth, the solitary eye is accompanied by Francis Bacon's phrase *Scientia est Potentia* — "Knowledge is Power." The logo's meaning is clear: total global surveillance.

It should not be surprising that *Sputnik* and *Apollo* pointed the way toward planetary surveillance. Since the Soviet satellite orbited Earth in 1957 and American astronauts captured the "Earthrise" image in 1968, there has been a nonstop technological and cultural imperative to place the entirety of Spaceship Earth within the expanding global media environments. There is a clear trajectory from Earthrise to Spaceship Earth to Google Earth.

From cave painting to cyberspace to outer space, the human drive for representation is visible wherever people seek to communicate and make meaning of the world. History tells the story of state, church, and corporation, be it kings, monarchs, theologians, dictators, bureaucrats, corporate executives, or any other type of censor, seeking to suppress and eliminate that which brought to light their oppression and superstitions, crimes and corruption. In the twenty-first century, this struggle continues in many parts of the world (Chomsky, 2010) and in the controversy surrounding the 2010 WikiLeaks reports on the Terror War.

Overcoming this struggle was the Enlightenment-inspired ambition of the First Amendment to the Bill of Rights of the United States Constitution, however imperfect the amendment has been in practice and despite the federal and local governments' never-ending attempts to override freedom of speech and press in the name of war, national security, social order, family values, religious beliefs, and so on. That freedom of expression is recognized as a human right by the United Nations attests to this Enlightenment ambition. The ultimate ground for the right to freedom of expression is the inherent human drive to *represent the world* and *to see the world* represented via art, language, and media, in all its forms.

The cultural trajectory toward total representation and planetary surveillance has evolved with the expansion of media technologies around the world, especially the global proliferation of satellites, cameras, computers, cell phones, databases, and the Internet, all powered by microprocessors and Moore's Law (ever more miniaturization, decreasing costs, increasing technological powers). No wonder there are already 2 billion users on the Internet. Maybe cell phones, Facebook, Twitter, and the Terror War merely offer early glimpses of a planetary culture moving toward total surveillance by its citizens in the dreams of total representation and nonstop personal expression.

Black Holes in Cosmology

Perhaps no recent scientific concept has exploded into the popular imagination like black holes (Table 13.1, Column 2). Though the term "black hole" appeared in 1967, the cosmology of black holes has its foundations in Albert Einstein's theory of general relativity (Greene, 2003, pp. 53–84). In its most general sense, relativity shows that mass with sufficient gravity effects a curvature in the fabric of space-time. Visualize a bowling ball sitting on a sheet of foam rubber, thus creating a curved indention. Large masses act the same way, with gravity curving space and bending the light passing through the curvature. The larger the mass, the larger the curve, and the greater the warping of space-time. Empirical proof of relativity came via a total solar eclipse in 1919, where photographs of distant stars revealed that the light waves had been curved by the gravity of the sun. In 1939, Robert Oppenheimer published an article suggesting that dying stars with sufficient mass collapse inward, generating a curvature in space so severe that the stars' own light rays would bend inward, effectively sealing off the event of the star's demise from any external observers (Hawking, 2007, pp. 47–48).

In 1963, John Wheeler announced that Oppenheimer had been correct; new electronic computers created simulations showing how dying stars would collapse inward. After Wheeler coined the term "black hole" (much more evocative than "gravitationally collapsed star"), the poetic name soon began to permeate popular culture (Hawking, 2007, p. 83).

When stars (with roughly three times the mass of the sun) burn up their fuel, they can enter a complete collapse, creating a curvature in space so severe that nothing escapes its gravitational pull, not even light. A black hole apparently collapses to a point of near-infinite density and curvature. This is the point of singularity, the region of space-time where the laws of relativity break down. Though nothing can escape a black hole, anything can enter a black hole. The "event horizon" is the point of no return, the point where the attraction is so strong that the object will eventually be pulled to the center of the black hole and crushed into a subatomic string of particles. Once inside the event horizon, the edge of the horizon is defined by light rays hovering upon the horizon but unable to escape (Greene, 2003, pp. 79-81).

By the 1970s, Stephen Hawking (1988) used black holes to integrate relativity (macro cosmology) with quantum mechanics (micro cosmology) and thermodynamics (the science of energy), thus yielding insights into the big bang and the expansion and fate of the universe (pp. 83-101). As poetically described by Hawking, "the singularities produced by gravitational collapse occur only in places, like black holes, where they are decently hidden from outside view by an event horizon. Strictly, this is what is known as the weak cosmic censorship hypothesis" (p. 91). Gravity's efforts at cosmic censorship seem to be just less than 100% effective, for Hawking (2007) also showed that black holes are not completely black (pp. 59-74).

It seems black holes range across the scales of the universe. As stars collapse into black holes, they may give off a shock wave in the form of a blast of bright light known as a "supernova." Some stars may collapse and simply disappear with no blast of light in an "unnova." In addition to the conventional stellar black hole, astronomers have identified supermassive black holes, comprised of the mass of millions or billions of stars, existing at the center of galaxies, including the Milky Way. Scientists now speculate that "micro black holes" might exist at the quantum level and may be temporarily created by the Large Hadron Collider (Greene, 2008).

Black holes exist at the cutting edge of current topics in cosmology. It seems that black holes do not permit information to escape from the universe, as Hawking had once theorized. Information is not lost, because when an object disappears into a black hole, the object's information is simultaneously smeared across the surface of the event horizon, smeared because of the massive distortion of space-time. In other words, a black hole's event horizon provides a two-dimensional representation of the three-dimensional world being distorted inside the black hole. This means black holes are holographic, as might be the entire universe (Susskind, 2008, pp. 290-306).

Exits from "Light" in Film

Marshall McLuhan (1964) viewed art as a potential "early warning system" for culture, capable of prefiguring cultural shifts and transformations. Artists function like "antennae," offering intuitive perceptions of cultural change expressed through works of art. If McLuhan was correct, there would seem to be radical implications for specific art-works since the early 1960s—films that deal with exits from light precisely as black holes were emerging in popular culture.

George Orwell foresaw the dark side of electronic surveillance in the 1948 novel, *Nineteen Eighty-Four* (1984), which seems to have been inspired, in part, by Jean-Paul Sartre's 1944 play, *No Exit* (1989), the dystopian tale of three people negotiating existence and meaning in conditions of total light, total surveillance, total representation. While Sartre and Orwell anticipated dystopian possibilities in realms of total light and electronic media, the first film to embrace an exit from light appeared in 1963, the same year in which John Wheeler announced computers had verified black holes.

The film was Roger Corman's cult classic with the crazy title: *X: The Man with X-Ray Eyes*. Though Corman is a less prestigious filmmaker than Jean-Luc Godard, Stanley Kubrick, and Steven Spielberg, *X* anticipated key ideas that later appeared in the films of these directors and many others. From Hollywood to independent, low budget to big budget, action film to art film, numerous filmmakers have projected a dystopian future in which the "hero" or "antihero" must exit from light in a culture of total surveillance and total representation, an exit from the light of a mediated universe (Table 13.1, Column 3).

In *X*, a scientist named Dr. Xavier creates eye drops that provide an ever increasing power of "X-ray vision" in hopes of improved surgeries and increased scientific insights in medicine, only to discover that an accelerating X-ray vision is more dystopian than utopian. The once-famous scientist is reduced to wandering in Las Vegas, blinded by ever more intensifying light but further removed from reality. Eventually Xavier exits the world of total light by gouging his eyes out in the desert near Las Vegas. In effect, Corman's film counters Plato's Cave, suggesting that the pursuit of *total* light would eventually lead to blindness. The dream of total representation is countered by disappearance.

In 1965, Godard's *Alphaville* featured an anti-hero, named "Lemmy Caution," who must exit a space-age city of the future, a dystopian metropolis under complete computer surveillance. As Caution exits, he is blasted with bright light, apparently from the computer (or maybe also symbolizing a blast of light from a Cold War nuclear bomb). In Kubrick's 1968 masterpiece, *2001: A Space Odyssey*, the astronaut Dave Bowman must exit the computer surveillance of the HAL 9000, the all-seeing, all-knowing computer. Dave eventually exits the nonstop ambient light of the spacecraft, facing his future as an astral child in the darkness of deep space or an aging man amidst the glow of cyberspace.

Three decades after the astronaut's exit in deep space, *The Truman Show* presents an exit from light to darkness that perfectly illustrates the metaphor of a black hole. In the film, Jim Carrey stars as Truman Burbank, an average person whose entire existence, unbeknownst to him, is inside a simulacrum of a pastoral beach town that is the back-drop for a nonstop television show.

In the climax of the film, Truman tries to escape by manning a sailboat and setting out across the harbor of Seahaven, only to eventually crash into the outer wall of the studio television dome (looking like the horizon of a blue sky). Dumbfounded, Truman steps onto a stairway and ascends to a door with a handle, upon which is a circle containing the word "EXIT." The door opens to nothing but darkness. Staring into the dark, with his back to the television cameras, Truman is contemplating his fate when Christof (the creator of the show) whispers into his microphone: "Truman." The whisper is heard by Truman and the global audience viewing on television. Truman turns around and gazes up at the sky. The following dialog ensues:

Truman—Who are you?

Christof—I am the creator of a television show that gives hope and joy and inspiration to millions.

Truman—Then, who am I?

Christof—You're the star.

Truman—Was nothing real?

Christof—You were real. That is what made you so good to watch. Listen to me, Truman. There is no more truth out there than there is in the world I created for you. The same lies, the same deceit. But, in my world, you have nothing to fear. (...) Talk to me. Say something.

(Truman remained silent)

Christof —Well, say something God dammit! You're on television, live to the whole world!

Truman—Well, if I don't see you: Good afternoon, good evening, and good night!

Truman then turns away from the camera, steps through the doorway and disappears into a realm of darkness, never to be seen again in the movie. In effect, Seahaven is an electronic Cave, though the bright light is used for illusion and the prisoner's exit is into darkness. Truman is the existential "true man" of the information age, the prisoner inhabiting a mediated universe from which he felt he must exit. Finally, when informed he is "the star" of his universe, Truman exits into the darkness, into the void—becoming a black hole in the electronic galaxies.

Black Holes in Media Theory

The term "black hole" is used in metaphorical contexts in media theory, with the intended meaning generally referring to information that has disappeared, become unreachable, or is purposely hidden from access or purposely made inaccessible (Table 13.1 column 4).

In 1983, Jean Baudrillard argued that the masses and media effect a black hole through the implosion and absorption of all content and social meaning, while radiating out images in a culture of screens and signs without substance:

> [T]he masses function as a black hole which inexorably inflects, bends and distorts all energy and light radiation approaching it: an implosive sphere, in which the curvature of spaces accelerates, in which all dimensions curve back on themselves and 'involve' to the point of annihilation, leaving in their stead only a sphere of potential engulfment. (pp. 3-4, 9)

To summarize, for the masses viewing the spectacle on the screens, the two-dimensional image represents the three-dimensional reality warped by the media, holograms for hyperreality. (Baudrillard, 1994, pp. 105–110)

In 1996, David Edwards argued that the propaganda model of Noam Chomsky and Edward Herman can be understood in terms of "black holes" that protect entrenched economic and social powers. "Chomsky and Herman seek to explain not only distorted reporting of events, but also massive media black holes into which 'unsuitable' truths fall out of sight" (Edwards, 1996, p. 19). The recent massive expansion of the U.S. secrecy programs is an attempt to create black holes that hide information that apparently reveal military deceit and war crimes (Greenwald, September 8, 2010).

In 1998, Manuel Castells used the term "black hole" to refer to areas of socio-economic exclusion effected by informational capitalism and the digital divide. "These black holes concentrate in their density all the destructive forces that affect humanity from multiple sources," such that "there is no escape from the pain and destruction inflicted on the human condition for those who, in one way or another, enter these social landscapes" (Castells, 2001, p. 167). Castells believed that this exclusion can be marginalized in a way that actually improves the efficiency of the network. "They're not valuable as producers, consumers; in fact, if they would disappear, the logic of the overall system would improve. If you are outside the network, in other words, you don't even exist" (Ogilvy, 1998).

Black Holes in Media Technologies

The term "black hole" has also migrated from cosmology to technology, especially in relation to the growth of the Internet over the past 20 years (Table 13.1, column 5). In 2007, computer scientists at the University of Washington designed the "Hubble" program to identify and map the black holes in the Internet. Named after the space telescope, the Hubble program uncovered 1.97 million "reachability problems" caused when one Internet address cannot reach another, even though the physical link is operational and the pathway was known to work before (Cox, 2008). Apparently, the traffic "seems to simply disappear into a black hole" (Moskowitz, 2008). In 2009, scientists in China and America created the first "desktop black hole," effected by 60 concentric layers of special circuit board made from materials used for "invisibility cloaks" that absorb microwave radiation from all directions (Ananthaswamy, 2009). In 2010, Apple made available a software application that allows users to clear sensitive information from their Macintosh with a single click. The application is called "Black Hole."

Conclusion: Representation, Reversal, and Resistance in the Information Society

What do these patterns mean individually, collectively, and metaphorically?

1. Spaceship Earth exists within the electronic galaxies of the information society.

From Plato's Cave to cyberspace, the extension of light has encircled the planet in the dream of total representation and total surveillance, where Spaceship Earth is to be ordered within ever more galaxies of information. That's why the future of Spaceship Earth is to be under total surveillance by its passengers—governments and corporations, theologians and technologists, celebrities and citizens. This is not a utopian or futurist prophesy, merely an existential extrapolation of the dominant cultural and technological trends. How can this not be the mediated destiny for societies and citizens in the ever more connected global information society, given the emergence of phenomena such as Google Earth, Google Streetview, YouTube, Facebook, the blogosphere, hyperlocal journalism, weather satellites, spy satellites, the PATRIOT Act, IAO, and the Terror War? Combine the expanding technological powers with the longstanding cultural imperatives—political, commercial, ideological, theological, social, psychological, and personal—and it seems inevitable that life on Spaceship Earth is to be spinning within a 24/7, omnipresent, media universe of electronic galaxies. There will be no exit.

Total light serves two possible outcomes for global surveillance and total representation: 1). Total light and global surveillance express the panoptic powers first articulated by Jeremy Bentham, which were then extended to electronic media and "Big Brother" by George Orwell

(1984), and extended throughout the "power" relations of modern culture by Michel Foucault (1995). 2). Total light liberates information to undermine authoritarianism, thus making possible the digital democracy of a "transparent society" (Brin, 1999). In this view, total surveillance develops, but the power to serve authoritarianism is countered by the pervasive dispersal of surveillance technologies throughout society, made possible by the effects of Moore's Law. The idea is that "the people" can watch the institutions that are watching them, such as corporations, governments, and theocracies. In the democratized surveillance of "the transparent society," the panoptic powers extend in all directions, eliminating personal and institutional privacy in the proliferation of public information. Though it remains to be seen which of these outcomes will prevail, this view of social transparency seems naïve, given the massive expansion of secrecy programs by the U.S. government during the Terror War (Greenwald, September 8, 2010).

2. Black holes offer a new metaphor for resistance to total surveillance.

3. The Enlightenment project may have entered a strange reversal.

Mirroring the rise of black holes in popular culture, there has been a striking pattern across five decades of film, wherein filmmakers project a potentially dystopian future in which exits from artificial light have been an existential theme. Perhaps these films suggest that the Enlightenment project has reached its climax and entered a reversal, where resistance may no longer be about representation and democracy, but rather non-representation and disappearance. Light has joined dark as a force for domination in the postmodern world, requiring an exit from light as a mode of resistance. In other words, survival for the hero or antihero requires escape from the world of total information and total spectacle. The many cinematic exits include: exits from natural light, exits from artificial light (in spacecrafts, futurist metropolises, theme parks), exits from computer surveillance, exits from networks, exits from media spectacles, and exits from mass society entranced with mass media.

McLuhan (1964) believed that each medium and technology simultaneously extends our senses and retrieves something previously lost. At the same time, each technology contains the genetic code of its own *reversal*, the point when the technology is pushed to its limit, overextended or "overheated," and users lose the enthusiasm for its original functions and benefits (pp. 33-40). Radio and the cell phone extended our voice and ears around the world, while retrieving town criers and oral traditions lost to print media. Television extends our eyes and ears around the planet, while retrieving cave paintings and campfire tales. Satellites extend our eyes and ears into space, while retrieving ecology and environmentalism.

When acoustic radio was pushed to the limit, it became audio-visual television and reverted back to the visual image lost to print culture. Telescopes and space probes have extended our eyes and ears—and electronic light—around the planet and into deep space, across 13.8 billion light years, triggering a reversal that seeks to return humans to the center of the universe.

4. This chapter extends black hole media theory to include resistance and reversal.

There might be no better example of Baudrillard's media black hole than the Earthrise image and the *Apollo 8* television broadcast from the moon to a billion people back on Earth in December 1968. Precisely as Earthrise and *Apollo 8* confirmed the profound insights of Copernicus, Galileo, and Newton—Earth and its passengers are not at the center of the universe—the astronauts read from Genesis in an attempt to give the accomplishment philosophical meaning for those masses confronting the existential discoveries of the space age, revealed right before their eyes. In the text for Peter Granser's art photography book about President Bush's neoconservative Texas, *Signs*, the author writes:

> At the moment of humankind's greatest scientific and technological accomplishment, secular and modern philosophy were utterly absent as the astronauts recited creation myths to the humans on Earth, precisely as one billion humans were united in their gaze into the cosmic voids of the expanding universe. If the Apollo 11 moonwalk was a "giant leap for mankind," then the Apollo 8 space-talk was a great leap backward for the human mind, with the superstitions born of the premodern mind suggesting not scientific revolution but spiritual devolution. As creation myths echoed down from

the moon to Mission Control at the speed of light, the space age crashed in Texas. (Vacker, 2008, p. 7)

Traveling at the speed of light, the electronic information that should have revolutionized human thought about global civilization was not accelerating into the future but was being warped deep into the past, with its existential meanings disappearing into a mediated black hole. Though Earthrise surely helped retrieve ecology and inspire the Gaia hypothesis, for billions of people the content and meaning of the information have been absorbed and neutralized, while the form is radiated as an image to circulate in the media networks.

The real meanings of Earthrise and *Apollo 8* have largely disappeared into a black hole, where the space age is sucked into the Stone Age, and Earthrise is little more than a hologram floating in the electronic galaxies of cyberspace. The same is true for the Pale Blue Dot and the Hubble Deep Field images as the telescope, computer, and space probe soak up natural light and extend electronic light to the very edge of the observable universe. The existential conditions revealed by our most advanced media technologies show we are a species living in the biosphere of a borderless planet orbiting one of 100 billion stars in our galaxy, itself one of hundreds of billions of galaxies, all in a vast cosmos of which *we are not the center.*

Since *Apollo 8* and Earthrise enabled humans to personally and collectively see they are not the center of the universe, a massive McLuhan-like reversal has been underway. The technologies of the space age were greeted with global enthusiasm in the 1960s, yet the very meanings of the vast universe revealed by the technologies have been largely ignored precisely as the technologies pushed to the *very limit* all previous cosmologies, ideologies, and theologies. Humans had to rethink or reverse.

Since *Apollo 8* and Earthrise, technology and theology have been on a nonstop mission of reversal, seeking to return the masses to the center of the universe, be it mediated or material. In December 1968, hypertext made its public debut on computer screens, the very same time that sacred texts starred on television screens. Hypertext places users at the center of cyberspace, just as sacred texts place followers at the center of outer space. After all, Facebook and fundamentalism offer the same thing: they allow people to pretend they are the center of the universe. Hypertext or sacred text, technology and theology, both now provide a sense of personal identity amidst global surveillance by data-mining corporations or deities promising destinies. Facebook users place themselves under surveillance in exchange for the power to represent themselves to themselves and their "friends," to be a micro-celebrity, a star at the center of their personal media universe. Fundamentalists place themselves under "spiritual" surveillance in exchange for the power to save themselves and fellow followers, to be born again with a destiny at the center of their personal Creator's universe.

The drive to be at the center of the universe explains why the *majority* of the American populace has not accepted evolution, has little scientific knowledge (Mooney & Kirshenbaum, 2009), has abandoned reason in cultural discourses (Jacoby, 2008), and has elected born-again presidents who defend and expand the militaristic-theological-corporate empires, all of which are used to justify total global surveillance in the Terror War. For example, how else to explain the populist "ignorance chic" celebrated by Sarah Palin and the Tea Party (Dowd, 2010)? And this dumbed-down media spectacle is happening despite nothing less than an explosion of scientific, biological, cognitive, and humanist knowledge since *Apollo 8*. In contrast to the supernova of expanding scientific knowledge, how can this growing cultural ignorance not be a supermassive cultural black hole in America, where the light of science and humanism is disappearing into the cognitive voids of ignorance and superstition among millions of people?

Of course, the problem is not merely America and its fundamentalists, for this is a global phenomenon. War, terror, genocide, and superstition have spread around the planet, with fundamentalists and theologies of all kinds claiming their sacred texts place their empires and destinies at the center of their Creator's universe. Such beliefs, and the Terror War, necessarily reflect the ignorance and denial toward the most powerful and profound empirical observations provided by our electronic media technologies—we are a species living in the biosphere of a borderless planet in a vast cosmos of which we are not the center.

How are social justice and civil liberty furthered by the black holes of ignorance and superstition now being globalized by the masses and mass media? How can this expanding black hole not signal a massive reversal in the technologies of electric light, an implosion of the information age and contraction of the space age, a retreat from the Enlightenment and the expanding knowledge necessary for building a global, secular, humanist civilization? Where is mass enlightenment in the information society?

So, what is an *individual* to do? How can an individual resist these forces in a civilized and non-violent manner? Participate in the simulacrum of "democracy" that is the two-party system? Lead a protest for a sound-bite on CNN? Write a book? Submit op-eds to *The New York Times*? Form a group in Facebook? Create a blog? Post a video on YouTube? Isn't this exactly what the spectacle wants individuals to do?

If the Enlightenment project sought to liberate individuals, with representation via the mass media and democratic politics, then it seems representation and entertainment are overtaking liberation and enlightenment, like a map overtaking the territory it is supposed to represent. To be surveilled and represented as information is to exist and be "real" as patriot and citizen, while the *real* individual exists beyond the screens. The deeper message of total surveillance is not physical presence, but the representation of presence, to be observed and recorded in the databases. To have *real* presence would require that one *not be there*. In the future, perhaps the only way individuals can be real and free is to disappear, where existence as a private individual requires disappearance as a political subject. Maybe Mayer-Schonberger's *Delete* will be extended into a form of resistance, as a way of "erasing" one's self from the electronic galaxies (2009). Isn't that the very condition suggested by the cinematic exits from light?

5. Black holes have been created with information technologies and might be modes for future disappearance and resistance.

The films are artworks trying to imagine new modes of resistance. In countering the spectacle of total representation, the filmmakers suggest that persons should have the power or right to be not represented, the power to exit the scenes or disappear from the screens. There are two possible ways to effect a *nonviolent* nonrepresentation:

1. Reject all media and information technologies in a nonviolent Luddite resistance, choosing to quietly disconnect and disappear. Perhaps this is the "unnova" scenario.
2. Use cutting-edge media and information technologies to effect a disappearance, however imperfect or impermanent it might be. Perhaps this is the "micro-black hole" or "desktop black hole" scenario.

The first scenario will momentarily seem attractive to casual Luddites who get frustrated with the spectacle's inanities, the proliferating images, the information overload, or who just want to read a book in peace and quiet. The unnova scenario will be very attractive to serious Luddites, but either scenario will be less plausible over time in a future requiring total representation and no privacy.

The second scenario seems currently implausible, yet might be possible in the not-too-distant future. Some trends are moving in that direction. As listed in Table 13.1, the following information-related black holes have been created: artificial event horizons, fiber-optic black holes, and desktop black holes. Plus, scientists have slowed light to zero on a microchip and invented the blackest material ever. And then there are the wide-ranging possibilities for quantum encryption and the discovery of inexplicable black holes on the Internet. Though no one knows how these technologies will play out, Moore's Law will insure these kinds of technologies will be made more powerful, less expensive, and more accessible. This is another example of a McLuhan reversal, with extreme electric light pushing to the limits for individuals, only to effect a flip, a reversal into going dark, into the media technology of black holes. This is also a reversal or flip of Plato's Cave.

To effect a black hole, individuals could deploy future media technology to make information disappear or become inaccessible, to create a form of personal cosmic censorship within the electronic galaxies. Maybe the quantum encryption code would determine the artificial event horizon, that point at which no light or information can escape, and the point beyond which the information cannot be seen or accessed, remaining unreachable for outside observers. Since black holes apparently have an inner surface of curved light, as if light were circling the interior of a ball, we can imagine personal black holes as tiny spheres of privacy in the electronic galaxies. At the singularity in the black hole, normal relativity is replaced by quantum existence, a chaotic state where the person's information, position, momentum, energy, and time are unknown. The personal black hole is the point of social singularity, the region in electronic space-time where the laws of state, church, and corporation break down.

Since black holes are not entirely black, we can imagine that any exit will produce virtual particles leaving traces on the electronic screens. Or maybe the personal data will be smeared across the event horizon, rendering any exit as a temporary void and distortion in a holographic universe. No exit will ever be complete, no unconnection will be possible.

We are living in an age of exponential power in media technologies that empower (and not merely entertain) us in pursuing our individual and collective destinies and should provide the power to resist domination and exploitation. Though no one knows exactly how these ideas and technologies will play out, black-hole resistance is becoming a reality. Such tactics are meeting fierce opposition in the Terror War, with the U.S. government concealing apparent war crimes in their black holes, while wiretapping the Internet and going supernova on the entire planet.

If there is an early example of these conclusions, then perhaps it is the recent case of Julian Assange and WikiLeaks, the whistleblower Web site that seeks to effect "total transparency" on a global scale (Khatchadourian, 2010). In its most dramatic leak, WikiLeaks released hundreds of thousands of documents that apparently reveal the deceit, misinformation, war crimes, and human-rights abuses hidden by the Pentagon and White House. While the U.S. would prefer the information remain hidden, WikiLeaks is bringing the information to light—the U.S. black hole is countered by the WikiLeaks supernova. Yet, to function successfully in accessing and releasing information provided by whistleblowers, Assange and WikiLeaks must deploy "state-of-the-art encryption" to keep the information hidden prior to release (Anderson & Assange, 2010). Assange describes the WikiLeaks site as "an uncensorable system for untraceable mass document leaking and public analysis" (Khatchadourian, 2010). In effect, the documents are hidden in temporary black holes.

Naturally, the Pentagon denounced these leaks as "threats" to soldiers and American interests, while the mainstream media such as CNN and *The New York Times* smeared Assange's reputation across the event horizons of the electronic screens (Greenwald, October 24, 2010). For fear of being arrested or assassinated, Assange is constantly "going dark" by having no fixed address, constantly switching cell phones, avoiding credit card transactions, and so on. Welcome to the future, where resistance to domination requires that individuals and organizations become or create black holes in the electronic galaxies—even if no unconnection is permanent and no exit is perfect.

References

Ananthaswamy, A. (2009, October 14). First black hole created for light on earth. [Electronic version]. *New Scientist*. Retrieved from http://www. newscientist.com/article/dn17980-first-black-hole-for-light-created-on-earth.html

Anderson, C. (Interviewer), & Assange, J. (Interviewee). (2010). *Why the world needs WikiLeaks* [Interview audio file]. Retrieved from http://www.ted. com/talks/lang/eng/julian_assange_why_the_world_needs_wikileaks.html

Bacon, F. (1988). New Atlantis. In H. Morley (Ed.), *Ideal commonwealths* (pp. 103–140). New York, NY: Hippocrene Books.

Baudrillard, J. (1983). *In the shadow of the silent majorities*. New York, NY: Semiotext(e).

Baudrillard, J. (1994). *Simulacra and simulation*. (S.F. Glaser, Trans.). Ann Arbor, MI: University of Michigan Press. (Original work published in French, 1981).

Bell, G., & Gemmell, J. (2009). *Total recall: How the e-memory revolution will change everything*. New York, NY: Dutton.

Brin, D. (1999). *The transparent society: Will technology force us to choose between privacy and freedom?* New York, NY: Basic Books.

Castells, M. (2000). *End of the millennium: The information age: Economy, society, and culture* (2nd ed.). Malden, MA: Blackwell. (Original work published 1998).

Castells, M. (2001). *The internet galaxy*. Oxford, England: Oxford University Press.

Chomsky, N. (2010). *Hopes and prospects*. Chicago, IL: Haymarket Books.

Cox, J. (2008, April 10). Researchers map Internet's "black holes." [Electronic version]. *Network World*. Retrieved from http://www.networkworld.com/news/2008/041008-internet-black-holes.html

Debord, G. (1995). *The society of the spectacle*. New York, NY: Zone Books. (Original work published 1967).

Department of Computer Science and Engineering in University of Washington. (2008). Studying black holes in the internet with hubble. Retrieved from http://www.cs.washington.edu/homes/ethan/papers/hubble-nsdi08.pdf

Dowd, M. (2010, October 19). Making ignorance chic. [Electronic version]. *The New York Times*. Retrieved from http://www.nytimes.com/2010/10/20/opinion/20dowd.html

Edwards, D. (1996). *Burning all illusions: A guide to personal and political freedom*. Cambridge, MA: South End Press.

Foucault, M. (1995). *Discipline and punish: The birth of the prison*. New York, NY: Vintage.

Greene, B. (2003). *The elegant universe*. New York, NY: Vintage.

Greene, B. (2008, September 11). The origins of the universe: A crash course. [Electronic version]. *The New York Times*. Retrieved from http://www.nytimes.com/2008/09/12/opinion/12greene.html

Greenwald, G. (2010, September 8). Obama wins the right to invoke "state secrets" to protect Bush crimes. [Electronic version]. *Salon*. Retrieved from http://www.salon.com/2010/09/08/obama_138/

Greenwald, G. (2010, October 24). The Nixonian henchmen of today: at the NYT. [Electronic version]. *Salon*. Retrieved from http://www.salon.com/2010/10/24/assange_2/

Hawking, S. (1988). *A brief history of time*. New York, NY: Bantam.

Hawking, S. (2007). *The theory of everything: The origin and fate of the universe*. Beverly Hills, CA: Phoenix Books.

Jacoby, S. (2008). *The age of American unreason*. New York, NY: Pantheon.

Khatchadourian, R. (2010, June 7). No secrets: Julian Assange's mission for total transparency. [Electronic version]. *The New Yorker*. Retrieved from http://www.newyorker.com/reporting/2010/06/07/100607fa_fact_khatchadourian

Mayer-Schonberger, V. (2009). *Delete: the virtue of forgetting in the digital age*. Princeton, NJ: Princeton University Press.

Miller, A. I. (2001). *Einstein, Picasso: Space, time, and the beauty that causes havoc*. New York, NY: Basic Books

McLuhan, M. (1964). *Understanding media: The extensions of man.* New York, NY: New American Library.

Mooney, C., & Kirshenbaum, S. (2009). *Unscientific America: How scientific illiteracy threatens our future.* New York, NY: Basic Books.

Moskowitz, C. (2008, April 11). Internet full of "black holes." [Electronic version]. *Live Science.* Retrieved from http://www.livescience.com/technology/080411-cyber-black-holes.html

National Telecommunication and Information Administration (1995, July). Falling through the Net I: A survey of the "have nots" in rural and urban America. Washington DC: NTIA.

National Telecommunication and Information Administration (2002, February). A nation online: How Americans are expanding their use of the Internet. Washington DC: NTIA.

Ogilvy, J. (1998, November). Dark side of the boom. [Electronic version]. *Wired,* 6(11). Retrieved from http://www.wired.com/wired/archive/6.11/castells.html

Orwell, G. (1984). *Nineteen eighty-four.* New York, NY: Plume.

Plato. (1974). *The republic.* (G. M. A. Grube, Trans.). Indianapolis, IN: Hackett.

Sartre, J.-P. (1989). *No exit and three other plays.* New York, NY: Vintage International.

Savage, C. (2010, September 27). U.S. tries to make it easier to wiretap the Internet. [Electronic version]. *The New York Times.* Retrieved from http://www.nytimes.com/2010/09/27/us/27wiretap.html

Susskind, L. (2008). *The black hole war: My battle with Stephen Hawking to make the world safe for quantum mechanics.* New York, NY: Back Bay Books.

Vacker, B. (2008). Lost stars, lost amidst the big bang. In P. Granser: *Signs.* Stuttgart, Germany: Hatje Cantz.

Warshauer, M. (2003). Technology and social inclusion. Cambridge, MA: MIT Press.

Williams, M. (2006, April 26). The total information awareness project lives on. [Electronic version]. *Technology Review.* Retrieved from http://www.technologyreview.com/communications/16741/

Yin, R.K. (2002). Case study research: Design and methods. Newbury Park, CA: Sage.

Zetter, K. (2009, May 11). FBI "going dark" with new advanced surveillance program. [Electronic version]. *Wired.* Retrieved from http://www.wired.com/threatlevel/2009/05/fbi-going-dark-with-new-advanced-surveillance-program/

ABOUT THE CONTRIBUTORS

ABIY AGIRO is a Ph.D. candidate in Public Affairs with a concentration in Public Administration at the University of Central Florida. Mr. Agira is interested in the intersections among technology, particularly social media, and civic engagement. He also has an interest in international comparative studies and has worked for transnational entities.

PAUL M. A. BAKER, Ph.D., is Associate Director, Center for 21st Century Universities (C21U), Georgia Institute of Technology, and an Adjunct Professor at the Centre for Disability Law & Policy at the National University of Ireland, Galway. His research focuses on higher education policy, technology and universal accessibility goals for persons with disabilities; the operation of communities of practice and online communities, and state and local government policy on information and communication technologies (ICT's).

JOHN C. BRICOUT, Ph.D., is Professor and Associate Dean for research at The University of Texas at Arlington School of Social Work. His research focuses on the impact of social technologies on the community participation of people with disabilities. Professor Bricout also studies innovation in community-university research partnerships. He is especially interested in the role of collaborative structures and learning communities in fostering innovation-generative partnership networks.

ALEX CASIANO is a Ph.D. student in Social Work at The University of Texas at Arlington. Mr. Casiano studies how social media can positively impact the behavior and attitudes of justice-system involved youth. In addition, he studies related policy issues, particularly as they pertain to national and regional differences in approach to technology and interventions.

MARTHA FUENTES-BAUTISTA, Ph.D., is assistant professor of Communication and Public Policy at the University of Massachusetts Amherst. Her research focuses on social stratification of information and communication technologies, and the role of public policy and civil society actors in digital inclusion efforts in the U.S. and Latin America.

ENRICO FERRO is the head of the Business Model and Policy Innovation Unit at Mario Boella Institute (ISMB), a research team studying the economic, social and policy implications of information and communication technologies. Over the last ten years Dr. Ferro has worked in many projects financed by the European Commission with roles ranging from scientific supervisor to senior expert. He is also an adjunct professor at the Polytechnic of Turin and at the International Labour Bureau of the United Nations where he regularly lectures on information management and strategies in both the public and the private sector. His research work has produced over forty academic publications, one handbook of research and over fifty research reports.

J. RAMON GIL-GARCIA is an Associate Professor in the Department of Public Administration and the Director of the Data Center for Applied Research in Social Sciences at Centro de Investigación y Docencia Económicas (CIDE) in Mexico City. In 2009, Dr. Gil-Garcia was considered the most prolific author in the field of digital government research worldwide. Currently, he is also a Research Fellow at the Center for Technology in Government, University at Albany, State University of New York (SUNY) and a Faculty Affiliate at the National Center for Digital Government, University of Massachusetts Amherst. His research interests include collaborative electronic government, adoption and implementation of emergent technologies, digital divide policies, new public management, and multi-method research approaches.

GERARD GOGGIN is Professor and Chair of the Department of Media and Communications, the University of Sydney. He has a long standing interest in disability, technology, policy and social justice, with key publications including Disability and the Media (2013; with Katie Ellis), and, with Christopher Newell, Digital Disability (2003) and

Disability in Australia (2005). Gerard has also published extensively on mobile media and the Internet, with his books including Mobile Technology and Place (2012; with Rowan Wilken), New Technologies and the Media (2012), Global Mobile Media (2011), Internationalizing Internet Studies (2009; with Mark McLelland), and Cell Phone Culture (2006).

JARICE HANSON, Ph.D., is Professor of Communication at the University of Massachusetts, Amherst. Her research focuses on the social impact of digital technologies and policies of inclusion and exclusion. She has authored, co-authored, edited, and co-edited over 25 books and numerous articles in a variety of scholarly and popular periodicals. One of her most well-known books is 24/7: How Cell Phones and the Internet Change the Way We Live, Work, and Play (Praeger, 2007). She is also co-editor (with Alison Alexander) of the successful Taking Sides: Mass Media and Society series, now in its 14th edition. She looks forward to being plagiarized for years for her authorship of the "Internet" entry in The World Book Encyclopedia.

JAMES W. HARRINGTON, JR. is Professor of Geography, Interdisciplinary Arts & Sciences, and Urban Studies at the University of Washington, where he also serves as vice chancellor (academic affairs) for the UW Tacoma campus. His research focus is subnational, regional economic development in the US and Canada.

NATALIE C. HELBIG, Ph.D., is a Senior Research Associate at the Center for Technology in Government, University at Albany, an applied research center dedicated to public sector innovation examining the intersections of policy, management, data, and technology. Dr. Helbig's research focuses understanding information use and management in public organizations and examining the informational relationships between government and citizens. Natalie's interests also include examining the digital divide, open government and information-intensive transparency, and promoting research-practice partnerships. Dr. Helbig currently teaches courses in Public Administration and Public Management at Rockefeller College of Public Affairs and Policy.

JEREMY HUNSINGER holds a Ph.D. in Science and Technology Studies from Virginia Tech. He is an Assistant Professor in Communication Studies at Wilfrid Laurier University. His research agenda analyzes the transformations of knowledge in the modes of production in the information age. His current research project examines innovation, expertise, knowledge production and distributions in hack labs and hacker spaces.

SUSAN L. JACOBSON, Ph.D., is an Assistant Professor in the Department of Journalism at Temple University. Her research interests include the impact of new media/social media on journalism and political communication. She can be contacted at susanjacobson@gmail.com.

THOMAS JACOBSON, Ph.D. University of Washington, is Professor and Interim Dean at the School of Communications and Theater at Temple University in Philadelphia, where he also serves as founding director of the Center for Public Interest Journalism. Tom is Chair of the Scholarly Review Committee for the International Association for Media and Communication Research. Recent research addresses communicative action and cultural change, problems of democratic legitimation, and program assessment.

DAVID JENSEN received his undergraduate and graduate degrees from the University of Washington Geography Department. His primary interest is in the intersections of public spaces and Internet spaces. He is particularly interested in how public library systems are mediating these intersections.

DOUGLAS NOONAN is Associate Professor in the School of Public and Environmental Affairs at Indiana University-Purdue University Indianapolis, and Director of Research at Indiana University's Public Policy Institute. He received his Ph.D. from the University of Chicago and spent over ten years as a professor in the School of Public Policy at the Georgia Institute of Technology. His research focuses on applied econometrics, measurement theory, environmental justice, and the distribution of open source software.

COSTAS PANAGOPOULOS is Associate Professor of Political Science and Director of the Center for Electoral Politics and Democracy at Fordham University. His research has been published in the American Journal of Political Science, the Journal of Politics, Political Behavior and many other scholarly outlets.

BARRY VACKER, Ph.D., is an Associate Professor at Temple University, where he teaches courses on media and cultural studies. Author of many articles on art, film, media, and technology, his most recent books include: the anthology, Media Environments (San Diego: Cognella 2011), the text for Peter Granser's art photography book, Signs (Stuttgart: Hatje Cantz and the Chicago Museum of Contemporary Photography 2008). He is also founder of the non-profit think tank, the Center for Media and Destiny.

AGREEN WANG finished her Master's degree in Broadcasting Telecommunications and Mass Media in Temple University. Her research focuses on popular culture, intercultural communication, and new media technologies. She adopts a philosophical and scientific approach to theorize the intersection of media, culture, and technology, all of which help outline human existence in the post-modern society. Her essay regarding human electronic consciousness in media universe was published in the Proceedings of 2011 McLuhan Philosophy of Media Centennial Conference.

ANDREW C. WARD has a Ph.D. in Health Services Research, Policy and Administration, an MPH in Public Health Administration from University of Minnesota, and a Ph.D. in Philosophy from the University of Kansas. He is an Instructor in the School of Public Health, University of Minnesota; a Community Faculty Member at the Metropolitan State University Department of Practical Philosophy and Ethics, and an Adjunct Associate Professor, Department of Health Policy and Management, School of Medicine, University of Kansas.

General Editor: **Steve Jones**

Digital Formations is the best source for critical, well-written books about digital technologies and modern life. Books in the series break new ground by emphasizing multiple methodological and theoretical approaches to deeply probe the formation and reformation of lived experience as it is refracted through digital interaction. Each volume in **Digital Formations** pushes forward our understanding of the intersections, and corresponding implications, between digital technologies and everyday life. The series examines broad issues in realms such as digital culture, electronic commerce, law, politics and governance, gender, the Internet, race, art, health and medicine, and education. The series emphasizes critical studies in the context of emergent and existing digital technologies.

Other recent titles include:

Felicia Wu Song
    Virtual Communities: Bowling Alone, Online Together

Edited by Sharon Kleinman
    The Culture of Efficiency: Technology in Everyday Life

Edward Lee Lamoureux, Steven L. Baron, & Claire Stewart
    Intellectual Property Law and Interactive Media: Free for a Fee

Edited by Adrienne Russell & Nabil Echchaibi
    International Blogging: Identity, Politics and Networked Publics

Edited by Don Heider
    Living Virtually: Researching New Worlds

Edited by Judith Burnett, Peter Senker & Kathy Walker
    The Myths of Technology: Innovation and Inequality

Edited by Knut Lundby
    Digital Storytelling, Mediatized Stories: Self-representations in New Media

Theresa M. Senft
    Camgirls: Celebrity and Community in the Age of Social Networks

Edited by Chris Paterson & David Domingo
    Making Online News: The Ethnography of New Media Production

To order other books in this series please contact our Customer Service Department:

        (800) 770-LANG (within the US)
        (212) 647-7706 (outside the US)
        (212) 647-7707 FAX

To find out more about the series or browse a full list of titles, please visit our website:
        WWW.PETERLANG.COM